SCHILLER'S TRAGEDIES:

THE PICCOLOMINI;

AND

THE DEATH OF WALLENSTEIN.

Translated from the German,

BY S. T. COLERIDGE.

WITH

AN INTRODUCTORY HISTORICAL SKETCH.

THERE can be no doubt that this drama forms, in its original tongue, one of the most splendid specimens of tragic art the world has witnessed ; and none at all that the execution of the version, from which we have quoted so largely, places Mr. Coleridge in the very first rank of poetical translators. He is, perhaps, the solitary example of a man of very great original genius, submitting to *all* the labours, and reaping *all* the honours, of this species of literary exertion.—*Blackwood's Mag.*, vol. xiv.

INTRODUCTORY NOTICE.

At the period of the Reformation, when the world awoke from a sleep of ages at the trumpet-toned summons of the intrepid Luther, the inhabitants of Bohemia were among the first to embrace the doctrines he promulgated. Bohemia suffered, in common with other Protestant states, from the persecution of the Catholics; but, adhering closely to their religion, they absolutely refused to march against the Protestant princes who had associated together under the title of the Smalcaldic League, and, taking arms against their sovereign, Ferdinand of Austria, prepared to join their fellow Protestants; but so many delays took place, that the decisive battle of Muhlberg, fought in 1547, and in which Charles V. entirely defeated the princes of the League, occurred before the Bohemian troops had joined the army. They immediately dispersed, and supplicated the mercy of their incensed sovereign, but in vain. Ferdinand gladly seized the opportunity of establishing his power, and he abolished many of their privileges, abridged others, and new-modelled the constitution according to his pleasure. He punished many of the insurgents with death, others with confiscation of their goods, or perpetual banishment. He disarmed the whole population, established oppressive garrisons, and loaded his people with taxes; all which, although it produced the silence of terror, by no means served to extinguish the fire of freedom.

The peace of Augsburg, which was finally ratified by the Emperor in 1555, put an end for a time to the contest between the Protestants and Catholics, but only to break out again with redoubled violence. Tranquillity was maintained throughout the reigns of Ferdinand, King of Bohemia, the successor of Charles V., and Maximilian II., whose mild sway went far to calm the stormy spirits of the age; but under the feeble administration of his son Rudolph, disputes again ran high, and the princes again began to band themselves together. Frederick IV., Elector of the Palatinate, headed the Protestant "Union," and Maximilian of Bavaria was the chief of the Catholic "League." The better to strengthen himself against his brother Mathias, who had rebelled against him, and finally possessed himself of all the power of the empire, Rudolph granted to the Bohemians a charter, known as "The Letter of Majesty," confirming all their ancient privileges and granting them entire freedom in their religion. Mathias succeeded to the titles of emperor and king, on the death of Rudolph, (the power he was already possessed of,) and, having no children, adopted Ferdinand of Gratz, Archduke of Carniola and Styria—a disciple of the Jesuits, and a staunch Catholic—as his successor on the throne of Bohemia; and he succeeded in persuading the people to ratify this choice, but not before Ferdinand had signed a document, freeing them from their allegiance as subjects, in the event of his infringing any of those rights which the coronation oath would call upon him to maintain. The violation of this agreement produced "the Thirty Years' War."

The charter granted by Rudolph to the Bohemians provided that "the Protestants should have the full right to build new schools and churches, not only in the towns, but in the country." Two new churches, built at Brunau and Clostergraben, were violently seized upon by the Catholic clergy, who pulled down one and shut up the other. A complaint was made to the Lords of the Council, the Emperor's representatives at Prague, who threw the deputies into prison. The Protestant members of the states, then assembled at Prague, upon this sent a remonstrance to the Emperor, who refused all redress, and declared that the states had abused the charter, and that the deputies were rebels and traitors. A copy of the imperial letter, and permission to return the next day and deliver their reply, were conceded to the deputation from the Protestant states, who proposed to hold a meeting at the house of Count Thurn, where it was resolved to inform the Lords of the Council, "that after the signature of the great charter by the Emperor, no order or decree, tending to endanger the liberties of the Protestant religion, could be received or obeyed;" and eight of the principal members were deputed to deliver this answer.

On the next morning, the 23rd of May, 1618, the deputation, each man in full armour, proceeded to the castle, followed by an immense multitude, all in arms, calling aloud for vengeance, many of whom thrust themselves into the hall of audience along with the deputies. The discussion, although begun in a temperate tone, soon became stormy. There were present at the board two members particularly obnoxious, Slavata and Martines, whom it had been previously determined to remove, should they appear. Reproaches were showered upon them, which were retorted; and at length the fiery Neusel of Raspowna exclaimed, "Wherefore all this delay? Let them be thrown out of the window, according to the good old Bohemian fashion." The words were no sooner spoken than the deed was done; and not only Slavata and Martines, but Fabricius the secretary, who had crept under the table, were precipitated from the windows. Sternberg and Lob-Kowitz were saved by their friends, who hurried them into another room. Fortunately there was a large mound of loose rubbish under the windows, and the unlucky councillors received little damage from their tumble, and notwithstanding they were fired at, they all escaped. This unfortunate affair proved very injurious to the Protestant cause, and gave its enemies a handle against them which they did not fail to make use of.

A humble apology and justification was sent to Vienna, but the states were careful to put themselves in a posture of defence. Some of the Catholic clergy were banished, and all the Jesuits were expelled. Count Thurn was put at the head of the army, and alliances were formed with Silesia and Lusatia, and application made to other states ; negotiations were attempted without success, and hostilities commenced. The Catholics of Bohemia, being equally interested with the Protestants in the maintenance of the charter, joined in opposing the Emperor ; and Count Mansfeld, the celebrated Condottieri leader, brought 4000 men to their aid, and captured Pilsen, the second town in the country, and the last which adhered to the Austrians. They endeavoured to persuade the famous Wallenstein, the favourite hero of the Germans, and whose fortunes form the subject of the beautiful drama to which these remarks are introductory, and who at this time was in command of the provincial militia of Moravia, to declare in their favour, but he remained stedfast to the Emperor, and was in consequence obliged to withdraw from Olmutz, carrying with him, however, the public treasure, which he delivered to the Emperor at Vienna.

Here we must pause for a moment to take a retrospect of the career of this extraordinary man, of whose earlier life very little is known, and who had at this period only just begun to be known and esteemed as a commander. Albrecht Eusebius Wenzeslaus of Waldstein or Wallenstein, was born at Humanis in Bohemia, on the 15th of September 1583, of an ancient and noble but impoverished family ; and as he was the youngest of six sons, his share of patri mony was but small. He was originally bred a Protestant, but the early loss of his parents threw him upon the protection of a maternal uncle, a Catholic, who placed him at the College of Nobles at Olmutz, established by the Jesuits, who found him an easy convert. He was from his boyhood averse to learning, fond of arms, and ambitious of command ; his active, powerful, and inquiring mind was incessantly occupied in procuring a knowledge of men and manners, and before entering on any profession he was able to gratify this disposition by foreign travel. He early entered the army, in what capacity is not known, but he met with little encouragement ; and served several campaigns against the Turks, before he attained the command of a company of foot. The want of money was pro bably the cause of his bad success, for at that period military rank could, as with us at this day, be purchased. His first step to fortune was the marriage of a wealthy widow, somewhat advanced in years. He lived retired with her, upon her estates, which devolved to him upon her death, which happened within a few years, but at what precise time is not ascertained. He is entirely lost to history for ten years, from 1607 to 1617, when, in his thirty-third year, he reappeared, and raised at his own expense a corps of horsemen, whom he led to the assistance of Ferdinand of Gratz, who was then at war with the Venetians. His successful conduct on this occasion, the splendour of his troops, the liberality of their pay, and the magnificence of his style of living, drew all eyes upon him. The Emperor invited him to Vienna, created him a count, gave him a chamberlain's key, and the important command of the Moravian militia. He now married his second wife, Isabella Catherine, Countess of Harrach, daughter of Count Harrach the Imperial minister ; a lady who not only brought him a great accession of fortune, but of influence also. We may here remark that Mr. Coleridge has in his translation fallen into an error in making it appear that the Countess Tertsky was the sister of this lady. She was the sister of Wallenstein himself ; and the mistake appears to have crept into the manuscript copy used by Mr. Coleridge, by some inadvertency, as in the printed copies, which were not published when the translation was made, the fact is correctly stated.

Wallenstein had now begun his career of glory. On his return from Olmutz he raised a troop of cuirassiers, and joining General Bocquoi, took an active part in the contest.

Ferdinand of Gratz succeeded to the Austrian dominions on the 20th March 1618, but it was a troubled inhe ritance. The Bohemians had now two armies : one under Count Mansfeld, the other under Count Thurn ; which latter was closely investing Vienna, when news arrived of the total defeat of Mansfeld by Bocquoi and Wallen stein, which forced Thurn to withdraw, and Ferdinand was delivered from great jeopardy. On the 29th of August, Ferdinand was elected emperor, and about the same time the Bohemians openly renounced their allegiance to him, and called Frederick V., the Elector Palatine, and husband of Elizabeth of England, to the throne. His story is well known. Abandoned by the allies, who, by the treaty of Ulm, agreed to give him no assistance except in defence of his native dominions, Maximilian, the chief of the League, who had entered into strict alliance with Ferdinand, turned all his forces against him ; and the defeat of Bethlem Gabor by Bocquoi and Wallenstein left their troops at liberty to attack Bohemia, and their united forces routed the army of Prince Christian of Anhalt, on the 8th November, 1620, and drove Frederick from his throne, and the battle of Prague restored Ferdinand to his dominions, when he commenced a dreadful persecution of the Protestants.

Wallenstein retired to his estates, and occupied himself in the acquisition of the enormous wealth for which he was afterwards distinguished, and which he effected by the purchase of confiscated estates. The deaths of Bocquoi and Dampier, the two best generals in the Austrian service, again called Wallenstein to the field, and in 1621 and 1623 he distinguished himself by defeating the armies of Bethlem Gabor. In reward of his services he was created Count Palatine and Duke of Friedland, with the right of striking coin and granting patents of nobility. In pos session of vast estates, he occupied himself incessantly with their improvement ; and although he lived with princely magnificence, every detail of his expense was managed with the most scrupulous economy. Meantime Tilly was occupied in the reduction of the Palatinate, but when this had been effected, and Mansfeld and the Duke of Brunswick driven out, the states began to take the alarm at the growing power of Ferdinand, and taking arms, an army of 60,000 men was quickly brought together. They entered into an alliance with the King of Denmark, and called, though vainly, upon England for assistance. The war began, but with small success. Tilly called for rein forcements, but the Emperor could not respond. His resources were utterly exhausted, and Bethlem Gabor found employment for every man he could command. At this crisis Wallenstein came forward, and offered to raise and equip an army of 50,000 men at his own expense. His offer was accepted ; and it was stipulated that he should be allowed to nominate his own officers, and was besides empowered to reward himself and his followers out of the property that might be confiscated in the conquered countries,—powers that necessarily gave him a wonderful ascendancy over his troops. Adventurers hastened to the standard of the princely general, and 20,000 were collected in a month ; and he marched from Eger on the 3rd of September 1625, at the head of 30,000 men, upon the frontiers of Lower Saxony. This extraordinary achievement excites our surprise, and it seems hard to believe how a private individual could command sufficient means to raise, support, and pay such a body of troops. It is true they lived at free quarters and levied very heavy contributions wherever they went ; yet Wallenstein's private advances were also enormous, especially for the provision of supplies and military stores, to every detail of which he himself gave the most minute attention.

It is impossible here to give a history of the Thirty Years' War. Our object has been merely to recal to the recollection of the reader, such of its events as led to the position in which the Empire was at the opening of Schiller's drama, and to show the steps by which Wallenstein attained his perilous elevation. Our notice of the passing events can therefore only be cursory. The efforts of Wallenstein cleared Germany of hostile armies, and rendered Ferdinand sole master of the country. He pushed his conquests to the sea ; state after state submitted, and were compelled to support the troops, who tyrannized over them and levied the most unsparing contributions. A thick crop of confiscations was reaped by the conquerors, and their chief was rewarded by the rich duchy of Mecklenburg, whose legitimate sovereign was expelled to make way for the haughty soldier. He now prepared to prosecute the war by sea, and tempted the king of Sweden with the offer of both Denmark and Norway, if he would join the Emperor; but he was above temptation. A peace with Denmark was at length concluded at Lubeck, in January 1629, and peace might also have been enjoyed by Germany if Ferdinand had not issued a decree commanding all property formerly belonging to the church to be restored. The grievance also of supporting the lawless bands of troops scattered over the country, lax in discipline and accustomed to free quarters, was dreadful. Their excesses led to complaints against their chief, and a diet assembled at Ratisbon strongly urged the Emperor to deprive Wallenstein of his command. Ferdinand was extremely anxious to obtain the election of his son as King of Hungary, and prevailed on Wallenstein to comply. He retired in 1630 to Gitchen, where he resided in princely state and attended by a large retinue.

Meantime war was declared by Gustavus Adolphus, who entered Germany and was opposed by Tilly with various success. At length Tilly lost the famous battle of Breitenfeld, fought on the 7th December 1631, and was soon afterwards slain in another battle near Augsburg, and Gustavus traversed Germany victoriously. Wallenstein was now once more summoned to the field. He again came forward, but limited his service to three months, in which space he promised to raise an army, and his name gathered one amounting to 40,000 men in that short time. He then resigned his command, and the Emperor was reduced to entreaties, before he would comply with his request and lead the troops to action. At length, upon the terms that he should be made commander-in-chief, with absolute power over all the Austrian and Spanish troops in Germany; that neither the King of Hungary nor the Emperor were to appear with the army, still less to exercise over it any act of authority; that the Emperor was to dispose of no military appointment, to confer no reward; that no pardon which he might grant should be valid without the sanction of the Duke of Friedland; that whatever might be conquered and confiscated was to be appropriated at the sole will and pleasure of the commander-in-chief, without the interference of any other authority; that as a certain reward of his services one of the hereditary provinces of the house of Austria, as an extraordinary reward one of the provinces of the empire, should be conferred upon him; that all the Austrian dominions were to be open for the reception of the army, in case retreat should become necessary; that on the conclusion of a peace, he was to be confirmed in the possession of the duchy of Mecklenburg; and that timely notice was to be given him, should it again be thought expedient to remove him from the command, he consented to lead the troops to action.

Never before were such terms dictated by a subject to a sovereign; and deeply humiliated must Ferdinand have felt, when necessity compelled him to assent to them, and thus to render himself almost a cipher in the empire. Wallenstein was in very ill-health, suffering most severely from the gout, and there is little reason to doubt that his reluctance to assume the command was not feigned, although Schiller viewed his conduct in a different light. The very extravagance of his demands may have arisen from the hope that they would be denied. But when they were granted, he at once exerted himself with all his accustomed vigilance and energy. On the 4th of May 1632, he attacked Arnheim's army before Prague, defeated him, and, following up his successes, quickly drove out all the enemy's forces from Bohemia. He wished now to carry the war into Saxony, and thus draw Gustavus from the centre of Germany; but at the earnest request of the Emperor and the Elector of Bavaria, the haughty Maximilian, whose machinations had been the chief cause of his former dismissal from command, he consented to seek the Swedes instead of forcing the Swedes to seek him. At Egra he experienced a proud triumph; Maximilian joined him with his army, which was put under the sole command of Wallenstein, and a formal instrument was executed by which both parties bound themselves to forget and forgive the past

Wallenstein conducted the campaign with extraordinary prudence; and Gustavus first experienced defeat before Nurenberg, where he suffered a reverse in an attempt to escape from the blockade by which Wallenstein attempted to subdue him in his lines by starvation. After a campaign conducted with masterly skill on both sides, Gustavus took up a position at Naumberg, and Wallenstein judging that he intended to remain there, as he had before Nurenberg, ventured to dispatch Pappenheim to the relief of Cologne, and to distribute many other of his troops in distant quarters; and in consequence, he was but ill prepared to meet Gustavus when he advanced to the famous field of Lutzen. His energy was taxed to its uttermost, and the hard-fought battle of Lutzen (6th November 1632,) was, although he experienced defeat, glorious rather than dishonourable. After rallying his troops, he took up winter quarters and occupied this time so diligently, that by the spring his army amounted to 40,000 men well equipped. In the course of the ensuing campaign, Wallenstein appears to have endeavoured to effect a peace by detaching Saxony from the Swedes; and he proposed to Arnheim the Saxon general to join with him in expelling the Swedes, " and then," said he, " we shall be able to make a peace among ourselves."

The transactions of this period are involved in much obscurity, and our knowledge of them a good deal depends upon the statements of Arnheim, " in whom," said Cardinal Richelieu, " the court of Rome lost a most accomplished Jesuit." It is certain that Arnheim reported to Oxenstiern, the Swedish commander, that Wallenstein was determined to take vengeance on the house of Austria, for the affront he had suffered when he was deprived of his command; that he intended to seize on Bohemia, restore the ancient privileges of the people, and then march to Vienna, and compel the Emperor to make peace,—a story altogether improbable, and so treated by Oxenstiern; who said, if it was a jest, it was a very bad one. With the hope of effecting a peace, Wallenstein consented to repeated truces, and his communication with the enemy caused his fidelity to be suspected; the emperor was perhaps afraid of a peace which would leave his too powerful subject unemployed. Reports of his ambitious designs became so prevalent, that applications and offers of assistance were made to him from France, to which he returned no answer. The last truce expired, and hostilities were again actively commenced, and successfully carried on, by Wallenstein. He drove the Swedes into a corner, and was in a fair way of reducing them altogether, when he was recalled to the defence of Bavaria, which was attacked by the Duke of Weimar. The reports which had been circulated to the prejudice of Wallenstein were given credit to by Ferdinand, although, when Wallenstein complained of them, he denied having heard them. He began to interfere with the arrangements of the army, and by so doing caused not only Wallenstein, but the officers, to complain. They began to be discontented, and forwarded a remonstrance against the measures adopted by the court, referring to their own sacrifices, and the want of pay. The rest of the story it is needless to detail; it is the subject of Schiller's drama, and all the attendant circumstances are fully detailed there. He however gives credit to the reality of Wallenstein's guilt, and also to the substitution of the false paper at the banquet of Illo, both which circumstances are very doubtful, and are certainly not borne out by any sufficient evidence; and it should be remembered that it was at the earnest request of his officers, who without his aid thought their just claims would never be admitted, that he consented to abide by them, upon the condition that they would abide by him; a compact certainly not unjustifiable, under the very peculiar relations in which both army and general stood with their sovereign.

It is not our purpose here to enter into a discussion upon Wallenstein's designs or conduct; we have merely detailed the leading facts of his career, our only intention being to point out his position at the time the drama of "The Piccolomini" opens. Neither is it our province to proceed farther with an outline of the war. It is sufficient here to state, that upon the death of Wallenstein, the King of Hungary took the command of the forces, whose murmurings were pacified with money, whilst the active agents in the destruction of the dreaded chieftain were richly rewarded. After a continued struggle, in which each party alternately gained and lost the advantage, and in which both France and Spain took part, the disastrous war of thirty years, which reduced Germany from plenty and prosperity to the brink of ruin, and the miseries of disorder and poverty, was at length closed by the treaty of peace concluded at Munster on the 24th of October 1648, by which liberty of conscience was secured to the Protestants, and the states of Europe were settled, as respects territory, in nearly the same manner as they remained until the commencement of the French Revolution.

PREFACE.

THE two Dramas,—PICCOLOMINI, or the first part of WALLENSTEIN, and THE DEATH OF WALLENSTEIN, are introduced in the original manuscript by a Prelude in one Act, entitled WALLENSTEIN'S CAMP. This is written in rhyme, and in nine-syllable verse, in the same *tilting* metre (if that expression may be permitted) with the second Eclogue of Spenser's Shepherd's Calendar.

This prelude possesses a sort of broad humour, and is not deficient in character; but to have translated it into prose, or into any other metre than that of the original, would have given a false idea both of its style and purport; to have translated it into the same metre would have been incompatible with a faithful adherence to the sense of the German, from the comparative poverty of our language in rhymes; and it would have been unadvisable, from the incongruity of those lax verses with the present taste of the English Public. Schiller's intention seems to have been merely to have prepared his reader for the Tragedies by a lively picture of the laxity of discipline, and the mutinous dispositions, of Wallenstein's soldiery. It is not necessary as a preliminary explanation. For these reasons it has been thought expedient not to translate it.

The admirers of Schiller, who have abstracted their idea of that author from The Robbers, and The Cabal and Love, plays in which the main interest is produced by the excitement of curiosity, and in which the curiosity is excited by terrible and extraordinary incident, will not have perused without some portion of disappointment the Dramas, which it has been my employment to translate. They should, however, reflect that these are Historical Dramas, taken from a popular German History; that we must, therefore, judge of them in some measure with the feelings of Germans; or, by analogy, with the interest excited in us by similar Dramas in our own language. Few, I trust, would be rash or ignorant enough to compare Schiller with Shakspeare; yet, merely as illustration, I would say that we should proceed to the perusal of Wallenstein, not from Lear or Othello, but from Richard the Second, or the three parts of Henry the Sixth. We scarcely expect rapidity in an Historical Drama; and many prolix speeches are pardoned from characters, whose names and actions have formed the most amusing tales of our early life. On the other hand, there exist in these plays more individual beauties, more passages whose excellence will bear reflection, than in the former productions of Schiller. The description of the Astrological Tower, and the reflections of the Young Lover, which follow it, form in the original a fine poem; and my translation must have been wretched indeed, if it can have wholly overclouded the beauties of the Scene in the first Act of the first Play, between Questenberg, Max. and Octavio Piccolomini. If we except the Scene of the setting sun in the Robbers, I know of no part in Schiller's Plays which equals the first Scene of the fifth Act of the concluding Play. It would be unbecoming in me to be more diffuse on this subject. A Translator stands connected with the original Author by a certain law of subordination, which makes it more decorous to point out excellences than defects: indeed he is not likely to be a fair judge of either. The pleasure or disgust from his own labour will mingle with the feelings that arise from an after-view of the original. Even in the first perusal of a work in any foreign language which we understand, we are apt to attribute to it more excellence than it really possesses from our own pleasurable sense of difficulty overcome without effort. Translation of poetry into poetry is difficult, because the Translator must give a brilliancy to his language without that warmth of original conception, from which such brilliancy would follow of its own accord. But the Translator of a living Author is encumbered with additional inconveniences. If he render his original faithfully, as to the *sense* of each passage, he must, necessarily, destroy a considerable portion of the *spirit*; if he endeavour to give a work executed according to laws of *compensation*, he subjects himself to imputations of vanity, or misrepresentation. I have thought it my duty to remain bound by the sense of my original, with as few exceptions as the nature of the languages rendered possible.

S. T. C.

DRAMATIS PERSONÆ.

WALLENSTEIN, *Duke of Friedland, Generalissimo of the Imperial Forces in the Thirty-years' War.*

OCTAVIO PICCOLOMINI, *Lieutenant-General.*

MAX. PICCOLOMINI, *his Son, Colonel of a Regiment of Cuirassiers.*

COUNT TERTSKY, *the Commander of several Regiments, and Brother-in-law of Wallenstein.*

ILLO, *Field Marshal, Wallenstein's Confidant.*

ISOLANI, *General of the Croats.*

BUTLER, *an Irishman, Commander of a Regiment of Dragoons.*

TIEFENBACH,
DON MARADAS,
GOETZ,
KOLATTO, } *Generals under Wallenstein.*

NEUMANN, *Captain of Cavalry, Aide-de-camp to Tertsky.*

VON QUESTENBERG, *the War Commissioner, Imperial Envoy.*

GENERAL WRANGEL, *Swedish Envoy.*

BAPTISTA SENI, *an Astrologer.*

DUCHESS OF FRIEDLAND, *Wife of Wallenstein.*

THEKLA, *her daughter, Princess of Friedland.*

THE COUNTESS TERTSKY, *sister of the Duchess.*

A CORNET.

COLONELS and GENERALS (*several*).

PAGES and ATTENDANTS *belonging to Wallenstein.*

ATTENDANTS and HOBOISTS *belonging to Tertsky.*

MASTER OF THE CELLAR, *to Count Tertsky.*

VALET DE CHAMBRE *of Count Piccolomini.*

THE PICCOLOMINI.

ACT I.

SCENE I.

*An old Gothic Chamber in the Council House at Pilsen,
decorated with Colours and other War Insignia.*

ILLO *with* BUTLER *and* ISOLANI.

ILLO.

Ye have come too late—but ye are come ! The
Count Isolan, excuses your delay.   [distance,

ISOLANI.

Add this too, that we come not empty-handed.
At Donauwerth [1] it was reported to us,   ,
A Swedish caravan was on its way
Transporting a rich cargo of provision,
Almost six hundred waggons.   This my Croats
Plunged down upon and seized, this weighty prize !—
We bring it hither——

ILLO.

Just in time to banquet
The illustrious company assembled here.

BUTLER.

'Tis all alive ! a stirring scene here !

ISOLANI.

Ay !
The very churches are all full of soldiers.
                         [*Casts his eye round.*
And in the Council-house too, I observe,
You're settled, quite at home ! Well, well ! we sol-
Must shift and suit us in what way we can. [diers

ILLO.

We have the colonels here of thirty regiments.
You'll find Count Tertsky here, and Tiefenbach,
Kolatto, Goetz, Maradas, Hinnersam,
The Piccolomini, both son and father——
You'll meet with many an unexpected greeting
From many an old friend and acquaintance. Only
Galas is wanting still, and Altringer.

BUTLER.

Expect not Galas.

ILLO (*hesitating*).

How so ! Do *you* know——

ISOLANI (*interrupting him*).

Max. Piccolomini here !—O bring me to him.
I see him yet ('tis now ten years ago,
We were engaged with Mansfeldt hard by Dessau,)
I see the youth, in my mind's eye I see him,
Leap his black war-horse from the bridge adown,
And t'ward his father, then in extreme peril,

---

[1] A town about twelve German miles N.E. of Ulm.

Beat up against the strong tide of the Elbe.
The down was scarce upon his chin ! I hear
He has made good the promise of his youth,
And the full hero now is finish'd in him.

ILLO.

You'll see him yet ere evening.   He conducts
The Duchess Friedland hither, and the Princess [2]
From Cärnthen.   We expect them here at noon.

BUTLER.

Both wife and daughter does the Duke call hither!
He crowds in visitants from all sides.

ISOLANI.

Hm !
So much the better ! I had framed my mind
To hear of nought but warlike circumstance,
Of marches, and attacks, and batteries :
And lo ! the Duke provides, that something too
Of gentler sort, and lovely, should be present
To feast our eyes.

ILLO (*who has been standing in the attitude of
meditation, to* BUTLER, *whom he leads a little on
one side*).
And how came you to know
That the Count Galas joins us not !

BUTLER.

Because
He importuned *me* to remain behind.

ILLO (*with warmth*).
And you !—You hold out firmly !
                [*Grasping his hand with affection.*
Noble Butler !

BUTLER.

After the obligation which the Duke
Had laid so newly on me——

ILLO.

I had forgotten
A pleasant duty—Major General,
I wish you joy !

ISOLANI.

What, you mean, of his regiment !
I hear, too, that to make the gift still sweeter,
The Duke has given him the very same
In which he first saw service, and since then, [ment,
Work'd himself, step by step, through each prefer-
From the ranks upwards.   And verily, it gives
A precedent of hope, a spur of action
To the whole corps, if once in their remembrance
An old deserving soldier makes his way.

---

[2] The Dukes in Germany being always reigning powers,
their sons and daughters are entitled Princes and Princesses.

B

BUTLER.

I am perplex'd and doubtful, whether or no
I dare accept this your congratulation.
The Emperor has not yet confirm'd the appointment.

ISOLANI.

Seize it, friend! Seize it! The hand which in that post
Placed you, is strong enough to keep you there,
Spite of the Emperor and his Ministers!

ILLO.

Ay, if we would but so consider it!—
If we would *all* of us consider it so!
The Emperor gives us nothing; from the Duke
Comes all—whate'er we hope, whate'er we have.

ISOLANI (*to* ILLO).

My noble brother! did I tell you how
The Duke will satisfy my creditors!
Will be himself my banker for the future,
Make me once more a creditable man!—
And this is now the third time, think of that!
This kingly-minded man has rescued me
From absolute ruin, and restored my honour.

ILLO.

O that his power but kept pace with his wishes!
Why, friend! he'd give the whole world to his soldiers.
But at Vienna, brother!—here's the grievance.—
What politic schemes do they not lay to shorten
His arm, and where they can, to clip his pinions.
Then these new dainty requisitions! these,
Which this same Questenberg brings hither!—

BUTLER.

Ay!

These requisitions of the Emperor,—
I too have heard about them; but I hope
The Duke will not draw back a single inch!

ILLO.

Not from his right most surely, unless first
—From office!

BUTLER (*shocked and confused*).

Know you *aught* then! You alarm me.

ISOLANI (*at the same time with* BUTLER, *and
in a hurrying voice*).

We should be ruin'd, every one of us!

ILLO.

No more!

Yonder I see *our worthy friend* [1] approaching
With the Lieutenant-General, Piccolomini.

BUTLER (*shaking his head significantly*).

I fear we shall not go hence as we came.

———◆———

SCENE II.

Enter OCTAVIO PICCOLOMINI *and* QUESTENBERG.

OCTAVIO (*still in the distance*.)

Ay, ay! more still! Still more new visitors!
Acknowledge, friend! that never was a camp,
Which held at once so many heads of heroes.
[*Approaching nearer.*
Welcome, Count Isolani!

ISOLANI.

My noble brother,
Even now am I arrived; it had been else my duty—

OCTAVIO.

And Colonel Butler—trust me, I rejoice
Thus to renew acquaintance with a man
Whose worth and services I know and honour.

[1] Spoken with a sneer.

See, see, my friend!
There might we place at once before our eyes
The sum of war's whole trade and mystery—
[*To* QUESTENBERG, *presenting* BUTLER *and* ISOLANI
at the same time to him.
These two the total sum—Strength and Dispatch.

QUESTENBERG (*to* OCTAVIO).

And lo! betwixt them both experienced Prudence!

OCTAVIO (*presenting* QUESTENBERG *to* BUTLER
and ISOLANI).

The Chamberlain and War-commissioner Questen-
The bearer of the Emperor's behests, [berg,
The long-tried friend and patron of all soldiers,
We honour in this noble visitor. [*Universal silence.*

ILLO (*moving towards* QUESTENBERG).

'Tis not the first time, noble Minister,
You have shown our camp this honour.

QUESTENBERG.

Once before
I stood before these colours.

ILLO.

Perchance too you remember *where* that was.
It was at Znäim [2] in Moravia, where
You did present yourself upon the part
Of the Emperor, to supplicate our Duke
That he would straight assume the chief command.

QUESTENBERG.

To *supplicate?* Nay bold General!
So far extended neither my commission
(At least to my own knowledge) nor my zeal.

ILLO.

Well, well, then—to *compel* him, if you choose.
I can remember it well, Count Tilly
Had suffer'd total rout upon the Lech.
Bavaria lay all open to the enemy,
Whom there was nothing to delay from pressing
Onwards into the very heart of Austria.
At that time you and Werdenberg appear'd
Before our General, storming him with prayers,
And menacing the Emperor's displeasure,
Unless he took compassion on this wretchedness.

ISOLANI (*steps up to them*).

Yes, yes, 'tis comprehensible enough,
Wherefore with your commission of to-day
You were not all too willing to remember
Your former one.

QUESTENBERG.

Why not, Count Isolan?
No contradiction sure exists between them.
It was the urgent business of that time
To snatch Bavaria from her enemy's hand;
And my commission of to-day instructs me
To free her from her good friends and protectors.

ILLO.

A worthy office! After with our blood
We have wrested this Bohemia from the Saxon,
To be swept *out* of it is all our thanks,
The sole reward of all our hard-won victories.

QUESTENBERG.

Unless that wretched land be doomed to suffer
Only a change of evils, it must be
Freed from the scourge alike of friend and foe.

ILLO.

What! 'Twas a favourable year; the boors
Can answer fresh demands already.

[2] A town not far from the Mine-mountains, on the high
road from Vienna to Prague.

QUESTENBERG.
Nay,
If *you* discourse of herds and meadow-grounds—

ISOLANI.
The war maintains the war. Are the boors ruin'd?
The Emperor gains so many more new soldiers.

QUESTENBERG.
And is the poorer by even so many subjects.

ISOLANI.
Poh! we are all his subjects.

QUESTENBERG.
Yet with a difference, General! The one fill
With profitable industry the purse,
The others are well skill'd to empty it.
The sword has made the Emperor poor; the plough
Must reinvigorate his resources.

ISOLANI.
Sure!
Times are not yet so bad. Methinks I see
[*Examining with his eye the dress and ornaments
of* QUESTENBERG.
Good store of gold that still remains uncoin'd.

QUESTENBERG.
Thank Heaven! that means have been found out to
Some little from the fingers of the Croats. [hide

ILLO.
There! The Stawata and the Martinitz,
On whom the Emperor heaps his gifts and graces,
To the heart-burning of all good Bohemians—
Those minions of court favour, those court harpies,
Who fatten on the wrecks of citizens
Driven from their house and home—who reap no
Save in the general calamity—   [harvests
Who now, with kingly pomp, insult and mock
The desolation of their country—these,
Let these, and such as these, support the war,
The fatal war, which they alone enkindled!

BUTLER.
And those state-parasites, who have their feet
So constantly beneath the Emperor's table,
Who cannot let a benefice fall, but they
Snap at it with dogs' hunger—they, forsooth, [ing!
Would pare the soldier's bread, and cross his reckon-

ISOLANI.
My life long will it anger me to think,
How when I went to court seven years ago,
To see about new horses for our regiment,
How from one antechamber to another
They dragg'd me on, and left me by the hour
To kick my heels among a crowd of simpering
Feast-fatten'd slaves, as if I had come thither
A mendicant suitor for the crumbs of favour
That fall beneath their tables. And, at last,
Whom should they send me but a capuchin!
Straight I began to muster up my sins
For absolution—but no such luck for *me!*
This was the man, this capuchin, with whom
I was to treat concerning the army horses:
And I was forced at last to quit the field,
The business unaccomplish'd. Afterwards
The Duke procured me in three days, what I
Could not obtain in thirty at Vienna.

QUESTENBERG.
Yes, yes! your travelling bills soon found their
way to us:
Too well I know we have still accounts to settle.

ILLO.
War is a violent trade: one cannot always

Finish one's work by soft means; every trifle
Must not be blacken'd into sacrilege.
If we should wait till you, in solemn council,
With due deliberation had selected
The smallest out of four-and-twenty evils,
I' faith we should wait long.—
"Dash! and through with it!"—That's the better
watch-word.
Then after come what may come. 'Tis man's nature
To make the best of a bad thing once past.
A bitter and perplex'd "what shall I do!"
Is worse to man than worst necessity.

QUESTENBERG.
Ay, doubtless, it is true: the Duke *does* spare us
The troublesome task of choosing.

BUTLER.
Yes, the Duke
Cares with a father's feelings for his troops;
But how the Emperor feels for us, we see.

QUESTENBERG.
His cares and feelings all ranks share alike,
Nor will he offer one up to another.

ISOLANI.
And therefore thrusts he us into the deserts
As beasts of prey, that so he may preserve
His dear sheep fattening in his fields at home.

QUESTENBERG (*with a sneer*).
Count! this comparison you make, not I.

BUTLER.
Why, were we all the Court supposes us,
'Twere dangerous, sure, to give us liberty.

QUESTENBERG.
You have taken liberty—it was not given you.
And therefore it becomes an urgent duty
To rein it in with curbs.

OCTAVIO (*interposing and addressing* QUESTENBERG).
My noble friend,
This is no more than a remembrancing
That you are now in camp, and among warriors.
The soldier's boldness constitutes his freedom.
Could he *act* daringly, unless he dared
Talk even so! One runs into the other.
The boldness of this worthy officer,
[*Pointing to* BUTLER.
Which now has but mistaken in its mark,
Preserved, when nought but boldness could pre-
serve it,
To the Emperor his capital city, Prague,
In a most formidable mutiny
Of the whole garrison. [*Military music at a distance.*
Hah! here they come!

ILLO.
The sentries are saluting them: this signal
Announces the arrival of the Duchess.

OCTAVIO (*to* QUESTENBERG).
Then my son Max. too has returned. 'Twas he
Fetch'd and attended them from Cärnthen hither.

ISOLANI (*to* ILLO).
Shall we not go in company to greet them!

ILLO.
Well, let us go.—Ho! Colonel Butler, come.
[*To* OCTAVIO.
You'll not forget, that yet ere noon we meet
The noble Envoy at the General's palace.

[*Exeunt all but* QUESTENBERG *and* OCTAVIO.
B 2

SCENE III.

QUESTENBERG and OCTAVIO.

QUESTENBERG (*with signs of aversion and astonishment*).
What have I not been forced to hear, Octavio !
What sentiments ! what fierce, uncurb'd defiance !
And were this spirit universal—

OCTAVIO.
          Hm !   [army.
You are now acquainted with three-fourths of the

QUESTENBERG.
Where must we seek then for a second host
To have the custody of this ? That Illo
Thinks worse, I fear me, than he speaks. And then
This Butler too—he cannot even conceal
The passionate workings of his ill intentions.

OCTAVIO.
Quickness of temper—irritated pride ;
'Twas nothing more. I cannot give up Butler.
I know a spell that will soon dispossess
The evil spirit in *him*.

QUESTENBERG (*walking up and down in evident disquiet*).
          Friend, friend !
O ! this is worse, far worse, than we had suffer'd
Ourselves to dream of at Vienna. There
We saw it only with a courtier's eyes,
Eyes dazzled by the splendour of the throne.
We had not seen the War-chief, the Commander,
The man all-powerful in his camp. Here, here,
'T is quite another thing.
Here is no Emperor more—the Duke is Emperor.
Alas, my friend ! alas, my noble friend !
This walk which you have ta'en me through the camp
Strikes my hopes prostrate.   [camp

OCTAVIO.
          Now you see yourself
Of what a perilous kind the office is,
Which you deliver to me from the Court.
The least suspicion of the General
Costs me my freedom and my life, and would
But hasten his most desperate enterprise.

QUESTENBERG.
Where was our reason sleeping when we trusted
This madman with the sword; and placed such
In such a hand ! I tell you, he 'll refuse, [power
Flatly refuse, to obey the Imperial orders.
Friend, he *can* do 't, and what he can, he will.
And then the impunity of his defiance—
Oh ! what a proclamation of our weakness !

OCTAVIO.
D' ye think too, he has brought his wife and daughter
Without a purpose hither ? Here in camp !
And at the very point of time, in which
We 're arming for the war ? That he has taken
These, the last pledges of his loyalty,
Away from out the Emperor's domains—
This is no doubtful token of the nearness
Of some eruption ?

QUESTENBERG.
          How shall we hold footing
Beneath this tempest, which collects itself
And threats us from all quarters ? The enemy
Of the empire on our borders, now already
The master of the Danube, and still farther,
And farther still, extending every hour !

In our interior the alarum-bells
Of insurrection—peasantry in arms—
All orders discontented—and the army,
Just in the moment of our expectation
Of aidance from it—lo ! this very army
Seduced, run wild, lost to all discipline,
Loosen'd, and rent asunder from the state
And from their sovereign, the blind instrument
Of the most daring of mankind, a weapon
Of fearful power, which at his will *he* wields !

OCTAVIO.
Nay, nay, friend ! let us not despair too soon.
Men's words are ever bolder than their deeds :
And many a resolute, who now appears
Made up to all extremes, will, on a sudden
Find in his breast a heart he wot not of,
Let but a single honest man speak out
The true name of his crime ! Remember too,
We stand not yet so wholly unprotected.
Counts Altringer and Galas have maintain'd
Their little army faithful to its duty,
And daily it becomes more numerous.
Nor can he take us by surprise : you know
I hold him all encompass'd by my listeners.
Whate'er he does, is mine, even while 't is doing—
No step so small, but instantly I hear it ;
Yea, his own mouth discloses it.

QUESTENBERG.
          'T is quite
Incomprehensible, that he detects not
The foe so near !

OCTAVIO.
          Beware, you do not think,
That I by lying arts, and complaisant
Hypocrisy, have skulked into his graces :
Or with the substance of smooth professions
Nourish his all-confiding friendship ! No—
Compell'd alike by prudence, and that duty
Which we all owe our country, and our sovereign,
To hide my genuine feelings from him, yet
Ne'er have I duped him with base counterfeits !

QUESTENBERG.
It is the visible ordinance of Heaven.

OCTAVIO.
I know not what it is that so attracts
And links him both to me and to my son.
Comrades and friends we always were—long habit,
Adventurous deeds performed in company,
And all those many and various incidents
Which store a soldier's memory with affections,
Had bound us long and early to each other—
Yet I can name the day, when all at once
His heart *rose* on me, and his confidence
Shot out into sudden growth. It was the morning
Before the memorable fight at Lützner.
Urged by an ugly dream, I sought him out,
To press him to accept another charger.
At distance from the tents, beneath a tree,
I found him in a sleep. When I had waked him,
And had related all my bodings to him,
Long time he stared upon me, like a man
Astounded : thereon fell upon my neck,
And manifested to me an emotion
That far outstripped the worth of that small service.
Since then his confidence has follow'd me
With the same pace that mine has fled from him.

QUESTENBERG.
You lead your son into the secret ?

OCTAVIO.
No !

QUESTENBERG.
What ! and not warn him either what bad hands
His lot has placed him in ?

OCTAVIO.
I must perforce
Leave him in wardship to his innocence.
His young and open soul—dissimulation
Is foreign to its habits ! Ignorance
Alone can keep alive the cheerful air,
The unembarrass'd sense and light free spirit,
That make the Duke secure.

QUESTENBERG (anxiously).
My honour'd friend ! most highly do I deem
Of Colonel Piccolomini—yet—if——
Reflect a little——

OCTAVIO.
I must venture it.
Hush !—There he comes !

SCENE IV.

MAX. PICCOLOMINI, OCTAVIO PICCOLOMINI, QUESTENBERG.

MAX.
Ha ! there he is himself. Welcome, my father !
[He embraces his father. As he turns round, he
observes QUESTENBERG, and draws back with a
cold and reserved air.
You are engaged, I see. I'll not disturb you.

OCTAVIO.
How, Max. ! Look closer at this visitor.
Attention, Max. an old friend merits—Reverence
Belongs of right to the envoy of your sovereign.

MAX. (drily).
Von Questenberg !—Welcome—if you bring with
Aught good to our head-quarters. [you

QUESTENBERG (seizing his hand).
Nay, draw not
Your hand away, Count Piccolomini !
Not on mine own account alone I seized it,
And nothing common will I say therewith.
[Taking the hands of both.
Octavio—Max. Piccolomini !
O saviour names, and full of happy omen !
Ne'er will her prosperous genius turn from Austria,
While two such stars, with blessed influences
Beaming protection, shine above her hosts.

MAX.
Heh !—Noble minister ! You miss your part.
You came not here to act a panegyric.
You 're sent, I know, to find fault and to scold us—
I must not be beforehand with my comrades.

OCTAVIO (to MAX.).
He comes from court, where people are not quite
So well contented with the Duke, as here.

MAX.
What now have they contrived to find out in him !
That he alone determines for himself
What he himself alone doth understand !
Well, therein he does right, and will persist in 't.
Heaven never meant him for that passive thing
That can be struck and hammer'd out to spit
Another's taste and fancy. He 'll not dance
To every tune of every minister :

It goes against his nature—he can't do it.
He is possess'd by a commanding spirit,
And his too is the station of command.
And well for us it is so ! There exist
Few fit to rule themselves, but few that use
Their intellects intelligently.—Then
Well for the whole, if there be found a man,
Who makes himself what nature destined him,
The pause, the central point to thousand thousands—
Stands fixed and stately, like a firm-built column,
Where all may press with joy and confidence.
Now such a man is Wallenstein ; and if
Another better suits the court—no other
But such a one as he can serve the army.

QUESTENBERG.
The army ! Doubtless !

OCTAVIO (to QUESTENBERG).
Hush ! Suppress it friend !
Unless some end were answer'd by the utterance.—
Of him there you 'll make nothing.

MAX. (continuing).
In their distress
They call a spirit up, and when he comes,
Straight their flesh creeps and quivers, and they
dread him
More than the ills for which they call'd him up.
The uncommon, the sublime, must seem and be
Like things of every day.—But in the field,
Ay, there the Present Being makes itself felt.
The personal must command, the actual eye
Examine. If to be the chieftain asks
All that is great in nature, let it be
Likewise his privilege to move and act
In all the correspondencies of greatness.
The oracle within him, that which lives,
He must invoke and question—not dead books,
Not ordinances, not mould-rotted papers.

OCTAVIO.
My son ! of those old narrow ordinances
Let us not hold too lightly. They are weights
Of priceless value, which oppress'd mankind
Tied to the volatile will of their oppressors.
For always formidable was the league
And partnership of free power with free will.
The way of ancient ordinance, though it winds,
Is yet no devious way. Straight forward goes
The lightning's path, and straight the fearful path
Of the cannon-ball. Direct it flies and rapid,
Shattering that it may reach, and shattering what
it reaches.
My son ! the road, the human being travels,
That, on which BLESSING comes and goes, doth
follow
The river's course, the valley's playful windings,
Curves round the corn-field and the hill of vines,
Honouring the holy bounds of property !
And thus secure, though late, leads to its end.

QUESTENBERG.
O hear your father, noble youth ! hear him,
Who is at once the hero and the man.

OCTAVIO.
My son, the nurseling of the camp spoke in thee !
A war of fifteen years
Hath been thy education and thy school.
Peace hast thou never witness'd ! There exists
An higher than the warrior's excellence.
In war itself war is no ultimate purpose.
The vast and sudden deeds of violence,

Adventures wild, and wonders of the moment,
These are not they, my son, that generate
The Calm, the Blissful, and the enduring Mighty!
Lo there ! the soldier, rapid architect !
Builds his light town of canvas, and at once
The whole scene moves and bustles momently,
With arms, and neighing steeds, and mirth and
      quarrel
The motley market fills ; the roads, the streams
Are crowded with new freights, trade stirs and hur-
But on some morrow morn, all suddenly,   [ries !
The tents drop down, the horde renews its march.
Dreary, and solitary as a church-yard
The meadow and down-trodden seed-plot lie,
And the year's harvest is gone utterly.

                    MAX.
O let the Emperor make peace, my father !
Most gladly would I give the blood-stained laurel
For the first violet[1] of the leafless spring,
Pluck'd in those quiet fields where I have journey'd !

                  OCTAVIO.
What ails thee ! What so moves thee all at once !

                    MAX.
Peace have I ne'er beheld ! I *have* beheld it.
From thence am I come hither : O ! that sight,
It glimmers still before me, like some landscape,
Left in the distance,—some delicious landscape !
My road conducted me through countries where
The war has not yet reach'd. Life, life, my father—
My venerable father, Life has charms
Which *we* have ne'er experienced. We have been
But voyaging along its barren coasts,
Like some poor ever-roaming horde of pirates,
That, crowded in the rank and narrow ship,
House on the wild sea with wild usages,
Nor know aught of the main land, but the bays
Where safeliest they may venture a thieves' landing.
Whate'er in the inland dales the land conceals
Of fair and exquisite, O ! nothing, nothing,
Do we behold of that in our rude voyage.

OCTAVIO, (*attentive, with an appearance of
                  uneasiness*).
And so your journey has reveal'd this to you !

                    MAX.
'Twas the first leisure of my life. O tell me,
What is the meed and purpose of the toil,
The painful toil, which robb'd me of my youth,
Left me a heart unsoul'd and solitary,
A spirit uninform'd, unornamented !
For the camp's stir and crowd and ceaseless larum,
The neighing war-horse, the air-shattering trumpet,
The unvaried, still returning hour of duty,
Word of command, and exercise of arms—
There's nothing here, there's nothing in all this,
To satisfy the heart, the gasping heart !
Mere bustling nothingness, where the soul is not—
This cannot be the sole felicity,
These cannot be man's best and only pleasures !

                  OCTAVIO.
Much hast thou learnt, my son, in this short journey.

                    MAX.
O ! day thrice lovely ! when at length the soldier
Returns home into life ; when he becomes
A fellow-man among his fellow-men.

      [1] In the original,
      Den blut'gen Lorbeer geb'ich hin mit Freuden
      Fürs erste Veilchen, das der März uns bringt,
      Das dürftige Pfand der neuverjüngten Erde.

The colours are unfurl'd, the cavalcade
Marshals, and now the buzz is hush'd, and hark !
Now the soft peace-march beats, home, brothers,
The caps and helmets are all garlanded   [home !
With green boughs, the last plundering of the fields.
The city gates fly open of themselves,
They need no longer the petard to tear them.
The ramparts are all filled with men and women,
With peaceful men and women, that send onwards
Kisses and welcomings upon the air,
Which they make breezy with affectionate gestures.
From all the towers rings out the merry peal,
The joyous vespers of a bloody day.
O happy man, O fortunate ! for whom
The well-known door, the faithful arms are open,
The faithful tender arms with mute embracing.

QUESTENBERG (*apparently much affected*).
              O that you should speak
Of such a distant, distant time, and not
Of the to-morrow, not of this to-day.

MAX. (*turning round to him, quick and vehement*).
Where lies the fault but on you in Vienna !
I will deal openly with you, Questenberg.
Just now, as first I saw you standing here,
(I'll own it to you freely) indignation
Crowded and press'd my inmost soul together.
'Tis ye that hinder peace, *ye !*—and the warrior,
It is the warrior that must force it from you.
Ye fret the General's life out, blacken him,
Hold him up as a rebel, and Heaven knows
What else still worse, because he spares the Saxons,
And tries to awaken confidence in the enemy ;
Which yet's the only way to peace : for if
War intermit not during war, *how* then
And *whence* can peace come !—Your own plagues
      fall on you !
Even as I love what's virtuous, hate I you.
And here make I this vow, here pledge myself ;
My blood shall spurt out for this Wallenstein,
And my heart drain off, drop by drop, ere ye
Shall revel and dance jubilee o'er his ruin. [*Exit.*

                  SCENE V.
        QUESTENBERG, OCTAVIO PICCOLOMINI.
                  QUESTENBERG.
Alas, alas ! and stands it so !
        [*Then in pressing and impatient tones.*
What friend ! and do we let him go away
In this delusion—let him go away !
Not call him back immediately, not open
His eyes upon the spot !

OCTAVIO (*recovering himself out of a deep study*).
                  He has now open'd mine,
And I see more than pleases me.
                  QUESTENBERG.
                              What is it !
                  OCTAVIO.
Curse on this journey !
                  QUESTENBERG.
                  But why so ! What is it !
                  OCTAVIO.
Come, come along, friend ! I must follow up
The ominous track immediately. Mine eyes
Are open'd now, and I must use them. Come !
              [*Draws QUESTENBERG on with him.*
                  QUESTENBERG.
What now ! *Where* go you then !

OCTAVIO.
To her herself.

QUESTENBERG.
To——

OCTAVIO (*interrupting him, and correcting himself*).
To the Duke. Come let us go—'Tis done, 'tis done,
I see the net that is thrown over him.
Oh! he returns not to me as he went.

QUESTENBERG.
Nay, but explain yourself.

OCTAVIO.
And that I should not
Foresee it, not prevent this journey! Wherefore
Did I keep it from him!—You were in the right.
I should have warn'd him! Now it is too late.

QUESTENBERG.
But *what's* too late! Bethink yourself, my friend,
That you are talking absolute riddles to me.

OCTAVIO (*more collected*).
Come! to the Duke's. 'Tis close upon the hour
Which he appointed you for audience. Come!
A curse, a threefold curse, upon this journey!
[*He leads* QUESTENBERG *off.*

SCENE VI.

Changes to a spacious Chamber in the House of the Duke of Friedland.—Servants employed in putting the tables and chairs in order. During this enters SENI, *like an old Italian doctor, in black, and clothed somewhat fantastically. He carries a white staff, with which he marks out the quarters of the heavens.*

FIRST SERVANT.
Come—to it, lads, to it! Make an end of it. I hear the sentry call out, "Stand to your arms!" They will be here in a minute.

SECOND SERVANT.
Why were we not told before that the audience would be held here? Nothing prepared—no orders —no instructions.

THIRD SERVANT.
Ay, and why was the balcony-chamber countermanded, that with the great worked carpet!— there one can look about one.

FIRST SERVANT.
Nay, that you must ask the mathematician there. He says it is an unlucky chamber.

SECOND SERVANT.
Poh! stuff and nonsense! That's what I call a *hum*. A chamber is a chamber; what much can the place signify in the affair!

SENI (*with gravity*).
My son, there's *nothing* insignificant, *Nothing!* But yet in every earthly thing First and most principal is place and time.

FIRST SERVANT (*to the second*).
Say nothing to him, Nat. The Duke himself must let him have his own will.

SENI (*counts the chairs, half in a loud, half in a low voice, till he comes to eleven, which he repeats*).
Eleven! an evil number! Set twelve chairs.
Twelve! twelve signs hath the zodiac: five and seven,
The holy numbers, include themselves in twelve.

SECOND SERVANT.
And what may you have to object against eleven? I should like to know that now.

SENI.
Eleven is transgression; eleven oversteps
The ten commandments.

SECOND SERVANT.
That's good! and why do you call five an holy number!

SENI.
Five is the soul of man: for even as man
Is mingled up of good and evil, so
The five is the first number that's made up
Of even and odd.

SECOND SERVANT.
The foolish old coxcomb!

FIRST SERVANT.
Ay! let him alone though. I like to hear him; there is more in his words than can be seen at first sight.

THIRD SERVANT.
Off, they come.

SECOND SERVANT.
There! Out at the side-door.
[*They hurry off.* SENI *follows slowly. A Page brings the staff of command on a red cushion, and places it on the table near the Duke's chair. They are announced from without, and the wings of the door fly open.*

SCENE VII.

WALLENSTEIN, DUCHESS.

WALLENSTEIN.
You went then through Vienna, were presented
To the Queen of Hungary!

DUCHESS.
Yes; and to the Empress too,
And by both Majesties were we admitted
To kiss the hand.

WALLENSTEIN.
And how was it received,
That I had sent for wife and daughter hither
To the camp, in winter-time!

DUCHESS.
I did even that
Which you commission'd me to do. I told them,
You had determined on our daughter's marriage,
And wish'd, ere yet you went into the field,
To show the elected husband his betrothed.

WALLENSTEIN.
And did they guess the choice which I had made!

DUCHESS.
They only hoped and wish'd it may have fallen
Upon no foreign nor yet Lutheran noble.

WALLENSTEIN.
And you—what do *you* wish, Elizabeth!

DUCHESS.
Your will, you know, was always mine.

WALLENSTEIN (*after a pause*).
Well then!
And in all else, of what kind and complexion
Was your reception at the court!
[*The* DUCHESS *casts her eyes on the ground, and remains silent.*
Hide nothing from me. How were you received!

DUCHESS.
O! my dear lord, all is not what it was.

A canker-worm, my lord, a canker-worm
Has stolen into the bud.

WALLENSTEIN.
Ay! is it so!
What, they were lax! they fail'd of the old respect!

DUCHESS.
Not of respect. No honours were omitted,
No outward courtesy; but in the place
Of condescending, confidential kindness,
Familiar and endearing, there were given me
Only these honours and that solemn courtesy.
Ah! and the tenderness which was put on,
It was the guise of pity not of favour.   [wife,
No! Albrecht's wife, Duke Albrecht's princely
Count Harrach's noble daughter, should not so—
Not wholly so should she have been received.

WALLENSTEIN.
Yes, yes; they have ta'en offence. My latest
They rail'd at it, no doubt.   [conduct,

DUCHESS.
O that they had!
I have been long accustomed to defend you,
To heal and pacify distemper'd spirits.
No; no one rail'd at you. They wrapp'd them up,
O Heaven! in such oppressive, solemn silence!—
Here is no every-day misunderstanding,
No transient pique, no cloud that passes over;
Something most luckless, most unhealable,
Has taken place. The Queen of Hungary
Used formerly to call me her dear aunt,
And ever at departure to embrace me—

WALLENSTEIN.
Now she omitted it!

DUCHESS (wiping away her tears after a pause).
She did embrace me,
But then first when I had already taken
My formal leave, and when the door already
Had closed upon me, then did she come out
In haste, as she had suddenly bethought herself,
And press'd me to her bosom, more with anguish
Than tenderness.

WALLENSTEIN (seizes her hand soothingly).
Nay, now collect yourself.
And what of Eggenberg and Lichtenstein,
And of our other friends there?

DUCHESS (shaking her head).
I saw none.

WALLENSTEIN.
The Ambassador from Spain, who once was wont
To plead so warmly for me!—

DUCHESS.
Silent, silent!

WALLENSTEIN.
These suns then are eclipsed for us. Henceforward
Must we roll on, our own fire, our own light.

DUCHESS.
And were it—were it, my dear lord, in that
Which moved about the court in buzz and whis-
But in the country let itself be heard   [per,
Aloud—in that which Father Lamormain
In sundry hints and——

WALLENSTEIN (eagerly).
Lamormain! what said he?

DUCHESS.
That you 're accused of having daringly
O'erstepp'd the powers entrusted to you, charged

With traitorous contempt of the Emperor
And his supreme behests. The proud Bavarian,
He and the Spaniards stand up your accusers—
That there's a storm collecting over you
Of far more fearful menace than that former one
Which whirl'd you headlong down at Regensburg.
And people talk, said he, of——Ah!—
[Stifling extreme emotion.

WALLENSTEIN.
Proceed!

DUCHESS.
I cannot utter it!

WALLENSTEIN.
Proceed!

DUCHESS.
They talk——

WALLENSTEIN.
Well!

DUCHESS.
Of a second——(catches her voice and hesitates).

WALLENSTEIN.
Second——

DUCHESS.
More disgraceful
——Dismission.

WALLENSTEIN.
Talk they?
[Strides across the Chamber in vehement agitation.
O! they force, they thrust me
With violence, against my own will, onward!

DUCHESS (presses near to him, in entreaty.)
O! if there yet be time, my husband! if
By giving way and by submission, this
Can be averted—my dear lord, give way!
Win down your proud heart to it! Tell that heart,
It is your sovereign lord, your Emperor
Before whom you retreat. O let no longer
Low tricking malice blacken your good meaning
With abhorr'd venomous glosses. Stand you up
Shielded and helm'd and weapon'd with the truth,
And drive before you into uttermost shame [we—
These slanderous liars! Few firm friends have
You know it!—The swift growth of our good for-
It hath but set us up a mark for hatred.   [tune,
What are we, if the sovereign's grace and favour
Stand not before us!

SCENE VIII.

Enter the Countess TERTSKY, leading in her hand the
Princess THEKLA, richly adorned with Brilliants.

COUNTESS, THEKLA, WALLENSTEIN, DUCHESS.

COUNTESS.
How, sister! What, already upon business;
[Observing the countenance of the DUCHESS.
And business of no pleasing kind I see,
Ere he has gladden'd at his child. The first
Moment belongs to joy. Here, Friedland! father!
This is thy daughter.
[THEKLA approaches with a shy and timid air, and
bends herself as about to kiss his hand. He receives
her in his arms, and remains standing for some
time lost in the feeling of her presence.

WALLENSTEIN.
Yes! pure and lovely hath hope risen on me:
I take her as the pledge of greater fortune.

DUCHESS.

'T was but a little child when you departed
To raise up that great army for the Emperor:
And after, at the close of the campaign,
When you return'd home out of Pomerania,
Your daughter was already in the convent,
Wherein she has remain'd till now.

WALLENSTEIN.

The while
We in the field here gave our cares and toils
To make her great, and fight her a free way
To the loftiest earthly good; lo! mother Nature
Within the peaceful silent convent walls
Has done her part, and out of her free grace
Hath she bestow'd on the beloved child
The godlike; and now leads her thus adorn'd
To meet her splendid fortune, and my hope.

DUCHESS (to THEKLA).

Thou wouldst not have recognised thy father,
Wouldst thou, my child! She counted scarce eight
When last she saw your face.   [years,

THEKLA.

O yes, yes, mother!
At the first glance!—My father is not alter'd.
The form that stands before me falsifies
No feature of the image that hath lived
So long within me!

WALLENSTEIN.

The voice of my child!
            [Then after a pause.
I was indignant at my destiny,
That it denied me a man-child to be
Heir of my name and of my prosperous fortune,
And re-illume my soon extinguish'd being
In a proud line of princes.
I wrong'd my destiny. Here upon this head,
So lovely in its maiden bloom, will I
Let fall the garland of a life of war,
Nor deem it lost, if only I can wreath it,
Transmitted to a regal ornament,
Around these beauteous brows,
            [He clasps her in his arms as PICCOLOMINI enters.

SCENE IX.

Enter MAX. PICCOLOMINI, *and some time after* COUNT
TERTSKY, *the others remaining as before.*

COUNTESS.

There comes the Paladin who protected us.

WALLENSTEIN.

Max.! Welcome, ever welcome! Always wert thou
The morning star of my best joys!

MAX.

My General——

WALLENSTEIN.

Till now it was the Emperor who rewarded thee,
I but the instrument. This day thou hast bound
The father to thee, Max.! the fortunate father,
And this debt Friedland's self must pay.

MAX.

My prince!
You made no common hurry to transfer it.
I come with shame: yes, not without a pang!
For scarce have I arrived here, scarce deliver'd
The mother and the daughter to your arms,
But there is brought to me from your equerry

A splendid richly-plated hunting dress
So to remunerate me for my troubles——
Yes, yes, remunerate me! Since a trouble
It must be, a mere office, not a favour
Which I leapt forward to receive, and which
I came already with full heart to thank you for.
No! 't was not so intended, that my business
Should be my highest best good-fortune!
            [TERTSKY enters, and delivers letters to the DUKE,
            which he breaks open hurryingly.

COUNTESS (to MAX.).

Remunerate your trouble! For his joy
He makes you recompense. 'T is not unfitting
For you, Count Piccolomini, to feel
So tenderly—my brother it beseems
To show himself for ever great and princely.

THEKLA.

Then I too must have scruples of his love:
For his munificent hands did ornament me
Ere yet the father's heart had spoken to me.

MAX.

Yes; 't is his nature ever to be giving
And making happy.
            [He grasps the hand of the DUCHESS with still in-
            creasing warmth.
            How my heart pours out
Its all of thanks to him! O! how I seem
To utter all things in the dear name Friedland.
While I shall live, so long will I remain
The captive of this name: in it shall bloom
My every fortune, every lovely hope.
Inextricably as in some magic ring
In this name hath my destiny charm-bound me!

COUNTESS (who during this time has been anxiously
watching the DUKE, and remarks that he is lost
in thought over the letters.)

My brother wishes us to leave him. Come.

WALLENSTEIN (turns himself round quick, collects
himself, and speaks with cheerfulness to the
DUCHESS.)

Once more I bid thee welcome to the camp,
Thou art the hostess of this court. You, Max.,
Will now again administer your old office,
While we perform the sovereign's business here.
            [MAX. PICCOLOMINI offers the DUCHESS his arm; the
            COUNTESS accompanies the PRINCESS.

TERTSKY (calling after him).

Max., we depend on seeing you at the meeting.

SCENE X.

WALLENSTEIN, COUNT TERTSKY.

WALLENSTEIN (in deep thought, to himself).

She hath seen all things as they are—It is so,
And squares completely with my other notices.
They have determined finally in Vienna,
Have given me my successor already;
It is the king of Hungary, Ferdinand,
The Emperor's delicate son! he's now their saviour,
He 's the new star that 's rising now! Of us
They think themselves already fairly rid,
And as we were deceased, the heir already
Is entering on possession—Therefore—despatch!
            [As he turns round he observes TERTSKY, and gives
            him a letter.

Count Altringer will have himself excused,
And Galas too—I like not this!

TERTSKY.

                    And if
Thou loiterest longer, all will fall away,
One following the other.

WALLENSTEIN.

                    Altringer
Is master of the Tyrol passes. I must forthwith
Send some one to him, that he let not in
The Spaniards on me from the Milanese.
——Well, and the old Sesin, that ancient trader
In contraband negociations, he
Has shown himself again of late. What brings he
From the Count Thur!

TERTSKY.

            The Count communicates,
He has found out the Swedish chancellor
At Halberstadt, where the convention's held,
Who says, you've tired him out, and that he'll have
No further dealings with you.

WALLENSTEIN.

                    And why so!

TERTSKY.

He says, you are never in earnest in your speeches;
That you decoy the Swedes—to make fools of them;
Will league yourself with Saxony against them,
And at last make yourself a riddance of them
With a paltry sum of money.

WALLENSTEIN.

                    So then, doubtless,
Yes, doubtless, this same modest Swede expects
That I shall yield him some fair German tract
For his prey and booty, that ourselves at last
On our own soil and native territory
May be no longer our own lords and masters!
An excellent scheme! No, no! They must be off,
Off, off! away! we want no such neighbours.

TERTSKY.

Nay, yield them up that dot, that speck of land—
It goes not from your portion. If you win
The game, what matters it to you who pays it!

WALLENSTEIN.

Off with them, off! Thou understand'st not this.
Never shall it be said of me, I parcell'd
My native land away, dismember'd Germany,
Betray'd it to a foreigner, in order
To come with stealthy tread, and filch away
My own share of the plunder—Never! never!
No foreign power thall strike root in the empire,
And least of all, these Goths! these hunger-wolves!
Who send such envious, hot and greedy glances
Toward the rich blessings of our German lands!
I'll have their aid to cast and draw my nets,
But not a single fish of all the draught
Shall they come in for.

TERTSKY.

                    You will deal, however,
More fairly with the Saxons! they lose patience
While you shift ground and make so many curves.
Say, to what purpose all these masks! Your friends
Are plunged in doubts, baffled, and led astray in you.
There's Oxenstein, there's Arnheim—neither knows
What he should think of your procrastinations.
And in the end I prove the liar; all
Passes through me. I have not even your hand-
    writing.

I never give my hand-writing; thou knowest it.

TERTSKY.

But how can it be known that you're in earnest,
If the act follows not upon the word!
You must yourself acknowledge, that in all
Your intercourses hitherto with the enemy,
You might have done with safety all you have done,
Had you meant nothing further than to gull him
For the Emperor's service.

WALLENSTEIN (after a pause, during which he looks
            narrowly on TERTSKY).

            And from whence dost thou know
That I'm not gulling him for the Emperor's service!
Whence knowest thou that I'm not gulling all of you!
Dost thou know me so well! When made I thee
The intendant of my secret purposes!
I am not conscious that I ever open'd
My inmost thoughts to thee. The Emperor, it is
Hath dealt with me amiss; and if I would, [true,
I could repay him with usurious interest
For the evil he hath done me. It delights me
To know my power; but whether I shall use it,
Of that, I should have thought that thou couldst
No wiselier than thy fellows.   [speak

TERTSKY.

So hast thou always played thy game with us.
                            [Enter ILLO.

————————

SCENE XI.

ILLO, WALLENSTEIN, TERTSKY.

WALLENSTEIN.

How stand affairs without! Are they prepared!

ILLO.

You'll find them in the very mood you wish.
They know about the Emperor's requisitions,
And are tumultuous.

WALLENSTEIN.

            How hath Isolan
Declared himself!

ILLO.

            He's your's, both soul and body,
Since you built up again his Faro-bank.

WALLENSTEIN.

And which way doth Kolatto bend! Hast thou
Made sure of Tiefenbach and Deodate!

ILLO.

What Piccolomini does, that they do too.

WALLENSTEIN.

You mean, then, I may venture somewhat with them!

ILLO.

—If you are assured of the Piccolomini.

WALLENSTEIN.

Not more assured of mine own self.

TERTSKY.

                    And yet
I would you trusted not so much to Octavio,
The fox!

WALLENSTEIN.

        Thou teachest me to know my man!
Sixteen campaigns I have made with that old
Besides, I have his horoscope: [warrior.
We both are born beneath like stars—in short,
                    [With an air of mystery.

To this belongs its own peculiar aspect,
If therefore thou canst warrant me the rest——

ILLO.

There is among them all but this one voice,
You *must* not lay down the command. I hear
They mean to send a deputation to you

WALLENSTEIN.

If I'm in aught to bind myself to them,
They too must bind themselves to me.

ILLO.
                                        Of course.

WALLENSTEIN.

Their words of honour they must give, their oaths,
Give them in writing to me, promising
Devotion to my service *unconditional.*

ILLO.

Why not?

TERTSKY.

Devotion *unconditional?*
The exception of their duties towards Austria
They'll always place among the premises.
With this reserve——

WALLENSTEIN (*shaking his head*).
                            All *unconditional!*
No premises, no reserves.

ILLO.
                  A thought has struck me.
Does not Count Tertsky give us a set banquet
This evening?

TERTSKY.
            Yes; and all the Generals
Have been invited.

ILLO (*to* WALLENSTEIN).
                  Say, will you here fully
Commission me to use my own discretion?
I'll gain for you the Generals' words of honour,
Even as you wish

WALLENSTEIN.
            Gain me their signatures!
How you come by them, that is *your* concern.

ILLO.

And if I bring it to you, black on white,
That all the leaders who are present here
Give themselves up to you, without condition;
Say, will you *then*—*then* will you show yourself
In earnest, and with some decisive action
Make trial of your luck?

WALLENSTEIN.
                  The signatures!
Gain me the signatures.

ILLO.
            Seize, seize the hour,
Ere it slips from you. Seldom comes the moment
In life, which is indeed sublime and weighty.
To make a great decision possible,
O! many things, all transient and all repaid,
Must meet at once: and, haply, they thus met
May by that confluence be enforced to pause
Time long enough for wisdom, though too short,
Far, far too short a time for doubt and scruple!
This is that moment. See, our army chieftains,
Our best, our noblest, are assembled around you
Their king-like leader! On your nod they wait.
The single threads, which here your prosperous
Hath woven together in one potent web [fortune
Instinct with destiny, O let them not
Unravel of themselves. If you permit

These chiefs to separate, so unanimous
Bring you them not a second time together.
'Tis the high tide that heaves the stranded ship,
And every individual's spirit waxes
In the great stream of multitudes. Behold
They are still here, here still! But soon the war
Bursts them once more asunder, and in small
Particular anxieties and interests
Scatters their spirit, and the sympathy
Of each man with the whole. He, who to-day
Forgets himself, forced onward with the stream,
Will become sober, seeing but himself.
Feel only his own weakness, and with speed
Will face about, and march on in the old
High road of duty, the old broad-trodden road,
And seek but to make shelter in good plight.

WALLENSTEIN.

The time is not yet come.

TERTSKY.
                  So you say always.
But *when* will it be time?

WALLENSTEIN.
                  When I shall say it.

ILLO.

You'll wait upon the stars, and on their hours,
Till the earthly hour escapes you. O, believe me,
In your own bosom are your destiny's stars.
Confidence in yourself, prompt resolution,
This is your Venus! and the sole malignant,
The only one that harmeth you, is Doubt.

WALLENSTEIN.

Thou speakest as thou understand'st. How oft
And many a time I've told thee, Jupiter,
That lustrous god, was setting at thy birth.
Thy visual power subdues no mysteries;
Mole-eyed, thou mayest but burrow in the earth,
Blind as that subterrestrial, who with wan
Lead-colour'd shine lighted thee into life.
The common, the terrestrial, thou mayest see,
With serviceable cunning knit together
The nearest with the nearest; and therein
I trust thee and believe thee! but whate'er
Full of mysterious import Nature weaves,
And fashions in the depths—the spirit's ladder,
That from this gross and visible world of dust
Even to the starry world, with thousand rounds,
Builds itself up; on which the unseen powers
Move up and down on heavenly ministeries—
The circles in the circles, that approach
The central sun with ever-narrowing orbit—
These see the glance alone, the unsealed eye,
Of Jupiter's glad children born in lustre.

[*He walks across the Chamber, then returns, and
standing still, proceeds.*

The heavenly constellations make not merely
The day and nights, summer and spring, not merely
Signify to the husbandman the seasons
Of sowing and of harvest. Human action,
That is the seed too of contingencies,
Strew'd on the dark land of futurity
In hopes to reconcile the powers of fate.
Whence it behoves us to seek out the seed-time,
To watch the stars, select their proper hours,
And trace with searching eye the heavenly houses,
Whether the enemy of growth and thriving
Hide himself not, malignant, in his corner.
Therefore permit me my own time. Meanwhile
Do you your part. As yet I cannot say
What *I* shall do—only, give way I will not.

Depose me too they shall not. On these points
You may rely.

PAGE (entering).
My Lords, the Generals.

WALLENSTEIN.
Let them come in.

———

SCENE XII.

WALLENSTEIN, TERZKY, ILLO.—To them enter QUESTEN-
BERG, OCTAVIO and MAX. PICCOLOMINI, BUTLER, ISOLANI,
MARADAS, and three other Generals. WALLENSTEIN
motions QUESTENBERG, who in consequence takes the
chair directly opposite to him ; the others follow, arrang-
ing themselves according to their rank. There reigns a
momentary silence.

WALLENSTEIN.
I have understood, 't is true, the sum and import
Of your instructions, Questenberg ; have weighed
And formed my final, absolute resolve :   [them,
Yet it seems fitting, that the Generals
Should hear the will of the Emperor from your
mouth.
May't please you then to open your commission
Before these noble Chieftains ?

QUESTENBERG.
                    I am ready
To obey you ; but will first entreat your Highness,
And all these noble Chieftains, to consider,
The Imperial dignity and sovereign right   [tion.
Speaks from my mouth, and not my own presump-

WALLENSTEIN.
We excuse all preface.

QUESTENBERG.
                When his Majesty
The Emperor to his courageous armies
Presented in the person of Duke Friedland
A most experienced and renown'd commander,
He did it in glad hope and confidence
To give thereby to the fortune of the war
A rapid and auspicious change. The onset
Was favourable to his royal wishes.
Bohemia was delivered from the Saxons,   [lands
The Swede's career of conquest check'd ! These
Began to draw breath freely, as Duke Friedland
From all the streams of Germany forced hither
The scattered armies of the enemy ;
Hither invoked as round one magic circle
The Rhinegrave, Bernhard, Banner, Oxenstein,
Yea, and that never-conquer'd King himself ;
Here finally, before the eye of Nürnberg,
The fearful game of battle to decide.

WALLENSTEIN.
May't please you, to the point.

QUESTENBERG.
In Nürnberg's camp the Swedish monarch left
His fame—in Lützen's plains his life. But who
Stood not astounded, when victorious Friedland
After this day of triumph, this proud day,
March'd toward Bohemia with the speed of flight,
And vanish'd from the theatre of war !
While the young Weimar hero forced his way
Into Franconia, to the Danube, like
Some delving winter-stream, which, where it rushes,
Makes its own channel, with such sudden speed
He marched, and now at once 'fore Regensburg
Stood to the affright of all good Catholic Christians.
Then did Bavaria's well-deserving Prince

Entreat swift aidance in his extreme need ; [land,
The Emperor sends seven horsemen to Duke Fried-
Seven horsemen couriers sends he with the entreaty :
He superadds his own, and supplicates
Where as the sovereign lord he can command.
In vain his supplication ! At this moment
The Duke hears only his old hate and grudge,
Barters the general good to gratify
Private revenge—and so falls Regensburg.

WALLENSTEIN.
Max., to what period of the war alludes he ?
My recollection fails me here.

MAX.
                He means
When we were in Silesia.

WALLENSTEIN.
                Ay ! is it so !
But what had we to do there ?

MAX.
                To beat out
The Swedes and Saxons from the province.

WALLENSTEIN.
                True ;
In that description which the Minister gave,
I seemed to have forgotten the whole war.
                    [To QUESTENBERG.
Well, but proceed a little.

QUESTENBERG.
                Yes ; at length
Beside the river Oder did the Duke
Assert his ancient fame. Upon the fields
Of Steinau did the Swedes lay down their arms,
Subdued without a blow. And here, with others,
The righteousness of Heaven to his avenger
Deliver'd that long-practised stirrer-up
Of insurrection, that curse-laden torch
And kindler of this war, Matthias Thur.
But he had fallen into magnanimous hands ;
Instead of punishment he found reward,
And with rich presents did the Duke dismiss
The arch-foe of his Emperor.

WALLENSTEIN (laughs).
                I know,
I know you had already in Vienna
Your windows and balconies all forestall'd
To see him on the executioner's cart.
I might have lost the battle, lost it too
With infamy, and still retain'd your graces—
But, to have cheated them of a spectacle,
Oh ! that the good folks of Vienna never,
No, never can forgive me !

QUESTENBERG.
                So Silesia
Was freed, and all things loudly called the Duke
Into Bavaria, now press'd hard on all sides.
And he did put his troops in motion : slowly,
Quite at his ease, and by the longest road
He traverses Bohemia ; but ere ever
He hath once seen the enemy, faces round,
Breaks up the march, and takes to winter-quarters.

WALLENSTEIN.
The troops were pitiably destitute
Of every necessary, every comfort.
The winter came. What thinks his Majesty
His troops are made of ! An't we men ? subjected
Like other men to wet, and cold, and all
The circumstances of necessity !

O miserable lot of the poor soldier!
Wherever he comes in, all flee before him,
And when he goes away, the general curse
Follows him on his route.   All must be seized,
Nothing is given him.   And compell'd to seize
From every man, he's every man's abhorrence.
Behold, here stand my Generals.   Karaffa!
Count Deodate! Butler! Tell this man
How long the soldiers' pay is in arrears.

BUTLER.
Already a full year.

WALLENSTEIN.
And 't is the hire
That constitutes the hireling's name and duties,
The soldier's *pay* is the soldier's *covenant*[1].

QUESTENBERG.
Ah! this is a far other tone from that,
In which the Duke spoke eight, nine years ago.

WALLENSTEIN.
Yes! 't is my fault, I know it: I myself
Have spoilt the Emperor by indulging him.
Nine years ago, during the Danish war,
I raised him up a force, a mighty force,
Forty or fifty thousand men, that cost him
Of his own purse no doit.   Through Saxony
The fury goddess of the war march'd on,
E'en to the surf-rocks of the Baltic, bearing
The terrors of his name.   That was a time!
In the whole Imperial realm no name like mine
Honour'd with festival and celebration—
And Albrecht Wallenstein, it was the title
Of the third jewel in his crown!
But at the Diet, when the Princes met
At Regensburg, there, there the whole broke out,
There 't was laid open, there it was made known,
Out of what money-bag I had paid the host.
And what was now my thank, what had I now,
That I, a faithful servant of the Sovereign,
Had loaded on myself the people's curses,
And let the Princes of the empire pay
The expenses of this war, that aggrandizes
The Emperor alone—What thanks had I!
What! I was offer'd up to their complaints,
Dismiss'd, degraded!

QUESTENBERG.
But your Highness knows
What little freedom he possess'd of action
In that disastrous diet.

WALLENSTEIN.
Death and hell!
I had that which could have procured him freedom.
No! Since 't was proved so inauspicious to me
To serve the Emperor at the empire's cost,
I have been taught far other trains of thinking
Of the empire, and the diet of the empire.
From the Emperor, doubtless, I received this staff,
But now I hold it as the empire's general—
For the common weal, the universal interest,

---

[1] The original is not translatable into English :
——Und sein Sold
Muss dem *Soldaten* werden, darnach heisst er.
It might perhaps have been thus rendered :
And that for which he sold his services,
The soldier must receive—
but a false or doubtful etymology is no more than a dull
pun.

And no more for that one man's aggrandizement!
But to the point.   What is it that's desired of me!

QUESTENBERG.
First, his Imperial Majesty hath will'd
That without pretexts of delay the army
Evacuate Bohemia.

WALLENSTEIN.
In this season!
And to what quarter wills the Emperor
That we direct our course!

QUESTENBERG.
To the enemy.
His Majesty resolves, that Regensburg
Be purified from the enemy ere Easter,
That Lutheranism may be no longer preach'd
In that cathedral, nor heretical
Defilement desecrate the celebration
Of that pure festival.

WALLENSTEIN.
My generals,
Can this be realised!

ILLO.
'T is not possible.

BUTLER.
It can't be realised.

QUESTENBERG.
The Emperor
Already hath commanded colonel Suys
To advance toward Bavaria.

WALLENSTEIN.
What did Suys!

QUESTENBERG.
That which his duty prompted.   He advanced!

WALLENSTEIN.
What! he advanced! And I, his general,
Had given him orders, peremptory orders,
Not to desert his station! Stands it thus
With my authority! Is this the obedience
Due to my office, which being thrown aside,
No war can be conducted!   Chieftains, speak!
You be the judges, generals!   What deserves
That officer who, of his oath neglectful,
Is guilty of contempt of orders!

ILLO.
Death.

WALLENSTEIN (*raising his voice, as all, but* ILLO
had remained silent, and seemingly scrupulous).
Count Piccolomini! what has he deserved!

MAX. PICCOLOMINI (*after a long pause*).
According to the letter of the law,
Death.

ISOLANI.
Death.

BUTLER.
Death, by the laws of war.
[QUESTENBERG *rises from his seat,* WALLENSTEIN *follows ; all the rest rise.*

WALLENSTEIN.
To this the law condemns him, and not I.
And if I show him favour, 't will arise
From the reverence that I owe my Emperor.

QUESTENBERG.
If *so*, I can say nothing further—*here!*

WALLENSTEIN.

I accepted the command but on conditions:
And this the first, that to the diminution
Of my authority no human being,
Not even the Emperor's self, should be entitled
To do aught, or to say aught, with the army.
If I stand warranter of the *event*,
Placing my honour and my head in pledge,
Needs must I have full mastery in all
The means thereto. What render'd this Gustavus
Resistless, and unconquer'd upon earth?
This—that he was the monarch in his army!
A monarch, one who is indeed a monarch,
Was never yet subdued but by his equal.
But to the point! The best is yet to come.
Attend now, generals!

QUESTENBERG.
                    The Prince Cardinal
Begins his route at the approach of spring
From the Milanese; and leads a Spanish army
Through Germany into the Netherlands.
That he may march secure and unimpeded,
'Tis the Emperor's will you grant him a detachment,
Of eight horse-regiments from the army here.

WALLENSTEIN.

Yes, yes! I understand!—Eight regiments! Well,
Right well concerted, father Lamormain!
Eight thousand horse! Yes, yes! 'Tis as it should
I see it coming.   [be!

QUESTENBERG.
                There is nothing coming.
All stands in front: the counsel of state-prudence,
The dictate of necessity!——

WALLENSTEIN.
                What then!
What, my Lord Envoy! May I not be suffer'd
To understand, that folks are tired of seeing
The sword's hilt in *my* grasp: and that your court
Snatch eagerly at this pretence, and use
The Spanish title, to drain off my forces,
To lead into the empire a new army
Unsubjected to my control? To throw me
Plumply aside,—I am still too powerful for you
To venture that. My stipulation runs,
That all the Imperial forces shall obey me
Where'er the German is the native language.
Of Spanish troops and of Prince Cardinals
That take their route as visitors, through the empire,
There stands no syllable in my stipulation.
No syllable! And so the politic court
Steals in a tiptoe, and creeps round behind it;
First makes me weaker, then to be dispensed with,
Till it dares strike at length a bolder blow
And make short work with me.
What need of all these crooked ways, Lord Envoy?
Straight-forward, man! His compact with me pinches
The Emperor. He would that I moved off!—
Well!—I will gratify him!
      [*Here there commences an agitation among the
       Generals, which increases continually.*
It grieves me for my noble officers' sakes!
I see not yet, by what means they will come at
The moneys they have advanced, or how obtain
The recompense their services demand.
Still a new leader brings new claimants forward,
And prior merit superannuates quickly.
There serve here many foreigners in the army,
And were the man in all else brave and gallant,

I was not wont to make nice scrutiny
After his pedigree or catechism.
This will be otherwise, i' the time to come.
Well—me no longer it concerns.   [*He seats himself.*

MAX. PICCOLOMINI.
Forbid it Heaven, that it should come to this!
Our troops will swell in dreadful fermentation—
The Emperor is abused—it cannot be.

ISOLANI.
It cannot be; all goes to instant wreck.

WALLENSTEIN.
Thou hast said truly, faithful Isolani!
What *we* with toil and foresight have built up,
Will go to wreck—all go to instant wreck.
What then! another chieftain is soon found,
Another army likewise (who dares doubt it?)
Will flock from all sides to the Emperor,
At the first beat of his recruiting drum.
      [*During this speech, ISOLANI, TERTSKY, ILLO, and
       MARADAS talk confusedly with great agitation.*

MAX. PICCOLOMINI (*busily and passionately going
from one to another, and soothing them*).

Hear, my commander! Hear me, generals!
Let me conjure you, Duke! Determine nothing,
Till we have met and represented to you
Our joint remonstrances.—Nay, calmer! Friends!
I hope all may yet be set right again.

TERTSKY.
Away! let us away! in the antechamber
Find we the others.   [*They go.*

BUTLER (*to* QUESTENBERG).
            If good counsel gain
Due audience from your wisdom, my Lord Envoy!
You will be cautious how you show yourself
In public for some hours to come—or hardly
Will that gold key protect you from mal-treatment.
      [*Commotions heard from without.*

WALLENSTEIN.
A salutary counsel——Thou, Octavio!
Wilt answer for the safety of our guest.
Farewell, Von Questenberg.
      [QUESTENBERG *is about to speak.*
                    Nay, not a word.
Not one word more of that detested subject!
You have perform'd your duty—We know how
To separate the office from the man.
      [*As* QUESTENBERG *is going off with* OCTAVIO; GORTZ,
       TIEFENBACH, KOLATTO, *press in; several other
       Generals following them.*

GOETZ.
Where's he who means to rob us of our general?

TIEFENBACH (*at the same time*).
What are we forced to hear! That thou wilt leave us?

KOLATTO (*at the same time*).
We will live with thee, we will die with thee.

WALLENSTEIN (*with stateliness, and pointing to
ILLO*).

There! the Field-Marshal knows our will. [*Exit.*
      [*While all are going off the stage, the curtain drops.*

————

ACT II.

SCENE I.

A small Chamber.

ILLO *and* TERTSKY.

TERTSKY.

Now for this evening's business ! How intend you
To manage with the generals at the banquet !

ILLO.

Attend ! We frame a formal declaration,
Wherein we to the Duke consign ourselves
Collectively, to be and to remain
His both with life and limb, and not to spare
The last drop of our blood for *him,* provided
So doing we infringe no oath or duty,
We may be under to the Emperor.—Mark !
This reservation we expressly make
In a particular clause, and save the conscience.
Now hear ! this formula so framed and worded
Will be presented to them for perusal
Before the banquet. No one will find in it
Cause of offence or scruple. Hear now further !
After the feast, when now the vap'ring wine
Opens the heart, and shuts the eyes, we let
A counterfeited paper, in the which
This one particular clause has been left out,
Go round for signatures.

TERTSKY.

How ! think you then
That they'll believe themselves bound by an oath,
Which we had trick'd them into by a juggle !

ILLO.

We shall have caught and caged them ! Let them
then
Beat their wings bare against the wires, and rave
Loud as they may against our treachery ;
At court their signatures will be believed
Far more than their most holy affirmations.
Traitors they are, and must be ; therefore wisely
Will make a virtue of necessity.

TERTSKY.

Well, well, it shall content me ; let but something
Be *done,* let only some decisive blow
Set us in motion.

ILLO.

Besides, 'tis of subordinate importance
How, or how far, we may thereby propel
The generals. 'Tis enough that we persuade
The Duke that they are his—Let him but act
In his determined mood, as if he had them,
And he *will* have them. Where he plunges in,
He makes a whirlpool, and all stream down to it.

TERTSKY.

His policy is such a labyrinth,
That many a time when I have thought myself
Close at his side, he's gone at once, and left me
Ignorant of the ground where I was standing.
He lends the enemy his ear, permits me
To write to them, to Arnheim ; to Sesina
Himself comes forward blank and undisguised ;
Talks with us by the hour about his plans.
And when I think I have him—off at once——
He has slipp'd from me, and appears as if
He had no scheme, but to retain his place.

ILLO.

He give up his old plans ! I'll tell you, friend !
His soul is occupied with nothing else, [dreams,
Even in his sleep—They are his thoughts, his
That day by day he questions for this purpose
The motions of the planets——

TERTSKY.

Ay ! you know
This night, that is now coming, he with SENI
Shuts himself up in the astrological tower
To make joint observations—for I hear,
It is to be a night of weight and crisis ;
And something great, and of long expectation,
Is to make its procession in the heaven.

ILLO.

Come ! be we bold and make despatch. The work
In this next day or two must thrive and grow
More than it has for years. And let but only
Things first turn up auspicious here below——
Mark what I say—the right stars too will show
themselves.
Come, to the generals. All is in the glow,
And must be beaten while 'tis malleable.

TERTSKY.

Do you go thither, Illo. I must stay
And *wait* here for the Countess Tertsky. Know,
That we too are not idle. Break one string,
A second is in readiness.

ILLO.

Yes ! yes !
I saw your lady smile with such sly meaning.
What's in the wind !

TERTSKY.

A secret. Hush ! she comes.
[*Exit* ILLO.

SCENE II.

(*The* COUNTESS *steps out from a Closet.*)

COUNT *and* COUNTESS TERTSKY.

TERTSKY.

Well—is she coming—I can keep him back
No longer.

COUNTESS.

She will be here instantly,
You only send him.

TERTSKY.

I am not quite certain
I must confess it, Countess, whether or not
We are earning the Duke's thanks hereby. You
know,
No ray has broke out from him on this point.
You have o'er-ruled me, and yourself know best,
How far you dare proceed.

COUNTESS.

I take it on me.
[*Talking to herself while she is advancing.*
Here's no need of full powers and commissions——
My cloudy Duke ! we understand each other—
And without words. What, could I not unriddle,
Wherefore the daughter should be sent for hither,
Why first *he,* and no other, should be chosen

To fetch her hither! This sham of betrothing her
To a bridegroom,[1] whom no one knows—No! no!—
This may blind others! I see through thee, Brother!
But it beseems thee not, to draw a card
At such a game.   Not yet!—It all remains
Mutely delivered up to my finessing——
Well—thou shalt not have been deceived, Duke
In her who is thy-sister.——   [Friedland!

SERVANT (*enters*).
                    The commanders!

TERTSKY (*to the* COUNTESS).
Take care you heat his fancy and affections—
Possess him with a reverie, and send him,
Absent and dreaming, to the banquet; that
He may not boggle at the signature.

COUNTESS.
Take you care of your guests!—Go, send him hither.

TERTSKY.
All rests upon his undersigning.

COUNTESS (*interrupting him*).
Go to your guests! Go——

ILLO (*comes back*).
                    Where art staying, Tertsky!
The house is full, and all expecting you.

TERTSKY.
Instantly! instantly!   [*To the* COUNTESS.
                    And let him not
Stay here too long.   It might awake suspicion
In the old man——

COUNTESS.
                A truce with your precautions!
                    [*Exeunt* TERTSKY *and* ILLO.

SCENE III.

COUNTESS, MAX. PICCOLOMINI.

MAX. (*peeping in on the stage shily.*)
Aunt Tertsky! may I venture!
    [*Advances to the middle of the stage, and looks
        around him with uneasiness.*
                    She's not here!
Where is she!

COUNTESS.
Look but somewhat narrowly
In yonder corner, lest perhaps she lie
Conceal'd behind that screen.

MAX.
                    There lie her gloves!
[*Snatches at them, but the* COUNTESS *takes them herself.*
You unkind Lady! You refuse me this—
You make it an amusement to torment me.

COUNTESS.
And this the thank you give me for my trouble!

MAX.
O, if you felt the oppression at *my* heart!
Since we've been here, so to constrain myself—
With such poor stealth to hazard words and
These, these are not my habits!   [*glances—*

[1] In Germany, after honourable addresses have been
paid and formally accepted, the lovers are called Bride
and Bridegroom, even though the marriage should not
take place till years afterwards.

COUNTESS.
                    You have still
Many new habits to acquire, young friend!
But on this proof of your obedient temper
I must continue to insist; and only
On this condition can I play the agent
For your concerns.

MAX.
        But wherefore comes she not!
Where is she!

COUNTESS.
            Into *my* hands you must place it
Whole and entire.   Whom could you find, indeed,
More zealously affected to your interest!
No soul on earth must know it—not your father.
He must not, above all.

MAX.
                Alas! what danger!
Here is no face on which I might concentre
All the enraptured soul stirs up within me.
O Lady! tell me.   Is all changed around me!
Or is it only I.!
            I find myself,
As among strangers!   Not a trace is left
Of all my former wishes, former joys.
Where has it vanish'd to!   There was a time
When even, methought, with such a world, as this,
I was not discontented.   Now how flat!
How stale! No life, no bloom, no flavour in it!
My comrades are intolerable to me.
My father—Even to him I can say nothing.
My arms, my military duties—O!
They are such wearying toys!

COUNTESS.
            But, gentle friend!
I must entreat it of your condescension,
You would be pleased to sink your eye, and favour
With one short glance or two this poor stale world,
Where even now much, and of much moment,
Is on the eve of its completion.

MAX.
            Something,
I can't but know, is going forward round me.
I see it gathering, crowding, driving on,
In wild uncustomary movements.   Well,
In due time, doubtless, it will reach even me.
Where think you I have been, dear lady! Nay,
No raillery.   The turmoil of the camp,
The spring-tide of acquaintance rolling in,
The pointless jest, the empty conversation,
Oppress'd and stifled me.   I gasp'd for air—
I could not breathe—I was constrain'd to fly,
To seek a silence out for my full heart;
And a pure spot wherein to feel my happiness.
No smiling, Countess!   In the church was I.
There is a cloister here to the heaven's gate,[2]
Thither I went, there found myself alone.
Over the altar hung a holy mother;
A wretched painting 'twas, yet 'twas the friend
That I was seeking in this moment.   Ah,
How oft have I beheld that glorious form
In splendour, 'mid ecstatic worshippers;
Yet, still it moved me not! and now at once
Was my devotion cloudless as my love.

[2] I am doubtful whether this be the dedication of the
cloister or the name of one of the city gates, near which it
stood. I have translated it in the former sense; but fearful
of having made some blunder, I add the original.—Es ist
ein Kloster hier *zur Himmelspforte*.

COUNTESS.

Enjoy your fortune and felicity !
Forget the world around you. Meantime, friendship
Shall keep strict vigils for you, anxious, active.
Only be manageable when that friendship
Points you the road to full accomplishment.
How long may it be since you declared your
    passion ?

MAX.

This morning did I hazard the first word.

COUNTESS.

This morning the first time in twenty days !

MAX.

'T was at that hunting-castle, betwixt here
And Nepomuck, where *you* had join'd us, and—
That was the last relay of the whole journey !
In a balcony we were standing mute,
And gazing out upon the dreary field :
Before us the dragoons were riding onward,
The safe-guard which the Duke had sent us—heavy
The inquietude of parting lay upon me,
And trembling ventured I at length these words :
This all reminds me, noble maiden, that
To-day I must take leave of my good fortune.
A few hours more, and you will find a father,
Will see yourself surrounded by new friends,
And I henceforth shall be but as a stranger,
Lost in the many—"Speak with my aunt Tertsky !"
With hurrying voice she interrupted me.
She falter'd. I beheld a glowing red
Possess her beautiful cheeks, and from the ground
Raised slowly up her eye met mine—no longer
Did I control myself.

[*The Princess* THEKLA *appears at the door, and
    remains standing, observed by the* COUNTESS,
    but not by PICCOLOMINI.

With instant boldness
I caught her in my arms, my mouth touch'd hers ;
There was a rustling in the room close by ;
It parted us—'Twas you. What since has hap-
You know.   [pen'd,

COUNTESS (*after a pause, with a stolen glance at*
    THEKLA).

And is it your excess of modesty ;
Or are you so incurious, that you do not
Ask me too of my secret ?

MAX.

Of *your* secret ?

COUNTESS.

Why, yes ! When in the instant after you
I stepp'd into the room, and found my niece there,
What she in this first moment of the heart
Ta'en with surprise—

MAX. (*with eagerness*).

Well ?

———————

SCENE IV.

THEKLA *hurries forward*), COUNTESS, MAX. PICCOLOMINI.

THEKLA (*to the* COUNTESS).

Spare yourself the trouble :
That hears he better from myself.

MAX. (*stepping backward*).

My Princess !
What have you let her hear me say, aunt Tertsky !

THEKLA (*to the* COUNTESS).

Has he been here long ?

COUNTESS.

Yes ; and soon must go.
Where have *you* stay'd so long ?

THEKLA.

Alas ! my mother
Wept so again ! and I—I see her suffer,
Yet cannot keep myself from being happy.

MAX.

Now once again I have courage to look on you.
To-day at noon I could not.
The dazzle of the jewels that play'd round you
Hid the beloved from me.

THEKLA.

Then you saw me
With your eye only—and not with your heart !

MAX.

This morning, when I found you in the circle
Of all your kindred, in your father's arms,
Beheld myself an alien in this circle,
O ! what an impulse felt I in that moment
To fall upon his neck, to call him *father !*
But his stern eye o'erpower'd the swelling passion,
It dared not but be silent. And those brilliants,
That like a crown of stars enwreathed your brows,
They scared me too ! O wherefore, wherefore should
At the first meeting spread as 'twere the ban [he
Of excommunication round you,—wherefore
Dress up the angel as for sacrifice,
And cast upon the light and joyous heart
The mournful burthen of *his* station ! Fitly
May love dare woo for love ; but such a splendour
Might none but monarchs venture to approach.

THEKLA.

Hush ! not a word more of this mummery ;
You see how soon the burthen is thrown off.
                              [*To the* COUNTESS.
He is not in spirits. Wherefore is he not ?
'T is you, aunt, that have made him all so gloomy !
He had quite another nature on the journey—
So calm, so bright, so joyous eloquent. [*To* MAX.
It was my wish to see you always so,
And never otherwise !

MAX.

You find yourself
In your great father's arms, beloved lady !
All in a new world, which does homage to you,
And which, were't only by its novelty,
Delights your eye.

THEKLA.

Yes ; I confess to you
That many things delight me here : this camp,
This motley stage of warriors, which renews
So manifold the image of my fancy,
And binds to life, binds to reality,
What hitherto had but been present to me
As a sweet dream !

MAX.

Alas ! not so to me.
It makes a dream of my reality.
Upon some island in the ethereal heights
I've lived for these last days. This mass of men
Forces me down to earth. It is a bridge
That, reconducting to my former life,
Divides me and my heaven.

THEKLA.

The game of life
Looks cheerful, when one carries in one's heart

c

The unalienable treasure. 'Tis a game,
Which having once review'd, I turn more joyous
Back to my deeper and appropriate bliss.
[Breaking off, and in a sportive tone.
In this short time that I've been present here,
What new unheard-of things have I not seen !
And yet they all must give place to the wonder
Which this mysterious castle guards.

COUNTESS (recollecting).
                              And what
Can this be then ! Methought I was acquainted
With all the dusky corners of this house.

THEKLA (smiling).
Ay, but the road thereto is watch'd by spirits,
Two griffins still stand sentry at the door.

COUNTESS (laughs).
The astrological tower !—How happens it
That this same sanctuary, whose access
Is to all others so impracticable,
Opens before you even at your approach !

THEKLA.
A dwarfish old man with a friendly face
And snow-white hairs, whose gracious services
Were mine at first sight, open'd me the doors.

MAX.
That is the Duke's astrologer, old Seni.

THEKLA.
He question'd me on many points ; for instance,
When I was born, what month, and on what day,
Whether by day or in the night.

COUNTESS.
                           He wish'd
To erect a figure for your horoscope.

THEKLA.
My hand too he examined, shook his head
With much sad meaning, and the lines, methought,
Did not square over truly with his wishes.

COUNTESS.
Well, Princess, and what found you in this tower !
My highest privilege has been to snatch
A side-glance, and away !

THEKLA.
              It was a strange
Sensation that came o'er me, when at first
From the broad sunshine I stepp'd in ; and now
The narrowing line of daylight, that ran after
The closing door, was gone ; and all about me
'T was pale and dusky night, with many shadows
Fantastically cast. Here six or seven
Colossal statues, and all kings, stood round me
In a half-circle. Each one in his hand
A sceptre bore, and on his head a star ;
And in the tower no other light was there
But from these stars: all seem'd to come from them.
" These are the planets," said that low old man,
" They govern worldly fates, and for that cause
Are imaged here as kings. He farthest from you,
Spiteful, and cold, an old man melancholy,
With bent and yellow forehead, he is Saturn.
He opposite, the king with the red light,
An arm'd man for the battle, that is Mars ;
And both these bring but little luck to man."
But at his side a lovely lady stood,
The star upon her head was soft and bright,
On that was Venus, the bright star of joy.
And the left hand, lo ! Mercury, with wings.

Quite in the middle glitter'd silver bright
A cheerful man, and with a monarch's mien ;
And this was Jupiter, my father's star :
And at his side I saw the Sun and Moon.

MAX.
O never rudely will I blame his faith
In the might of stars and angels ! 'T is not merely
The human being's Pride that peoples space
With life and mystical predominance ;
Since likewise for the stricken heart of Love
This visible nature, and this common world,
Is all too narrow ; yea, a deeper import
Lurks in the legend told my infant years
Than lies upon that truth, we live to learn.
For fable is Love's world, his home, his birth-place
Delightedly dwells he 'mong fays and talismans,
And spirits ; and delightedly believes
Divinities, being himself divine.
The intelligible forms of ancient poets,
The fair humanities of old religion,
The Power, the Beauty, and the Majesty,
That had her haunts in dale, or piny mountain,
Or forest by slow stream, or pebbly spring,
Or chasms and wat'ry depths ; all these have
    vanish'd.
They live no longer in the faith of reason !
But still the heart doth need a language, still
Doth the old instinct bring back the old names,
And to yon starry world they now are gone,
Spirits or gods, that used to share this earth
With man as with their friend ;[1] and to the lover
Yonder they move, from yonder visible sky
Shoot influence down : and even at this day
'T is Jupiter who brings whate'er is great,
And Venus who brings every thing that 's fair !

THEKLA.
And if this be the science of the stars,
I too, with glad and zealous industry,
Will learn acquaintance with this cheerful faith.
It is a gentle and affectionate thought,
That in immeasurable heights above us,
At our first birth, the wreath of love was woven,
With sparkling stars for flowers.

COUNTESS.
                    Not only roses,
But thorns too hath the heaven, and well for you
Leave they your wreath of love inviolate :
What Venus twined, the bearer of glad fortune,
The sullen orb of Mars soon tears to pieces.

MAX.
Soon will his gloomy empire reach its close.
Blest be the General's zeal : into the laurel
Will he inweave the olive-branch, presenting
Peace to the shouting nations. Then no wish
Will have remain'd for his great heart ! Enough
Has he perform'd for glory, and can now
Live for himself and his. To his domains
Will he retire ; he has a stately seat
Of fairest view at Gitschin ; Reichenberg,
And Friedland Castle, both lie pleasantly—
Even to the foot of the huge mountains here
Stretches the chase and covers of his forests :
His ruling passion, to create the splendid
He can indulge without restraint ; can give
A princely patronage to every art,

---
[1] No more of talk, where god or angel guest
      With man, as with his friend familiar, used
      To sit indulgent.   *Paradise Lost*, B. IX.

And to all worth a Sovereign's protection.
Can build, can plant, can watch the starry courses—

COUNTESS.
Yet I would have you look, and look again,
Before you lay aside your arms, young friend !
A gentle bride, as she is, is well worth it,
That you should woo and win her with the sword.

MAX.
O, that the sword could win her !

COUNTESS.
What was that !
Did you hear nothing ! Seem'd, as if I heard
Tumult and larum in the banquet-room.
[*Exit* COUNTESS.

———◆———

SCENE V.

THEKLA *and* MAX. PICCOLOMINI.

THEKLA (*as soon as the* COUNTESS *is out of sight, in
a quick low voice to* PICCOLOMINI).
Don't trust them ! They are false !

MAX.
Impossible !

THEKLA.
Trust no one here but me. I saw at once,
They had a *purpose.*

MAX.
Purpose ! but what purpose !
And how can we be instrumental to it ?

THEKLA.
I know no more than you ; but yet believe me :
There's some design in this ! to make us happy,
To realise our union—trust me, love !
They but pretend to wish it.

MAX.
But these Tertskys—
Why use we them at all ! Why not your mother !
Excellent creature ! she deserves from us
A full and filial confidence.

THEKLA.
She doth love you,
Doth rate you high before all others—but—
But such a secret—she would never have
The courage to conceal it from my father.
For her own peace of mind we must preserve it
A secret from her too.

MAX.
Why any secret !
I love not secrets. Mark, what I will do.
I'll throw me at your father's feet—let *him*
Decide upon my fortunes !—He is true,
He wears no mask—he hates all crooked ways—
He is so good, so noble !

THEKLA (*falls on his neck*).
That are you !

MAX.
You knew him only since this morn ! but I
Have lived ten years already in his presence.
And who knows whether in this very moment
He is not merely waiting for us both
To own our loves, in order to unite us !
You are silent !—
You look at me with such a hopelessness !
What have you to object against your father !

THEKLA.
I ! Nothing. Only he's so occupied—
He has no leisure time to think about
The happiness of us two. [*Taking his hand tenderly.*
Follow me !
Let us not place too great a faith in men.
These Tertskys—we will still be grateful to them
For every kindness, but not trust them further
Than they deserve ;—and in all else rely—
On our own hearts !

MAX.
O ! shall we *e'er* be happy !

THEKLA.
Are we not happy now ! Art thou not mine !
Am I not thine ! There lives within my soul
A lofty courage—'t is love gives it me !
I ought to be less open—ought to hide
My heart more from thee—so decorum dictates :
But where in this place couldst thou seek for truth,
If in my mouth thou didst not find it !

SCENE VI.

To them enters the Countess TERTSKY.

COUNTESS (*in a pressing manner*).
Come !
My husband sends me for you—It is now
The latest moment.
[*They not appearing to attend to what she says, she
steps between them.*
Part you !

THEKLA.
O, not yet !
It has been scarce a moment.

COUNTESS.
Ay ! Then time
Flies swiftly with your Highness, Princess niece !

MAX.
There is no hurry, aunt.

COUNTESS.
Away ! away !
The folks begin to miss you. Twice already
His father has ask'd for him.

THEKLA.
Ha ! his father !

COUNTESS.
You understand *that*, niece !

THEKLA.
Why needs he
To go at all to that society !
'T is not his proper company. They may
Be worthy men, but he's too young for them.
In brief. he suits not such society.

COUNTESS.
You mean, you'd rather keep him wholly here !

THEKLA (*with energy*).
Yes ! you have hit it, aunt ! That is my meaning.
Leave him here wholly ! Tell the company—

COUNTESS.
What ! have you lost your senses, niece !—
Count, you remember the conditions. Come !

MAX. (*to* THEKLA).
Lady, I must obey, Farewell, dear lady !
[THEKLA *turns away from him with a quick motion.*
What say you then, dear lady !
c 2

THEKLA (*without looking at him*).
Nothing. Go!

MAX.

Can I, when you are angry—
[*He draws up to her, their eyes meet, she stands
silent a moment, then throws herself into his
arms; he presses her fast to his heart.*

COUNTESS.

Off! Heavens! if any one should come!
Hark! What's that noise! It comes this way.—Off!
[*MAX. tears himself away out of her arms, and goes.
The COUNTESS accompanies him. THEKLA follows him with her eyes at first, walks restlessly
across the room, then stops, and remains standing, lost in thought. A guitar lies on the table,
she seizes it as by a sudden emotion, and after
she has played a while an irregular and melancholy symphony, she falls gradually into the
music and sings.*

THEKLA (*plays and sings*).

The cloud doth gather, the greenwood roar,
The damsel paces along the shore;
The billows they tumble with might, with might;
And she flings out her voice to the darksome night;
   Her bosom is swelling with sorrow;
The world it is empty, the heart will die,
There's nothing to wish for beneath the sky:
Thou Holy One, call thy child away!
I 've lived and loved, and that was to-day—
   Make ready my grave-clothes to-morrow.[1]

[1] I found it not in my power to translate this song with
literal fidelity, preserving at the same time the Alcaic
movement; and have therefore added the original with a
prose translation. Some of my readers may be more fortunate.

THEKLA (*spielt und singt*).

Der Eichwald brauset, die Wolken ziehn,
Das Mägdlein wandelt an Ufers Grün;
Es bricht sich die Welle mit Macht, mit Macht,
Und sie singt hinaus in die finstre Nacht,
   Das Auge von Weinen getrübet:
Das Herz ist gestorben, die Welt ist leer,
Und weiter giebt sie dem Wunsche nichts mehr.
Du Heilige, rufe dein Kind zurück,
Ich habe genossen das irdische Glück,
   Ich habe gelebt und geliebet.

LITERAL TRANSLATION.

THEKLA (*plays and sings*).

The oak-forest bellows, the clouds gather, the damsel
walks to and fro on the green of the shore; the wave
breaks with might, with might, and she sings out into
the dark night, her eye discoloured with weeping: the
heart is dead, the world is empty, and further gives it
nothing more to the wish. Thou Holy One, call thy child
home. I have enjoyed the happiness of this world, I have
lived and have loved.

I cannot but add here an imitation of this song, with
which the author of "The Tale of Rosamund Gray and
Blind Margaret" has favoured me, and which appears to
me to have caught the happiest manner of our old ballads.

The clouds are blackening, the storms threat'ning,
   The cavern doth mutter, the greenwood moan!
Billows are breaking, the damsel's heart aching,
   Thus in the dark night she singeth alone,
      Her eye upward roving:
The world is empty, the heart is dead surely,
   In this world plainly all seemeth amiss;
To thy heaven, Holy One, take home thy little one,
   I have partaken of all earth's bliss,
      Both living and loving.

SCENE VII.

COUNTESS (*returns*), THEKLA.

COUNTESS.

Fie, lady niece! to throw yourself upon him,
Like a poor gift to one who cares not for it,
And so must be flung after him! For you,
Duke Friedland's only child, I should have thought,
It had been more beseeming to have shown your-
More chary of your person.   [self

THEKLA (*rising*).
                      And what mean you!

COUNTESS.

I mean, niece, that you should not have forgotten
Who *you* are, and who he is. But perchance
That never once occurr'd to you.

THEKLA.
              What then!

COUNTESS.

That you 're daughter of the Prince Duke Friedland.

THEKLA.

Well—and what farther!

COUNTESS.
              What! a pretty question!

THEKLA.

He was *born* that which we have but *become*.
He 's of an ancient Lombard family,
Son of a reigning princess.

COUNTESS.
              Are you dreaming!
Talking in sleep! An excellent jest, forsooth!
We shall no doubt right courteously *entreat* him
To honour with his hand the richest heiress
In Europe.

THEKLA.
That will not be necessary.

COUNTESS.

Methinks 't were well though not to run the hazard.

THEKLA.

His father loves him; Count Octavio
Will interpose no difficulty——

COUNTESS.
                          His!
His father! *his!* But yours niece, what of yours!

THEKLA.

Why I begin to think you fear his father.
So anxiously you hide it from the man!
His father, *his*, I mean.

COUNTESS (*looks at her as scrutinising*).
              Niece, you are *false*.

THEKLA.

Are you then wounded! O, be friends with me!

COUNTESS.

You hold your game for won already. Do not
Triumph too soon!—

THEKLA (*interrupting her, and attempting to
              soothe her.*)
              Nay now, be friends with me.

COUNTESS.

It is not yet so far gone.

THEKLA.
              I believe you.

COUNTESS.

Did you suppose your father had laid out
His most important life in toils of war,
Denied himself each quiet earthly bliss,
Had banish'd slumber from his tent, devoted
His noble head to care, and for this only,
To make a happier pair of you! At length
To draw you from your convent, and conduct
In easy triumph to your arms the man   [thinks,
That chanced to please your eyes! All this, me-
He might have purchased at a cheaper rate.

THEKLA.

That which he did not plant for me might yet
Bear me fair fruitage of its own accord.
And if my friendly and affectionate fate,
Out of his fearful and enormous being,
Will but prepare the joys of life for me—

COUNTESS.

Thou seest it with a lovelorn maiden's eyes.
Cast thine eye round, bethink thee who thou art.
Into no house of joyance hast thou stepp'd,
For no espousals dost thou find the walls
Deck'd out, no guests the nuptial garland wearing.
Here is no splendour but of arms. Or think'st thou
That all these thousands are here congregated
To lead up the long dances at thy wedding!
Thou see'st thy father's forehead full of thought,
Thy mother's eye in tears: upon the balance
Lies the great destiny of all our house.
Leave now the puny wish, the girlish feeling,
O thrust it far behind thee! Give thou proof,
Thou'rt the daughter of the Mighty—his
Who where he moves creates the wonderful.
Not to herself the woman must belong,
Annex'd and bound to alien destinies.
But she performs the best part, she the wisest,
Who can transmute the alien into self,
Meet and disarm necessity by choice;
And what must be, take freely to her heart,
And bear and foster it with mother's love.

THEKLA.

Such ever was my lesson in the convent.
I had no loves, no wishes, knew myself
Only as his—his daughter—his, the Mighty!
His fame, the echo of whose blast drove to me
From the far distance, waken'd in my soul
No other thought than this—I am appointed
To offer up myself in passiveness to him.

COUNTESS.

That is thy fate. Mould thou thy wishes to it.
I and thy mother gave thee the example.

THEKLA.

My fate hath shown me him, to whom behoves it
That I should offer up myself. In gladness
Him will I follow.

COUNTESS.

                 Not thy fate hath shown him!
Thy heart, say rather—'t was thy heart, my child!

THEKLA.

Fate hath no voice but the heart's impulses.
I am all his! His present—his alone,
Is this new life, which lives in me! He hath
A right to his own creature. What was I
Ere his fair love infused a soul into me!

COUNTESS.

Thou wouldst oppose thy father then, should he
Have otherwise determined with thy person!

[THEKLA remains silent. The COUNTESS continues.

Thou mean'st to force him to thy liking!—Child,
His name is Friedland.

THEKLA.

           My name too is Friedland.
He shall have found a genuine daughter in me.

COUNTESS.

What! he has vanquish'd all impediment,
And in the wilful mood of his own daughter
Shall a new struggle rise for him! Child! child!
As yet thou hast seen thy father's smiles alone;
The eye of his rage thou hast not seen. Dear child,
I will not frighten thee. To that extreme,
I trust, it ne'er shall come. His will is yet
Unknown to me: 't is possible his aims
May have the same direction as thy wish.
But this can never, never be his will
That thou, the daughter of his haughty fortunes,
Should'st e'er demean thee as a love-sick maiden;
And like some poor cost-nothing, fling thyself
Toward the man, who, if that high prize ever
Be destined to await him, yet, with sacrifices
The highest love can bring, must pay for it.

[Exit COUNTESS.

THEKLA (who during the last speech had been
     standing evidently lost in her reflections).
I thank thee for the hint. It turns
My sad presentiment to certainty.
And it is so!—Not one friend have we here,
Not one true heart! we 've nothing but ourselves!
O she said rightly—no auspicious signs
Beam on this covenant of our affections.
This is no theatre, where hope abides:
The dull thick noise of war alone stirs here;
And Love himself, as he were arm'd in steel,
Steps forth, and girds him for the strife of death.

[Music from the banquet-room is heard.

There 's a dark spirit walking in our house,
And swiftly will the Destiny close on us.
It drove me hither from my calm asylum,
It mocks my soul with charming witchery,
It lures me forward in a seraph's shape,
I see it near, I see it nearer floating,
It draws it pulls me with a god-like power —
And lo! the abyss—and thither am I moving—
I have no power within me not to move!

[The music from the banquet-room becomes louder.

O when a house is doom'd in fire to perish,
Many and dark heaven drives his clouds together,
Yea, shoots his lightnings down from sunny heights,
Flames burst from out the subterraneous chasms,
[1]And fiends and angels, mingling in their fury,
Sling fire-brands at the burning edifice.

[Exit THEKLA.

——◆——

SCENE VIII.

*A large Saloon lighted up with festal Splendour ; in the
midst of it, and in the centre of the Stage, a Table richly
set out, at which eight Generals are sitting, among whom
are OCTAVIO PICCOLOMINI, TERTSKY, and MARADAS.
Right and left of this, but farther back, two other Tables,
at each of which six Persons are placed. The Middle
Door, which is standing open, gives to the Prospect a*

---

[1] There are few, who will not have taste enough to laugh
at the two concluding lines of this soliloquy; and still fewer,
I would fain hope, who would not have been more disposed
to shudder, had I given a *faithful* translation. For the
readers of German I have added the original:

Blind-wüthend schleudert selbst der Gott der Freude
Den Pechkranz in das brennende Gebäude.

fourth Table, with the same number of Persons. More forward stands the Sideboard. The whole front of the Stage is kept open for the Pages and Servants in waiting. All is in motion. The Band of Music belonging to TERTSKY'S *Regiment march across the Stage, and draw up round the Tables. Before they are quite off from the Front of the Stage,* MAX. PICCOLOMINI *appears,* TERTSKY *advances towards him with a Paper,* ISOLANI *comes up to meet him with a Beaker or Service-cup.*

TERTSKY, ISOLANI, MAX. PICCOLOMINI.

ISOLANI.

Here, brother, what we love ! Why, where hast
   been !
Off to thy place—quick ! Tertsky here has given
The mother's holiday wine up to free booty.
Here it goes on as at the Heidelberg castle.
Already hast thou lost the best.   They're giving
At yonder table ducal crowns in shares ;
There's Sternberg's lands and chattels are put up,
With Eggenberg's, Stawata's, Lichtenstein's,
And all the great Bohemian feodalities.
Be nimble, lad ! and something may turn up
For thee—who knows ! off—to thy place ! quick !
   march !

TIEFENBACH *and* GOETZ *(call out from the second
and third tables).*
Count Piccolomini !

TERTSKY.

Stop, ye shall have him in an instant.—Read
This oath here, whether as 'tis here set forth,
The wording satisfies you.   They've all read it,
Each in his turn, and each one will subscribe
His individual signature.

MAX. *(reads).*
" Ingratis servire nefas."

ISOLANI.

That sounds to my ears very much like Latin,
And being interpreted, pray what may't mean !

TERTSKY.

No honest man will serve a thankless master.

MAX.

" Inasmuch as our supreme Commander, the
illustrious Duke of Friedland, in consequence of
the manifold affronts and grievances which he has
received, had expressed his determination to quit
the Emperor, but on our unanimous entreaty has
graciously consented to remain still with the army,
and not to part from us without our approbation
thereof, so we, collectively and *each in particular*,
in the stead of an oath personally taken, do hereby
oblige ourselves—likewise by him honourably and
faithfully to hold, and in nowise whatsoever from
him to part, and to be ready to shed for his interests the last drop of our blood, so far, namely, as
our oath to the Emperor will permit it. (*These
last words are repeated by* ISOLANI.) In testimony
of which we subscribe our names."

TERTSKY.

Now !—are you willing to subscribe this paper !

ISOLANI.

Why should he not ! All officers of honour
Can do it, ay, must do it.—Pen and ink here !

TERTSKY.

Nay, let it rest till after meal.

ISOLANI *(drawing* MAX. *along).*
   Come, Max.
   [*Both seat themselves at their table.*

SCENE IX.

TERTSKY, NEUMANN.

TERTSKY *(beckons to* NEUMANN *who is waiting at
the side-table, and steps forward with him to the
edge of the stage).*
Have you the copy with you, Neumann ! Give it.
It may be changed for the other !

NEUMANN.
   I have copied it
Letter by letter, line by line ; no eye
Would e'er discover other difference,
Save only the omission of that clause,
According to your Excelleney's order.

TERTSKY.

Right ! lay it yonder, and away with this—
It has performed its business—to the fire with it—
   [NEUMANN *lays the copy on the table, and steps
   back again to the side-table.*

SCENE X.

ILLO *(comes out from the second Chamber),* TERTSKY.

ILLO.
How goes it with young Piccolomini !

TERTSKY.
All right, I think.   He has started no objection.

ILLO.
He is the only one I fear about—
He and his father.   Have an eye on both !

TERTSKY.
How looks it at your table : you forget not
To keep them warm and stirring !

ILLO.
   O, quite cordial,
They are quite cordial in the scheme.   We have
   them.
And 'tis as I predicted too.   Already
It is the talk, not merely to maintain
The Duke in station.   " Since we're once for all
Together and unanimous, why not,"
Says Montecuculi, " ay, why not onward,
And make conditions with the Emperor
There in his own Vienna ! "   Trust me, Count,
Were it not for these said Piccolomini,
We might have spared ourselves the cheat.

TERTSKY.
   And Butler !
How goes it there ! Hush !

SCENE XI.

To them enter BUTLER *from the second table.*

BUTLER.
   Don't disturb yourselves.
Field Marshal, I have understood you perfectly.
Good luck be to the scheme ; and as to me,
   [*With an air of mystery.*
You may depend upon me.

ILLO *(with vivacity).*
   May we, Butler !

BUTLER.

With or without the clause, all one to me !
You understand me ! My fidelity
The Duke may put to any proof—I'm with him !
Tell him so ! I'm the Emperor's officer,
As long as 'tis his pleasure to remain
The Emperor's general ! and Friedland's servant,
As soon as it shall please him to become
His own lord.

TERTSKY.

You would make a good exchange.
No stern economist, no Ferdinand,
Is he to whom you plight your services.

BUTLER (with a haughty look).

I do not put up my fidelity
To sale, Count Tertsky ! Half a year ago
I would not have advised you to have made me
An overture to that, to which I now
Offer myself of my own free accord.—
But that is past ! and to the Duke, Field Marshal,
I bring myself together with my regiment.
And mark you, 'tis my humour to believe,
The example which I give will not remain
Without an influence.

ILLO.

Who is ignorant,
That the whole army look to Colonel Butler,
As to a light that moves before them !

BUTLER.

Ey !
Then I repent me not of that fidelity
Which for the length of forty years I held,
If in my sixtieth year my old good name
Can purchase for me a revenge so full.
Start not at what I say, sir Generals !
My real motives—they concern not you.
And you yourselves, I trust, could not expect [or
That this your game had crook'd my judgment—
That fickleness, quick blood, or such like cause,
Has driven the old man from the track of honour,
Which he so long had trodden. Come, my friends !
I'm not thereto determined with less firmness,
Because I know and have looked steadily
At that on which I have determined.

ILLO.

Say,
And speak roundly, what are we to deem you ?

BUTLER.

A friend ! I give you here my hand ! I'm yours
With all I have. Not only men, but money
Will the Duke want.—Go, tell him, sirs !
I've earn'd and laid up somewhat in his service,
I lend it him ; and is he my survivor,
It has been already long ago bequeathed him.
He is my heir. For me, I stand alone
Here in the world ; nought know I of the feeling
That binds the husband to a wife and children.
My name dies with me, my existence ends.

ILLO.

'Tis not your money that he needs—a heart
Like yours weighs tons of gold down, weighs down
   millions !

BUTLER.

I came a simple soldier's boy from Ireland
To Prague—and with a master, whom I buried.
From lowest stable duty I climb'd up,
Such was the fate of war, to this high rank,

The plaything of a whimsical good fortune.
And Wallenstein too is a child of luck ;
I love a fortune that is like my own.

ILLO.

All powerful souls have kindred with each other.

BUTLER.

This is an awful moment ! to the brave,
To the determined, an auspicious moment.
The Prince of Weimar arms, upon the Maine
To found a mighty dukedom. He of Halberstadt,
That Mansfeldt, wanted but a longer life
To have mark'd out with his good sword a lordship
That should reward his courage. Who of these
Equals our Friedland ? there is nothing, nothing
So high, but he may set the ladder to it !

TERTSKY.

That's spoken like a man !

BUTLER.

Do you secure the Spaniard and Italian—
I'll be your warrant for the Scotchman Lesly.
Come, to the company !

TERTSKY.

Where is the master of the cellar ? Ho !
Let the best wines come up. Ho ! cheerly, boy !
Luck comes to-day, so give her hearty welcome.
                         [Exeunt, each to his table.

SCENE XII.

*The MASTER OF THE CELLAR advancing with NEUMANN,
Servants passing backwards and forwards.*

MASTER OF THE CELLAR.

The best wine ! O : if my old mistress, his lady
mother, could but see these wild goings on, she
would turn herself round in her grave. Yes, yes,
sir officer ! 'tis all down the hill with this noble
house ! no end, no moderation ! And this marriage
with the Duke's sister, a splendid connection, a
very splendid connection ! but I will tell you, sir
officer, it looks no good.

NEUMANN.

Heaven forbid ! Why, at this very moment the
whole prospect is in bud and blossom !

MASTER OF THE CELLAR.

You think so ?—Well, well ! much may be said
on that head.

FIRST SERVANT (comes).

Burgundy for the fourth table.

MASTER OF THE CELLAR.

Now, sir lieutenant, if this an't the seventieth
flask—

FIRST SERVANT.

Why, the reason is, that German lord, Tiefenbach, sits at that table.

MASTER OF THE CELLAR (continuing his discourse
to NEUMANN).

They are soaring too high. They would rival
kings and electors in their pomp and splendour ;
and wherever the Duke leaps, not a minute does
my gracious master, the count, loiter on the brink
—(to the Servants.)—What do you stand there
listening for ? I will let you know you have legs
presently. Off ! see to the tables, see to the flasks !

Look there! Count Palfi has an empty glass before him!

RUNNER (comes).

The great service-cup is wanted, sir; that rich gold cup with the Bohemian arms on it. The Count says you know which it is.

MASTER OF THE CELLAR.

Ay! that was made for Frederick's coronation by the artist William—there was not such another prize in the whole booty at Prague.

RUNNER.

The same!—a health is to go round in him.

MASTER OF THE CELLAR (*shaking his head while he fetches and rinses the cups*).

This will be something for the tale-bearers—this goes to Vienna.

NEUMANN.

Permit me to look at it.—Well, this is a cup indeed! How heavy! as well it may be, being all gold.—And what neat things are embossed on it! how natural and elegant they look!—There, on that first quarter, let me see. That proud Amazon there on horseback, she that is taking a leap over the crosier and mitres, and carries on a wand a hat together with a banner, on which there's a goblet represented. Can you tell me what all this signifies?

MASTER OF THE CELLAR.

The woman whom you see there on horseback, is the Free Election of the Bohemian Crown. That is signified by the round hat, and by that fiery steed on which she is riding. The hat is the pride of man; for he who cannot keep his hat on before kings and emperors is no free man.

NEUMANN.

But what is the cup there on the banner?

MASTER OF THE CELLAR.

The cup signifies the freedom of the Bohemian Church, as it was in our forefathers' times. Our forefathers in the wars of the Hussites forced from the Pope this noble privilege : for the Pope, you know, will not grant the cup to any layman. Your true Moravian values nothing beyond the cup; it is his costly jewel, and has cost the Bohemians their precious blood in many and many a battle.

NEUMANN.

And what says that chart that hangs in the air there, over it all?

MASTER OF THE CELLAR.

That signifies the Bohemian letter-royal, which we forced from the Emperor Rudolph—a precious, never to be enough valued parchment, that secures to the new Church the old privileges of free ringing and open psalmody. But since he of Steiermark has ruled over us, that is at an end; and after the battle at Prague, in which Count Palatine Frederick lost crown and empire, our faith hangs upon the pulpit and the altar—and our brethren look at their homes over their shoulders; but the letter-royal the Emperor himself cut to pieces with his scissars.

NEUMANN.

Why, my good Master of the Cellar! you are deep read in the chronicles of your country?

MASTER OF THE CELLAR.

So were my forefathers, and for that reason were they minstrels, and served under Procopius

and Ziska. Peace be with their ashes! Well, well! they fought for a good cause though—There! carry it up!

NEUMANN.

Stay! let me but look at this second quarter. Look *there!* That is, when at Prague Castle the Imperial Counsellors, Martinitz and Stawata, were hurled down head over heels. 'Tis even so! there stands Count Thur who commands it.

[*Runner takes the service-cup and goes off with it.*

MASTER OF THE CELLAR.

O let me never more hear of that day. It was the three-and-twentieth of May, in the year of our Lord one thousand, six hundred, and eighteen. It seems to me as it were but yesterday—from that unlucky day it all began, all the heart-aches of the country. Since that day it is now sixteen years, and there has never once been peace on the earth.

[*Health drank aloud at the second table.*

The Prince of Weimar! Hurra!

[*At the third and fourth table.*

Long live Prince William! Long live Duke Bernard! Hurra! [*Music strikes up.*

FIRST SERVANT.

Hear 'em! Hear 'em! What an uproar!

SECOND SERVANT (*comes in running*).

Did you hear? They have drank the Prince of Weimar's health.

THIRD SERVANT.

The Swedish Chief Commander!

FIRST SERVANT (*speaking at the same time*).

The Lutheran!

SECOND SERVANT.

Just before, when Count Deodate gave out the Emperor's health, they were all as mum as a nibbling mouse.

MASTER OF THE CELLAR.

Po, po! When the wine goes in, strange things come out. A good servant hears, and hears not! —You should be nothing but eyes and feet, except when you are called to.

SECOND SERVANT.

[*To the Runner, to whom he gives secretly a flask of wine, keeping his eye on the Master of the Cellar, standing between him and the Runner.*

Quick, Thomas! before the Master of the Cellar runs this way—'tis a flask of Frontignac! —Snapped it up at the third table.—Canst go off with it?

RUNNER (*hides it in his pocket*).

All right! [*Exit the Second Servant.*

THIRD SERVANT (*aside to the First*).

Be on the hark, Jack! that we may have right plenty to tell to father Quivoga—He will give us right plenty of absolution in return for it.

FIRST SERVANT.

For that very purpose I am always having something to do behind Illo's chair.—He is the man for speeches to make you stare with!

MASTER OF THE CELLAR (*to* NEUMANN).

Who, pray, may that swarthy man be, he with the cross, that is chatting so confidentially with Esterhats?

NEUMANN.

Ay! he too is one of those to whom they confide too much. He calls himself Maradas, a Spaniard is he.

MASTER OF THE CELLAR (*impatiently*).
Spaniard! Spaniard!—I tell you, friend, nothing good comes of those Spaniards. All these outlandish fellows [1] are little better than rogues.

NEUMANN.
Fy, fy! you should not say so, friend. There are among them our very best generals, and those on whom the Duke at this moment relies the most.

MASTER OF THE CELLAR.
[*Taking the flask out of the* Runner's *pocket.*
My son, it will be broken to pieces in your pocket.
[TERTSKY *hurries in, fetches away the Paper and calls to a Servant for Pen and Ink, and goes to the back of the Stage.*

MASTER OF THE CELLAR (*to the* Servants).
The Lieutenant-General stands up.—Be on the watch.—Now! They break up.—Off and move back the forms.
[*They rise at all the tables, the Servants hurry off the front of the Stage to the Tables; part of the guests come forward.*

SCENE XIII.

OCTAVIO PICCOLOMINI *enters in conversation with* MARADAS, *and both place themselves quite on the edge of the Stage on one side of the Proscenium. On the side directly opposite,* MAX. PICCOLOMINI, *by himself, lost in thought, and taking no part in any thing that is going forward. The middle space between both, but rather more distant from the edge of the Stage, is filled up by* BUTLER, ISOLANI, GOETZ, TIEFENBACH, *and* KOLATTO.

ISOLANI (*while the Company is coming forward*).
Good-night, good night, Kolatto! Good night, Lieutenant-General!—I should rather say, good morning.

GOETZ (*to* TIEFENBACH).
Noble brother! (*making the usual compliment after meals*).

TIEFENBACH.
Ay! 'twas a royal feast indeed.

GOETZ.
Yes, my Lady Countess understands these matters. Her mother-in-law, Heaven rest her soul, taught her!—Ah! that was a housewife for you!

TIEFENBACH.
There was not her like in all Bohemia for setting out a table.

OCTAVIO (*aside to* MARADAS).
Do me the favour to talk to me—talk of what you will—or of nothing. Only preserve the appearance at least of talking. I would not wish to stand by myself, and yet I conjecture that there will be goings on here worthy of our attentive observation. (*He continues to fix his eye on the whole following scene.*)

ISOLANI (*on the point of going*).
Lights! lights!

---

[1] There is a humour in the original which cannot be given in the translation. "Die *Welschen* alle," &c. which word in classical German means the *Italians* alone; but in its first sense, and at present in the *vulgar* use of the word, signifies foreigners in general. Our word wall-nuts, I suppose, means *outlandish* nuts—Wallæ nuces, in German "Welsche Nüsse."

TERTSKY (*advances with the Paper to* ISOLANI).
Noble brother; two minutes longer!—Here is something to subscribe.

ISOLANI.
Subscribe as much as you like—but you must excuse me from reading it.

TERTSKY.
There is no need. It is the oath which you have already read.—Only a few marks of your pen!
[ISOLANI *hands over the Paper to* OCTAVIO *respectfully.*

TERTSKY.
Nay, nay, first come first served. There is no precedence here. (OCTAVIO *runs over the Paper with apparent indifference.* TERTSKY *watches him at some distance.*)

GOETZ (*to* TERTSKY).
Noble Count! with your permission — Good night.

TERTSKY.
Where's the hurry? Come, one other composing draught. (*To the* Servants).—Ho!

GOETZ.
Excuse me—an't able.

TERTSKY.
A thimble-full!

GOETZ.
Excuse me.

TIEFENBACH (*sits down*).
Pardon me, nobles!—This standing does not agree with me.

TERTSKY.
Consult only your own convenience, General!

TIEFENBACH.
Clear at head, sound in stomach—only my legs won't carry me any longer.

ISOLANI (*pointing at his corpulence*).
Poor legs! how *should* they! Such an unmerciful load! (OCTAVIO *subscribes his name, and reaches over the Paper to* TERTSKY, *who gives it to* ISOLANI; *and he goes to the table to sign his name.*)

TIEFENBACH.
'Twas that war in Pomerania that first brought it on. Out in all weathers—ice and snow—no help for it.—I shall never get the better of it all the days of my life.

GOETZ.
Why, in simple verity, your Swede makes no nice inquiries about the season.

TERTSKY (*observing* ISOLANI, *whose hand trembles excessively so that he can scarce direct his pen.*)
Have you had that ugly complaint long, noble brother?—Dispatch it.

ISOLANI.
The sins of youth! I have already tried the chalybeate waters. Well—I must bear it.
[TERTSKY *gives the Paper to* MARADAS; *he steps to the table to subscribe.*

OCTAVIO (*advancing to* BUTLER).
You are not over fond of the orgies of Bacchus, Colonel! I have observed it. You would, I think, find yourself more to your liking in the uproar of a battle, than of a feast.

BUTLER.
I must confess, 'tis not in my way.

OCTAVIO (*stepping nearer to him friendlily*).
Nor in mine either, I can assure you ; and I am not a little glad, my much-honoured Colonel Butler, that we agree so well in our opinions. A half dozen good friends at most, at a small round table, a glass of genuine Tokay, open hearts, and a rational conversation—that's my taste !

BUTLER.
And mine too, when it can be had.
[*The paper comes to* TIEFENBACH, *who glances over it at the same time with* GOETZ *and* KOLATTO. MARADAS *in the mean time returns to* OCTAVIO. *All this takes place, the conversation with* BUTLER *proceeding uninterrupted.*

OCTAVIO (*introducing* MARADAS *to* BUTLER).
Don Balthasar Maradas ! likewise a man of our stamp, and long ago your admirer.
[BUTLER *bows.*

OCTAVIO (*continuing*).
You are a stranger here—'t was but yesterday you arrived—you are ignorant of the ways and means here. 'T is a wretched place—I know, at our age, one loves to be snug and quiet—What if you moved your lodgings ?—Come, be my visitor. (BUTLER *makes a low bow.*) Nay, without compliment !—For a friend like you, I have still a corner remaining.

BUTLER (*coldly*).
Your obliged humble servant, my Lord Lieutenant General !
[*The paper comes to* BUTLER, *who goes to the table to subscribe it. The front of the stage is vacant, so that both the* PICCOLOMINIS, *each on the side where he had been from the commencement of the scene, remain alone.*

OCTAVIO (*after having some time watched his son in silence, advances somewhat nearer to him*).
You were long absent from us, friend !

MAX.
I——urgent business detained me.

OCTAVIO.
And, I observe, you are still absent !

MAX.
You know this crowd and bustle always makes me silent.

OCTAVIO (*advancing still nearer*).
May I be permitted to ask what the business was that detained you ? *Tertsky* knows it without asking ?

MAX.
What does Tertsky know ?

OCTAVIO.
He was the only one who did not miss you.

ISOLANI (*who has been attending to them from some distance, steps up*).
Well done, father ! Rout out his baggage ! Beat up his quarters ! there is something there that should not be.

TERTSKY (*with the paper*).
Is there none wanting ? Have the whole subscribed ?

OCTAVIO.
All.

TERTSKY (*calling aloud*).
Ho ! Who subscribes ?

BUTLER (*to* TERTSKY).
Count the names. There ought to be just thirty.

TERTSKY.
Here is a cross.

TIEFENBACH.
That 's my mark.

ISOLANI.
He cannot write ; but his cross is a good cross, and is honoured by Jews as well as Christians.

OCTAVIO (*presses on to* MAX.).
Come, general ! let us go. It is late.

TERTSKY.
One Piccolomini only has signed.

ISOLANI (*pointing to* MAX.).
Look ! that is your man, that statue there, who has had neither eye, ear, nor tongue for us the whole evening. (MAX. *receives the paper from* TERTSKY, *which he looks upon vacantly*).

SCENE XIV.

To these enter ILLO *from the inner room. He has in his hand a golden service-cup, and is extremely distempered with drinking ;* GOETZ *and* BUTLER *follow him, endeavouring to keep him back.*

ILLO.
What do you want ? Let me go.

GOETZ *and* BUTLER.
Drink no more, Illo ! For Heaven's sake, drink no more.

ILLO (*goes up to* OCTAVIO, *and shakes him cordially by the hand, and then drinks*).
Octavio ! I bring this to you ! Let all grudge be drowned in this friendly bowl ! I know well enough, ye never loved me—Devil take me !—and I never loved you !—I am always even with people in that way !—Let what 's past be past—that is, you understand—forgotten ! I esteem you infinitely. (*Embracing him repeatedly.*) You have not a dearer friend on earth than I—but that you know. The fellow that cries rogue to you calls me villain —and I 'll strangle him !—my *dear* friend !

TERTSKY (*whispering to him*).
Art in thy senses ? For Heaven's sake, Illo, think where you are !

ILLO (*aloud*).
What do you mean ?—There are none but friends here, are there ? (*Looks round the whole circle with a jolly and triumphant air.*) Not a sneaker among us, thank Heaven !

TERTSKY (*to* BUTLER. *eagerly*).
Take him off with you, force him off, I entreat you, Butler !

BUTLER (*to* ILLO).
Field Marshal ! a word with you. (*Leads him to the side-board.*)

ILLO (*cordially*).
A thousand for one ; Fill—Fill it once more up to the brim.—To this gallant man's health !

ISOLANI (*to* MAX. *who all the while has been staring on the paper with fixed but vacant eyes*).
Slow and sure, my noble brother !—Hast parsed it all yet ?—Some words yet to go through ?—Ha !

MAX. (*waking as from a dream*).
What am I to do ?

TERTSKY, *and at the same time* ISOLANI.
Sign your name. (OCTAVIO *directs his eyes on him with intense anxiety.*)

MAX. (*returns the paper.*)
Let it stay till to-morrow. It is *business*—to-day I am not sufficiently collected. Send it to me to-morrow.

TERTSKY.
Nay, collect yourself a little.

ISOLANI.
Awake man! awake!—Come, thy signature, and have done with it! What! Thou art the youngest in the whole company, and wouldst be wiser than all of us together! Look there! thy father has signed—we have all signed.

TERTSKY (*to* OCTAVIO).
Use your influence. Instruct him.

OCTAVIO.
My son is at the age of discretion.

ILLO (*leaves the service-cup on the side-board.*)
What's the dispute?

TERTSKY.
He declines subscribing the paper.

MAX.
I say, it may as well stay till to-morrow.

ILLO.
It cannot stay. We have all subscribed to it—and so must you.—You must subscribe.

MAX.
Illo, good night!

ILLO.
No! You come not off so! The Duke shall learn who are his friends. (*All collect round* ILLO *and* MAX.)

MAX.
What my sentiments are towards the Duke, the Duke knows, every one knows—what need of this wild stuff?

ILLO.
This is the thanks the Duke gets for his partiality to Italians and foreigners.—Us Bohemians he holds for little better than dullards—nothing pleases him but what's outlandish.

TERTSKY (*in extreme embarrassment, to the Commanders, who at* ILLO'S *words give a sudden start, as preparing to resent them.*)
It is the wine that speaks, and not his reason. Attend not to him, I entreat you.

ISOLANI (*with a bitter laugh.*)
Wine invents nothing: it only *tattles.*

ILLO.
He who is not with me is against me. Your tender consciences! Unless they can slip out by a back-door, by a puny proviso—

TERTSKY (*interrupting him*).
He is stark mad—don't listen to him!

ILLO (*raising his voice to the highest pitch*).
Unless they can slip out by a *proviso.*—What of the proviso! The devil take this proviso!

MAX. (*has his attention roused, and looks again into the paper*).
What is there here then of such perilous import! You make me curious—I must look closer at it.

TERTSKY (*in a low voice to* ILLO).
What are you doing, Illo! You are ruining us.

TIEFENBACH (*to* KOLATTO).
Ay, ay! I observed, that before we sat down to supper, it was read differently.

GOETZ.
Why, I seemed to think so too.

ISOLANI.
What do I care for that! Where there stand other names, mine can stand too.

TIEFENBACH.
Before supper there *was* a certain proviso there-in, or short clause, concerning our duties to the Emperor.

BUTLER (*to one of the Commanders*).
For shame, for shame! Bethink you. What is the main business here! The question now is, whether we shall keep our General, or let him retire. One must not take these things too nicely and over-scrupulously.

ISOLANI (*to one of the Generals*).
Did the Duke make any of these provisos when he gave you your regiment?

TERTSKY (*to* GOETZ).
Or when he gave you the office of army-purveyancer, which brings you in yearly a thousand pistoles!

ILLO.
He is a rascal who makes us out to be rogues. If there be any one that wants satisfaction, let him say so,—I am his man.

TIEFENBACH.
Softly, softly! 'T was but a word or two.

MAX. (*having read the paper gives it back*).
Till to-morrow, therefore!

ILLO (*stammering with rage and fury, loses all command over himself, and presents the paper to* MAX. *with one hand, and his sword in the other*).
Subscribe—Judas!

ISOLANI.
Out upon you, Illo!

OCTAVIO, TERTSKY, BUTLER (*all together*).
Down with the sword!

MAX. (*rushes on him suddenly and disarms him, then to* COUNT TERTSKY).
Take him off to bed.
[MAX. *leaves the stage.* ILLO *cursing and raving is held back by some of the Officers, and amidst a universal confusion the Curtain drops.*

ACT III.

SCENE I.

A Chamber in PICCOLOMINI'S *Mansion.—It is Night.*

OCTAVIO PICCOLOMINI. *A* Valet de Chambre *with Lights.*

OCTAVIO.
——And when my son comes in, conduct him
What is the hour ?   [hither.

VALET.
              'T is on the point of morning.

OCTAVIO.
Set down the light. We mean not to undress.
You may retire to sleep.
    [*Exit* Valet. OCTAVIO *paces, musing, across the
    chamber ;* MAX. PICCOLOMINI *enters unobserved,
    and looks at his father for some moments in
    silence.*

MAX.
Art thou offended with me ? Heaven knows
That odious business was no fault of mine.
'T is true, indeed, I saw thy signature,
What *thou* hadst sanction'd, should not, it might
        seem,
Have come amiss to me. But—'t is my nature—
Thou know'st that in such matters I must follow
My own light, not another's.

OCTAVIO (*goes up to him and embraces him*).
              Follow it,
O follow it still further, my best son !
To-night, dear boy ! it hath more faithfully
Guided thee than the example of thy father.

MAX.
Declare thyself less darkly.

OCTAVIO.
              I will do so.
For after what has taken place this night,
There must remain no secrets 'twixt us two.
    [*Both seat themselves.*
Max. Piccolomini ! what thinkest thou of
The oath that was sent round for signatures ?

MAX.
I hold it for a thing of harmless import,
Although I love not these set declarations.

OCTAVIO.
And on no other ground hast thou refused
The signature they fain had wrested from thee ?

MAX.
It was a serious business——I was absent—
The affair itself seem'd not so urgent to me.

OCTAVIO.
Be open, Max. Thou hadst then no suspicion ?

MAX.
Suspicion ! what suspicion ? Not the least.

OCTAVIO.
Thank thy good angel, Piccolomini :
He drew thee back unconscious from the abyss.

MAX.
I know not what thou meanest.

OCTAVIO.
              I will tell thee.
Fain would they have extorted from thee, son,
The sanction of thy name to villany ;

Yea, with a single flourish of thy pen,
Made thee renounce thy duty and thy honour !

MAX. (*rises*).
Octavio !

OCTAVIO.
      Patience ! Seat yourself. Much yet
Hast thou to hear from me, friend !—hast for years
Lived in incomprehensible illusion.
Before thine eyes is Treason drawing out
As black a web as e'er was spun for venom :
A power of hell o'erclouds thy understanding.
I dare no longer stand in silence—dare
No longer see thee wandering on in darkness,
Nor pluck the bandage from thine eyes.

MAX.
                      My father !
Yet, ere thou speakest, a moment's pause of
If your disclosures should appear to be [thought !
Conjectures only—and almost I fear
They will be nothing further—spare them ! I
Am not in that collected mood at present,
That I could listen to them quietly.

OCTAVIO.
The deeper cause thou hast to hate this light,
The more impatient cause have I, my son,
To force it on thee. To the innocence
And wisdom of thy heart I could have trusted
With calm assurance—but I see the net   [thee
Preparing—and it is thy heart itself
Alarms me for thine innocence—that secret,
    [*Fixing his eye steadfastly on his son's face.*
Which thou concealest, forces mine from me.
    [MAX. *attempts to answer, but hesitates, and casts
    his eyes to the ground embarrassed.*

OCTAVIO (*after a pause*).
Know, then, they are duping thee !—a most foul
        game
With thee and with us all—nay, hear me calmly—
The Duke even now is playing. He assumes
The mask, as if he would forsake the army ;
And in this moment makes he preparations
That army from the Emperor to *steal,*
And carry it over to the enemy !

MAX.
That low Priest's legend I know well, but did not
Expect to hear it from thy mouth.

OCTAVIO.
                      That mouth,
From which thou hearest it at this present moment,
Doth warrant thee that it is no Priest's legend.

MAX.
How mere a maniac they supposed the Duke ;
What, he can meditate ?—the Duke ?—can dream
That he can lure away full thirty thousand
Tried troops and true, all honourable soldiers,
More than a thousand noblemen among them,
From oaths, from duty, from their honour lure
And make them all unanimous to do   [them,
A deed that brands them scoundrels ?

OCTAVIO.
                      Such a deed,
With such a front of infamy, the Duke
No ways desires—what he requires of us

Bears a far gentler appellation. Nothing
He wishes, but to give the Empire peace.
And so, because the Emperor hates this peace,
Therefore the Duke—the Duke will force him to it.
All parts of the Empire will he pacify,
And for his trouble will retain in payment
(What he has already in his gripe)—Bohemia !

MAX.

Has he, Octavio, merited of us,
That we—that we should think so vilely of him !

OCTAVIO.

What *we would* think is not the question here,
The affair speaks for itself—and clearest proofs !
Hear me, my son—'tis not unknown to thee,
In what ill credit with the Court we stand.
But little dost thou know, or guess, what tricks,
What base intrigues, what lying artifices,
Have been employed—for this sole end—to sow
Mutiny in the camp !   All bands are loosed—
Loosed all the bands, that link the officer
To his liege Emperor, all that bind the soldier
Affectionately to the citizen.
Lawless he stands, and threateningly beleaguers
The state he's bound to guard.   To such a height
'Tis swoln, that at this hour the Emperor
Before his armies—his own armies—trembles ;
Yea, in his capital, his palace, fears
The traitors' poniards, and is meditating
To hurry off and hide his tender offspring——
Not from ..e Swedes, not from the Lutherans—
No ! from his own troops hide and hurry them !

MAX.

Cease, cease ! thou torturest, shatterest me.   I know
That oft we tremble at an empty terror ;
But the false phantasm brings a real misery.

OCTAVIO.

It is no phantasm.   An intestine war,
Of all the most unnatural and cruel,
Will burst out into flames, if instantly
We do not fly and stifle it.   The Generals
Are many of them long ago won over ;
The subalterns are vacillating—whole
Regiments and garrisons are vacillating.
To foreigners our strongholds are entrusted ;
To that suspected Schafgotch is the whole
Force of Silesia given up : to Tertsky
Five regiments, foot and horse—to Isolani,
To Illo, Kinsky, Butler, the best troops.

MAX.

Likewise to both of us.

OCTAVIO.

Because the Duke
Believes he has secured us—means to lure us
Still further on by splendid promises.
To me he portions forth the princedoms, Glatz
And Sagan ; and too plain I see the angel
With which he doubts not to catch *thee.*

MAX.

No ! no !

I tell thee—no !

OCTAVIO.

O open yet thine eyes !
And to what purpose think'st thou he has called us
Hither to Pilsen !—to avail himself
Of our advice !—O when did Friedland ever
Need our advice !—Be calm, and listen to me.
To sell ourselves are we called hither, and
Decline we that—to be his hostages.

Therefore doth noble Galas stand aloof ;
Thy father, too, thou wouldst not have seen here,
If higher duties had not held him fetter'd.

MAX.

He makes no secret of it—needs make none—
That we're called hither for his sake—he owns it.
He needs our aidance to maintain himself—
He did so much for us ; and 'tis but fair
That we too should do somewhat now for him.

OCTAVIO.

And know'st thou what it is which we must do !
That Illo's drunken mood betray'd it to thee.
Bethink thyself—what hast thou heard, what seen !
The counterfeited paper—the omission
Of that particular clause, so full of meaning,
Does it not prove, that they would bind us down
To nothing good !

MAX.

That counterfeited paper
Appears to me no other than a trick
Of Illo's own device.   These underhand
Traders in great men's interests ever use
To urge and hurry all things to the extreme.
They see the Duke at variance with the court,
And fondly think to serve him, when they widen
The breach irreparably.   Trust me, father,
The Duke knows nothing of all this.

OCTAVIO.

It grieves me
That I must dash to earth, that I must shatter
A faith so specious ; but I may not spare thee !
For this is not a time for tenderness.
Thou must take measures, speedy ones—must act.
I therefore will confess to thee, that all
Which I've entrusted to thee now—that all
Which seems to thee so unbelievable,
That—yes, I will tell thee—(*a pause*)—Max. ! I
had it all
From his own mouth—from the Duke's mouth I
had it.

MAX. (*in excessive agitation*).

No !—no !—never !

OCTAVIO.

Himself confided to me
What I, 'tis true, had long before discover'd
By other means—himself confided to me,
That 'twas his settled plan to join the Swedes ;
And, at the head of the united armies,
Compel the Emperor——

MAX.

He is passionate,
The Court has stung him—he is sore all over
With injuries and affronts ; and in a moment
Of irritation, what if he, for once,
Forgot himself !   He's an impetuous man.

OCTAVIO.

Nay, in cold blood he did confess this to me :
And having construed my astonishment
Into a scruple of his power, he showed me
His written evidences—showed me letters,
Both from the Saxon and the Swede, that gave
Promise of aidance, and defined the amount.

MAX.

It cannot be !—can *not* be !—*can* not be !
Dost thou not see, it cannot !
Thou wouldst of necessity have shown him
Such horror, such deep loathing—that or he
Had taken thee for his better genius, or
Thou stood'st not now a living man before me—

OCTAVIO.

I have laid open my objections to him,
Dissuaded him with pressing earnestness ;
But my *abhorrence*, the full sentiment
Of my *whole* heart—that I have still kept sacred
To my own consciousness.

MAX.

          And *thou* hast been
So treacherous ! That looks not like my father !
I trusted not thy words, when thou didst tell me
Evil of him ; much less can I *now* do it,
That thou calumniatest thy own self.

OCTAVIO.

I did not thrust myself into his secrecy.

MAX.

Uprightness merited his confidence.

OCTAVIO.

He was no longer worthy of sincerity.

MAX.

Dissimulation, sure, was still less worthy
Of thee, Octavio !

OCTAVIO.

          Gave I him a cause
To entertain a scruple of my honour !

MAX.

That he did not, evinced his confidence.

OCTAVIO.

Dear son, it is not always possible
Still to preserve that infant purity
Which the voice teaches in our inmost heart,
Still in alarum, for ever on the watch
Against the wiles of wicked men : e'en Virtue
Will sometimes bear away her outward robes
Soiled in the wrestle with Iniquity.
This is the curse of every evil deed,
That, propagating still, it brings forth evil.
I do not cheat my better soul with sophisms :
I but perform my orders ; the Emperor
Prescribes my conduct to me. Dearest boy,
Far better were it, doubtless, if we all
Obey'd the heart at all times ; but so doing,
In this our present sojourn with bad men,
We must abandon many an honest object.
'Tis now our call to serve the Emperor ;
By what means he can best be served—the heart
May whisper what it will—this is our call !

MAX.

It seems a thing appointed, that to-day
I should not comprehend, not understand thee.
The Duke, thou say'st, did honestly pour out
His heart to thee, but for an evil purpose ;
And thou dishonestly hast cheated him
For a good purpose ! Silence, I entreat thee—
My friend, thou stealest not from me—
Let me not lose my father !

OCTAVIO (*suppressing resentment*).

As yet thou know'st not all, my son. I have
Yet somewhat to disclose to thee. [*After a pause.*
          Duke Friedland
Hath made his preparations. He relies
Upon his stars. He deems us unprovided,
And thinks to fall upon us by surprise.
Yes, in his dream of hope, he grasps already
The golden circle in his hand. He errs,
We too have been in action—he but grasps
His evil fate, most evil, most mysterious !

MAX.

O nothing rash, my sire ! By all that's good
Let me invoke thee—no precipitation !

OCTAVIO.

With light tread stole he on his evil way, [him.
And light tread hath Vengeance stolen on after
Unseen she stands already, dark behind him—
But one step more—he shudders in her grasp !
Thou hast seen Questenberg with me. As yet
Thou know'st but his ostensible commission :
He brought with him a *private* one, my son !
And that was for me only.

MAX.

          May I know it ?

OCTAVIO (*seizes the patent*).

               Max !
              [*A pause.*
——In this disclosure place I in thy hands
The Empire's welfare and thy father's life :
Dear to thy inmost heart is Wallenstein :
A powerful tie of love, of veneration,
Hath knit thee to him from thy earliest youth.
Thou nourishest the *wish*,—O let me still
Anticipate thy loitering confidence !
The *hope* thou nourishest to knit thyself
Yet closer to him——

MAX

          Father——

OCTAVIO.

          O my son !
I trust thy heart undoubtingly. But am I
Equally sure of thy collectedness ?
Wilt thou be able, with calm countenance,
To enter this man's presence, when that I
Have trusted to thee his whole fate !

MAX.

          According
As thou dost trust me, father, with his crime.
  [OCTAVIO *takes a paper out of his escrutoire, and*
    gives it to him.

MAX.

What ! how ! a full Imperial patent !

OCTAVIO.

          Read it.

MAX. (*just glances on it*).
Duke Friedland sentenced and condemn'd !

OCTAVIO.

          Even so.

MAX. (*throws down the paper*).
O this is too much ! O unhappy error !

OCTAVIO.

Read on. Collect thyself.

MAX. (*after he has read further, with a look of
    affright and astonishment on his father.*)
          How ! what ! Thou ! thou !

OCTAVIO.

But for the present moment, till the King,
Of Hungary may safely join the army,
Is the command assign'd to me.

MAX.

          And think'st thou,
Dost thou believe, that thou wilt tear it from him ?
O never hope it !—Father ! father ! father !
An inauspicious office is enjoin'd thee.
This paper here—this ! and wilt thou enforce it ?
The mighty in the middle of his host,

Surrounded by his thousands, him wouldst thou
Disarm—degrade! Thou art lost, both thou and all
[of us.

OCTAVIO.

What hazard I incur thereby, I know.
In the great hand of God I stand. The Almighty
Will cover with his shield the Imperial house,
And shatter, in his wrath, the work of darkness.
The Emperor hath true servants still; and even
Here in the camp, there are enough brave men
Who for the good cause will fight gallantly.
The faithful have been warn'd—the dangerous
Are closely watch'd. I wait but the first step,
And then immediately——

MAX.

What! on suspicion!
Immediately!

OCTAVIO.

The Emperor is no tyrant.
The deed alone he'll punish, not the wish.
The Duke hath yet his destiny in his power.
Let him but leave the treason uncompleted,
He will be silently displaced from office,
And make way to his Emperor's royal son.
An honourable exile to his castles
Will be a benefaction to him rather
Than punishment. But the first open step——

MAX.

What callest thou such a step! A wicked step
Ne'er will he take; but thou mightest easily,
Yea, thou hast done it, misinterpret him.

OCTAVIO.

Nay, howsoever punishable were
Duke Friedland's purposes, yet still the steps
Which he hath taken openly, permit
A mild construction. It is my intention
To leave this paper wholly uninforced
Till some act is committed which convicts him
Of high-treason, without doubt or plea,
And that shall sentence him.

MAX.

But who the judge!

OCTAVIO.

Thyself.

MAX.

For ever, then, this paper will lie idle.

OCTAVIO.

Too soon, I fear, its powers must all be proved.
After the counter-promise of this evening,
It cannot be but he must deem himself
Secure of the majority with us;
And of the army's general sentiment
He hath a pleasing proof in that petition,
Which thou deliver'st to him from the regiments.
Add this too—I have letters that the Rhinegrave
Hath changed his route, and travels by forced
marches
To the Bohemian forests. What this purports
Remains unknown; and, to confirm suspicion,
This night a Swedish nobleman arrived here.

MAX.

I have thy word. Thou'lt not proceed to action
Before thou hast convinced me—me myself.

OCTAVIO.

Is it possible! Still, after all thou know'st,
Canst thou believe still in his innocence!

MAX. (with enthusiasm).

Thy judgment may mistake; my heart can not.
[Moderates his voice and manner.

These reasons might expound thy spirit or mine;
But they expound not Friedland—I have faith:
For as he knits his fortunes to the stars,
Even so doth he resemble them in secret,
Wonderful, still inexplicable courses!
Trust me, they do him wrong. All will be solved.
These smokes at once will kindle into flame—
The edges of this black and stormy cloud
Will brighten suddenly, and we shall view
The Unapproachable glide out in splendour.

OCTAVIO.

I will await it.

SCENE II.

OCTAVIO and MAX. as before. To them the Valet of the
Chamber.

OCTAVIO.

How now, then!

VALET.

A despatch is at the door.

OCTAVIO.

So early! From whom comes he then! Who is it!

VALET.

That he refused to tell me.

OCTAVIO.

Lead him in:
And, hark you—let it not transpire.
[Exit Valet; the cornet steps in.

OCTAVIO.

Ha! Cornet—is it you! and from Count Galas!
Give me your letters.

CORNET.

The Lieutenant-general
Trusted it not to letters.

OCTAVIO.

And what is it!

CORNET.

He bade me tell you—Dare I speak openly here!

OCTAVIO.

My son knows all.

CORNET.

We have him.

OCTAVIO.

Whom!

CORNET.

Sesina,
The old negociator.

OCTAVIO (eagerly).

And you have him!

CORNET.

In the Bohemian Forest Captain Mohrbrand
Found and secured him yester morning early:
He was proceeding then to Regensburg,
And on him were despatches for the Swede.

OCTAVIO.

And the despatches——

CORNET.

The Lieutenant-general
Sent them that instant to Vienna, and
The prisoner with them.

OCTAVIO.

This is, indeed, a tiding!
That fellow is a precious casket to us,
Enclosing weighty things.—Was much found on
him!

CORNET.

I think, six packets, with Count Tertsky's arms.

OCTAVIO.

None in the Duke's own hand!

CORNET.

Not that I know.

OCTAVIO.

And old Sesina!

CORNET.

He was sorely frighten'd,
When it was told him he must to Vienna.
But the Count Altringer bade him take heart,
Would he but make a full and free confession.

OCTAVIO.

Is Altringer then with your Lord! I heard
That he lay sick at Linz.

CORNET.

These three days past
He's with my master, the Lieutenant-general,
At Frauenburg. Already have they sixty
Small companies together, chosen men;
Respectfully they greet you with assurances,
That they are only waiting your commands.

OCTAVIO.

In a few days may great events take place.
And when must you return!

CORNET.

I wait your orders.

OCTAVIO.

Remain till evening.

Cornet signifies his assent and obeisance, and is going.
No one saw you—ha!

CORNET.

No living creature. Through the cloister wicket
The Capuchins, as usual, let me in.

OCTAVIO.

Go, rest your limbs, and keep yourself conceal'd
I hold it probable, that yet ere evening
I shall despatch you. The development
Of this affair approaches : ere the day,
That even now is dawning in the heaven,
Ere this eventful day hath set, the lot
That must decide our fortunes will be drawn.

[Exit Cornet.

———◆———

SCENE III.

OCTAVIO *and* MAX. PICCOLOMINI.

OCTAVIO.

Well—and what now, son! All will soon be clear ;
For all, I'm certain, went through that Sesina.

MAX. (*who through the whole of the foregoing scene
has been in a violent and visible struggle of feelings, at length starts as one resolved*).
I will procure me light a shorter way.
Farewell.

OCTAVIO.

Where now!—Remain here.

MAX.

To the Duke.

OCTAVIO (*alarmed*).
What——

MAX. (*returning*).
If thou hast believed that I shall act
A part in this thy play——
Thou hast miscalculated on me grievously.
My way must be straight on. True with the tongue,

False with the heart—I may not, cannot be :
Nor can I suffer that a man should trust me—
As his friend trust me—and then lull my conscience
With such low pleas as these :—" I ask him not—
He did it all at his own hazard—and
My *mouth* has never lied to him."—No, no !
What a friend takes me for, that I must be.
—I'll to the Duke ; ere yet this day is ended
Will I demand of him that he do save
His good name from the world, and with one stride
Break through and rend this fine-spun web of yours.
He can, he will !—*I* still am his believer.
Yet I'll not pledge myself, but that those letters
May furnish you, perchance, with proofs against him.
How far may not this Tertsky have proceeded—
What may not he himself too have permitted
Himself to do, to snare the enemy,
The laws of war excusing ! Nothing, save
His own mouth shall convict him—nothing less !
And face to face will I go question him.

OCTAVIO.

Thou wilt !

MAX.

I will, as sure as this heart beats.

OCTAVIO.

I have, indeed, miscalculated on thee.
I calculated on a prudent son,
Who would have bless'd the hand beneficent
That pluck'd him back from the abyss—and lo !
A fascinated being I discover,
Whom his two eyes befool, whom passion wilders,
Whom not the broadest light of noon can heal.
Go, question him !—Be mad enough, I pray thee.
The purpose of thy father, of thy Emperor,
Go, give it up free booty !—Force me, drive me
To an open breach before the time. And now,
Now that a miracle of Heaven had guarded
My secret purpose even to this hour,
And laid to sleep Suspicion's piercing eyes,
Let me have lived to see that mine own son,
With frantic enterprise, annihilates
My toilsome labours and state-policy.

MAX.

Ay—this state-policy ! O how I curse it !
You will some time, with your state-policy,
Compel him to the measure : it may happen,
Because ye are *determined* that he is guilty,
Guilty ye'll *make* him. All retreat cut off,
You close up every outlet, hem him in
Narrower and narrower, till at length ye force him—
Yes, ye,—ye *force* him, in his desperation,
To set fire to his prison. Father ! father !
That never can end well—it cannot—will not !
And let it be decided as it may,
I see with boding heart the near approach
Of an ill-starr'd, unblest catastrophe.
For this great Monarch-spirit, if he fall,
Will drag a world into the ruin with him.
And as a ship (that midway on the ocean
Takes fire) at once, and with a thunder-burst
Explodes, and with itself shoots out its crew
In smoke and ruin betwixt sea and heaven ;
So will he, falling, draw down in his fall
All us, who 're fix'd and mortised to his fortune.
Deem of it what thou wilt ; but pardon me,
That I must bear me on in my own way.
All must remain pure betwixt him and me ;
And, ere the day-light dawns, it must be known
Which I must lose—my father, or my friend.

[During his exit the curtain drops.

ACT IV.

SCENE I.

A Room fitted up for astrological labours, and provided with celestial Charts, with Globes, Telescopes, Quadrants, and other mathematical Instruments.—Seven Colossal Figures, representing the Planets, each with a transparent Star of a different Colour on its Head, stand in a semicircle in the Back-ground, so that Mars and Saturn are nearest the Eye.—The Remainder of the Scene, and its Disposition, is given in the Fourth Scene of the Second Act.— There must be a Curtain over the Figures, which may be dropped, and conceal them on occasions.

[*In the Fifth Scene of this Act it must be dropped; but in the Seventh Scene, it must be again drawn up wholly or in part.*]

WALLENSTEIN *at a black Table, on which a Speculum Astrologicum is described with Chalk.* SENI *is taking Observations through a window.*

WALLENSTEIN.

All well—and now let it be ended, Seni.—Come,
The dawn commences, and Mars rules the hour.
We must give o'er the operation.   Come,
We know enough.

SENI.
          Your Highness must permit me
Just to contemplate Venus.   She's now rising:
Like as a sun, so shines she in the east.

WALLENSTEIN.

She is at present in her perigee,
And shoots down now her strongest influences.
          [*Contemplating the figure on the table.*
Auspicious aspect! fateful in conjunction,
At length the mighty three corradiate;
And the two stars of blessing, Jupiter
And Venus, take between them the malignant
Slily-malicious Mars, and thus compel
Into *my* service that old mischief-founder:
For long he view'd me hostilely, and ever
With beam oblique, or perpendicular,
Now in the Quartile, now in the Secundan,
Shot his red lightnings at my stars, disturbing
Their blessed influences and sweet aspects.
Now they have conquer'd the old enemy,
And bring him in the heavens a prisoner to me.

SENI (*who has come down from the window*).
And in a corner house, your Highness—think of
  that!
That makes each influence of double strength.

WALLENSTEIN:

And sun and moon, too, in the Sextile aspect,
The soft light with the vehement—so I love it.
SOL is the heart, LUNA the head of heaven,
Bold be the plan, fiery the execution.

SENI.
And both the mighty Lumina by no
Maleficus *affronted*.   Lo! Saturnus,
Innocuous, powerless, in cadente Domo.

WALLENSTEIN.

The empire of Saturnus is gone by;
Lord of the secret birth of things is he;
Within the lap of earth, and in the depths
Of the imagination dominates;
And his are all things that eschew the light.

The time is o'er of brooding and contrivance,
For Jupiter, the lustrous, lordeth now,
And the dark work, complete of preparation,
He draws by force into the realm of light.
Now must we hasten on to action, ere
The scheme, and most auspicious positure
Parts o'er my head, and takes once more its flight;
For the heavens journey still, and sojourn not.
         [*There are knocks at the door.*
There's some one knocking there.   See who it is.

TERTSKY (*from without*).
Open, and let me in.

WALLENSTEIN.
          Ay—'t is Tertsky.
What is there of such urgence!   We are busy.

TERTSKY (*from without*).
Lay all aside at present, I entreat you.
It suffers no delaying.

WALLENSTEIN.
         Open, Seni!
[*While SENI opens the door for TERTSKY, WALLENSTEIN draws the curtain over the figures*

TERTSKY (*enters*).
Hast thou already heard it!   He is taken.
Galas has given him up to the Emperor.
        [*SENI draws off the black table, and exit.*

SCENE II.

WALLENSTEIN, COUNT TERTSKY.

WALLENSTEIN (*to* TERTSKY).
Who has been taken!   Who is given up!

TERTSKY.
The man who knows our secrets, who knows every
Negotiation with the Swede and Saxon,
Through whose hands all and every thing has
  pass'd—

WALLENSTEIN (*drawing back*).
Nay, not Sesina!—Say, No!   I entreat thee.

TERTSKY.
All on his road for Regensburg to the Swede
He was plunged down upon by Galas' agent,
Who had been long in ambush, lurking for him.
There must have been found on him my whole packet
To Thur, to Kinsky, to Oxenstirn, to Arnheim:
All this is in their hands; they have now an insight
Into the whole—our measures, and our motives.

SCENE III.

To them enters ILLO.

ILLO (*to* TERTSKY).
Has he heard it!

TERTSKY.
        He has heard it.

ILLO (*to* WALLENSTEIN).
          Thinkest thou still
To make thy peace with the Emperor, to regain
His confidence!—E'en were it now thy wish
To abandon all thy plans, yet still they know

D

What thou hast wish'd : then forwards thou must
Retreat is now no longer in thy power.   [press ;

TERTSKY.

They have documents against us, and in hands,
Which show beyond all power of contradiction—

WALLENSTEIN.

Of my hand-writing—no iota.   Thee
I punish for thy lies.

ILLO.

And thou believest,
That what this man, that what thy sister's husband,
Did in thy name, will not stand on thy reck'ning !
His word must pass for thy word with the Swede,
And not with those that hate thee at Vienna !

TERTSKY.

In writing thou gavest nothing—But bethink thee,
How far thou ventured'st by word of mouth
With this Sesina ! And will he be silent !
If he can save himself by yielding up
Thy secret purposes, will he retain them !

ILLO.

Thyself dost not conceive it possible ;
And since they now have evidence authentic
How far thou hast already gone, speak !—tell us,
What art thou waiting for ! thou canst no longer
Keep thy command ; and beyond hope of rescue
Thou 'rt lost, if thou resign'st it.

WALLENSTEIN.

In the army
Lies my security. The army will not
Abandon me.   Whatever they may know,
The power is mine, and they must gulp it down—
And substitute I caution for my fealty,
They must be satisfied, at least appear so.

ILLO.

The army, Duke, *is* thine now—for this moment—
'T is thine : but think with terror on the slow,
The quiet power of time. From open violence
The attachment of thy soldiery secures thee
To-day—to-morrow : but grant'st thou them a
respite,
Unheard, unseen, they'll undermine that love
On which thou now dost feel so firm a footing,
With wily theft will draw away from thee
One after the other—

WALLENSTEIN.

'T is a cursed accident !

ILLO.

Oh ! I will call it a most blessed one,
If it work on thee as it ought to do,
Hurry thee on to action—to decision—
The Swedish General—

WALLENSTEIN.

He 's arrived ! Know'st thou
What his commission is—

ILLO.

To thee alone
Will he entrust the purpose of his coming.

WALLENSTEIN.

A cursed, cursed accident ! Yes, yes,
Sesina knows too much, and won't be silent.

TERTSKY.

He 's a Bohemian fugitive and rebel,
His neck is forfeit.   Can he save himself
At thy cost, think you he will scruple it !
And if they put him to the torture, will he,
Will *he*, that dastardling, have strength enough—

WALLENSTEIN (*lost in thought*).

Their confidence is lost—irreparably !
And I may act what way I will, I shall
Be and remain for ever in their thought
A traitor to my country.   How sincerely
Soever I return back to my duty,
It will no longer help me——

ILLO.

Ruin thee,
That it will do ! Not thy fidelity,
Thy weakness will be deem'd the sole occasion—

WALLENSTEIN (*pacing up and down in extreme
agitation*).

What ! I must realize it now in earnest,
Because I toy'd too freely with the thought !
Accursed he who dallies with a devil !
And must I—I *must* realize it now—
Now, while I have the power, it *must* take place !

ILLO.

Now—now—ere they can ward and parry it !

WALLENSTEIN (*looking at the paper of signatures*).

I have the Generals' word—a written promise !
Max. Piccolomini stands not here—how's that !

TERTSKY.

It was——he fancied——

ILLO.

Mere self-willedness.
There needed no such thing 'twixt him and you

WALLENSTEIN.

He is quite right—there needeth no such thing.
The regiments, too, deny to march for Flanders—
Have sent me in a paper of remonstrance,
And openly resist the imperial orders.
The first step to revolt 's already taken.

ILLO.

Believe me, thou wilt find it far more easy
To lead them over to the enemy
Than to the Spaniard.

WALLENSTEIN.

I will hear, however,
What the Swede has to say to me.

ILLO (*eagerly to* TERTSKY).

Go, call him !
He stands without the door in waiting.

WALLENSTEIN.

Stay !
Stay yet a little.   It hath taken me
All by surprise,—it came too quick upon me ;
'T is wholly novel, that an accident,
With its dark lordship, and blind agency,
Should force me on with it.

ILLO.

First hear him only,
And after weigh it.   [*Exeunt* TERTSKY *and* ILLO.

SCENE IV.

WALLENSTEIN (*in soliloquy*).
Is it possible !
Is 't so ! I can no longer what I *would* ?
No longer draw back at my liking ! I
Must *do* the deed, because I *thought* of it !
And fed this heart here with a dream ! Because
I did not scowl temptation from my presence,
Dallied with thoughts of possible fulfilment,

Commenced no movement, left all time uncertain,
And only kept the road, the access open !
By the great God of Heaven ! It was not
My serious meaning, it was ne'er resolve.
I but amused myself with thinking of it.
The free-will tempted me, the power to do
Or not to do it.—Was it criminal
To make the fancy minister to hope,
To fill the air with pretty toys of air,
And clutch fantastic sceptres moving t'ward me !
Was not the will kept free ! Beheld I not
The road of duty close beside me—but
One little step, and once more I was in it !
Where am I ! Whither have I been transported !
No road, no track behind me, but a wall,
Impenetrable, insurmountable,
Rises obedient to the spells I mutter'd
And meant not—my own doings tower behind me.
    [Pauses and remains in deep thought.
A punishable man I seem ; the guilt,
Try what I will, I cannot roll off from me
The equivocal demeanour of my life
Bears witness on my prosecutor's party.
And even my purest acts from purest motives
Suspicion poisons with malicious gloss.
Were I that thing for which I pass, that traitor,
A goodly outside I had sure reserved,
Had drawn the coverings thick and double round
Been calm and chary of my utterance ;   [me,
But being conscious of the innocence
Of my intent, my uncorrupted will,
I gave way to my humours, to my passion :
Bold were my words, because my deeds were *not.*
Now every planless measure, chance event,
The threat of rage, the vaunt of joy and triumph,
And all the May-games of a heart o'er-flowing,
Will they connect, and weave them all together
Into one web of treason ; all will be plan,
My eye ne'er absent from the far-off mark,
Step tracing step, each step a politic progress ;
And out of all they'll fabricate a charge
So specious, that I must myself stand dumb.
I am caught in my own net, and only force,
Nought but a sudden rent can liberate me.
    [Pauses again.
How else ! since that the heart 's unbiass'd instinct
Impell'd me to the daring deed, which now
Necessity, self-preservation, *orders.*
Stern is the On-look of Necessity,
Not without shudder may a human hand
Grasp the mysterious urn of destiny.
My deed was mine, remaining in my bosom :
Once suffer'd to escape from its safe corner
Within the heart, its nursery and birth-place,
Sent forth into the Foreign, it belongs
For ever to those sly malicious powers
Whom never art of man conciliated.
    *[Paces in agitation through the chamber, then pauses,
    and, after the pause, breaks out again into audible
    soliloquy.*
What is thy enterprise ! thy aim ! thy object !
Hast honestly confess'd it to thyself !
Power seated on a quiet throne thou 'dst shake,
Power on an ancient consecrated throne,
Strong in possession, founded in old custom ;
Power by a thousand tough and stringy roots
Fix'd to the people's pious nursery-faith.
This, this will be no strife of strength with strength.
That fear'd I not. I brave each combatant,
Whom I can look on, fixing eye to eye,

Who, full himself of courage, kindles courage
In me too. 'T is a foe invisible,
The which I fear—a fearful enemy,
Which in the human heart opposes me,
By its coward fear alone made fearful to me.
Not that, which full of life, instinct with power,
Makes known its present being ; that is not
The true, the perilously formidable.
O no ! it is the common, the quite common,
The thing of an eternal yesterday,
What ever was, and evermore returns,
Sterling to-morrow, for to-day 't was sterling !
For of the wholly common is man made,
And custom is his nurse ! Woe then to them,
Who lay irreverent hands upon his old
House furniture, the dear inheritance
From his forefathers ! For time consecrates ;
And what is grey with age becomes religion.
Be in possession, and thou hast the right,
And sacred will the many guard it for thee !
    [To the PAGE, who here enters.
The Swedish officer !—Well, let him enter.
    *[The PAGE exit, WALLENSTEIN fixes his eye in deed
    thought on the door*
Yet is it pure—as yet !—the crime has come
Not o'er this threshold yet—so slender is
The boundary that divideth life's two paths.

———•———

SCENE V.

WALLENSTEIN and WRANGEL.

WALLENSTEIN (*after having fixed a searching look
    on him.*)
Your name is Wrangel !

      WRANGEL.
      Gustave Wrangel, General
Of the Sudermanian Blues.

      WALLENSTEIN.
      It was a Wrangel
Who injured me materially at Stralsund,
And by his brave resistance was the cause
Of the opposition which that sea-port made.

      WRANGEL.
It was the doing of the element   [merit.
With which you fought, my Lord ! and not my
The Baltic Neptune did assert his freedom :
The sea and land, it seem'd, were not to serve
One and the same.

WALLENSTEIN (*makes the motion for him to take a
    seat, and seats himself.*)
      And where are your credentials !
Come you provided with full powers, Sir General !

      WRANGEL.
There are so many scruples yet to solve——

WALLENSTEIN (*having read the credentials.*)
An able letter !—Ay—he is a prudent
Intelligent master, whom you serve, Sir General !
The Chancellor writes me, that he but fulfils
His late departed Sovereign's own idea
In helping me to the Bohemian crown.

      WRANGEL.
He says the truth. Our great King, now in heaven,
Did ever deem most highly of your Grace's
Pre-eminent sense and military genius ;
And always the commanding Intellect,
He said, should have command, and be the King.

          D 2

WALLENSTEIN.

Yes, he *might* say it safely.—General Wrangel,
[*Taking his hand affectionately.*
Come, fair and open.—Trust me, I was always
A Swede at heart. Eh! that did you experience
Both in Silesia and at Nuremberg;
I had you often in my power, and let you
Always slip out by some back-door or other.
'Tis this for which the Court can ne'er forgive me,
Which drives me to this present step: and since
Our interests so run in one direction,
E'en let us have a thorough confidence
Each in the other.

WRANGEL.
Confidence will come
Has each but only first security.

WALLENSTEIN.

The Chancellor still, I see, does not quite trust me;
And, I confess—the gain does not lie wholly
To my advantage—Without doubt he thinks,
If I can play false with the Emperor,
Who is my Sov'reign, I can do the like
With the enemy, and that *the one* too were
Sooner to be forgiven me than the *other*.
Is not this your opinion too, Sir General?

WRANGEL.
I have here an office merely, no opinion.

WALLENSTEIN.

The Emperor hath urged me to the uttermost:
I can no longer honourably serve him.
For my security, in self-defence,
I take this hard step, which my conscience blames.

WRANGEL.

That I believe. So far would no one go
Who was not forced to it. [*After a pause.*
What may have impell'd
Your princely Highness in this wise to act
Toward your Sovereign Lord and Emperor,
Beseems not us to expound or criticise.
The Swede is fighting for his good old cause,
With his good sword and conscience. This con-
currence,
This opportunity, is in our favour,
And all advantages in war are lawful.
We take what offers without questioning;
And if all have its due and just proportions——

WALLENSTEIN.

Of what then are ye doubting? Of my will?
Or of my power? I pledged me to the Chancellor,
Would he trust *me* with sixteen thousand men,
That I would instantly go over to them
With eighteen thousand of the Emperor's troops.

WRANGEL.

Your Grace is known to be a mighty war-chief,
To be a second Attila and Pyrrhus.
'Tis talked of still with fresh astonishment,
How some years past, beyond all human faith,
You call'd an army forth, like a creation:
But yet——

WALLENSTEIN.
But yet?

WRANGEL.
But still the Chancellor thinks,
It might yet be an easier thing from nothing
To call forth sixty thousand men of battle,
Than to persuade one sixtieth part of them——

WALLENSTEIN.

What now? Out with it, friend?

WRANGEL.
To break their oaths.

WALLENSTEIN.

And he thinks so?—He judges like a Swede,
And like a Protestant. You Lutherans
Fight for your Bible. You are interested
About the cause; and with your *hearts* you follow
Your banners.—Among *you*, whoe'er deserts
To the enemy, hath broken covenant [fancies.
With two Lords at one time.—We've no such

WRANGEL.

Great God in Heaven! Have then the people here
No house and home, no fire-side, no altar?

WALLENSTEIN.

I will explain that to you, how it stands:—
The Austrian *has* a country, ay, and loves it,
And has good cause to love it—but this army,
That calls itself the Imperial, this that houses
Here in Bohemia, this has none—no country;
This is an outcast of all foreign lands,
Unclaim'd by town or tribe, to whom belongs
Nothing, except the universal sun.

WRANGEL.

But then the Nobles and the Officers?
Such a desertion, such a felony,
It is without example, my Lord Duke,
In the world's history.

WALLENSTEIN.

They are all mine—
Mine unconditionally—mine on all terms.
Not me, your own eyes you must trust.
[*He gives him the paper containing the written oath.*
WRANGEL *reads it through, and, having read it,
lays it on the table, remaining silent.*
So then?

Now comprehend you?

WRANGEL.
Comprehend who can!
My Lord Duke; I will let the mask drop—yes!
I've full powers for a final settlement.
The Rhinegrave stands but four days' march from
With fifteen thousand men, and only waits [here
For orders to proceed and join your army.
Those orders *I* give out, immediately
We're compromised.

WALLENSTEIN.
What asks the Chancellor?

WRANGEL (*considerately*).
Twelve regiments, every man a Swede—my head
The warranty—and all might prove at last
Only false play——

WALLENSTEIN (*starting*).
Sir Swede!

WRANGEL (*calmly proceeding*).
Am therefore forced
T' insist thereon, that he do formally,
Irrevocably break with the Emperor,
Else not a Swede is trusted to Duke Friedland.

WALLENSTEIN.
Come, brief, and open! What is the demand?

WRANGEL.
That he forthwith disarm the Spanish regiments
Attached to the Emperor, that he seize Prague,
And to the Swedes give up that city, with
The strong pass Egra.

WALLENSTEIN.

That is much indeed!
Prague!—Egra's granted—But—but Prague!—
I give you every security   ['Twon't do.
Which you may ask of me in common reason—
But Prague—Bohemia—these, sir General,
I can myself protect.

WRANGEL.
                We doubt it not.
But 'tis not the protection that is now
Our sole concern. We want security,
That we shall not expend our men and money
All to no purpose.

WALLENSTEIN.
          'Tis but reasonable.

WRANGEL.
And till we are indemnified, so long
Stays Prague in pledge.

WALLENSTEIN.
                Then trust you us so little!

WRANGEL (rising).
The Swede, if he would treat well with the German,
Must keep a sharp look-out. We have been call'd
Over the Baltic, we have saved the empire
From ruin—with our best blood have we sealed
The liberty of faith, and gospel truth.
But now already is the benefaction
No longer felt, the load alone is felt.—
Ye look askance with evil eye upon us,
As foreigners, intruders in the empire,
And would fain send us, with some paltry sum
Of money, home again to our old forests.
No, no! my Lord Duke! no!—it never was
For Judas' pay, for chinking gold and silver,
That we did leave our King by the Great Stone[1].
No, not for gold and silver have there bled
So many of our Swedish Nobles—neither
Will we, with empty laurels for our payment,
Hoist sail for our own country. Citizens
Will we remain upon the soil, the which
Our Monarch conquer'd for himself, and died.

WALLENSTEIN.
Help to keep down the common enemy,
And the fair border land must needs be yours.

WRANGEL.
But when the common enemy lies vanquish'd,
Who knits together our new friendship then!
We know, Duke Friedland! though perhaps the
       Swede
Ought not t' have known it, that you carry on
Secret negotiations with the Saxons.
Who is our warranty, that we are not
The sacrifices in those articles
Which 'tis thought needful to conceal from us!

WALLENSTEIN (rises).
Think you of something better, Gustave Wrangel!
Of Prague no more.

WRANGEL.
            Here my commission ends.

WALLENSTEIN.
Surrender up to you my capital!
Far liever would I face about, and step
Back to my Emperor.

---

[1] A great stone near Lützen, since called the Swede's
Stone, the body of their great king having been found at
the foot of it, after the battle in which he lost his life.

WRANGEL.
    If time yet permits—

WALLENSTEIN.
That lies with me, even now, at any hour.

WRANGEL.
Some days ago, perhaps. To-day, no longer;
No longer since Sesina's been a prisoner.
          [WALLENSTEIN is struck, and silenced.
My lord Duke, hear me—We believe that you
At present do mean honourably by us.
Since yesterday we're sure of that—and now
This paper warrants for the troops, there's nothing
Stands in the way of our full confidence.
Prague shall not part us. Hear! The Chancellor
Contents himself with Albstadt ; to your Grace
He gives up Ratschin and the narrow side.
But Egra above all must open to us,
Ere we can think of any junction.

WALLENSTEIN.
                    You,
You therefore must I trust, and you not me!
I will consider of your proposition.

WRANGEL.
I must entreat, that your consideration
Occupy not too long a time. Already
Has this negotiation, my Lord Duke!
Crept on into the second year. If nothing
Is settled this time, will the Chancellor
Consider it as broken off for ever.

WALLENSTEIN.
Ye press me hard. A measure such as this,
Ought to be thought of.

WRANGEL.
                Ay! but think of this too,
That sudden action only can procure it
Success—think first of this, your Highness.
                    [Exit WRANGEL.

SCENE VI.

WALLENSTEIN, TERTSKY, and ILLO (re-enter.)

ILLO.
Is't all right!

TERTSKY.
        Are you compromised!

ILLO.
                This Swede
Went smiling from you. Yes! you're compromised.

WALLENSTEIN.
As yet is nothing settled : and (well weighed)
I feel myself inclined to leave it so.

TERTSKY.
How! What is that!

WALLENSTEIN.
            Come on me what will come,
The doing evil to avoid an evil
Cannot be good!

TERTSKY.
        Nay, but bethink you, Duke.

WALLENSTEIN.
To live upon the mercy of these Swedes!   [it.
Of these proud-hearted Swedes!—I could not bear

ILLO.
Goest thou as fugitive, as mendicant!
Bringest thou not more to them than thou receivest!

SCENE VII.

To these enter the COUNTESS TERTSKY.

WALLENSTEIN.

Who sent for you? There is no business here
For women.

COUNTESS.

I am come to bid you joy.

WALLENSTEIN.

Use thy authority, Tertsky; bid her go.

COUNTESS.

Come I perhaps too early? I hope not.

WALLENSTEIN.

Set not this tongue upon me, I entreat you:
You know it is the weapon that destroys me.
I am routed, if a woman but attack me:
I cannot traffic in the trade of words
With that unreasoning sex.

COUNTESS.

                              I had already
Given the Bohemians a king.

WALLENSTEIN (*sarcastically*).

                              They have one,
In consequence, no doubt.

COUNTESS (*to the others*).

                              Ha! what new scruple?

TERTSKY.

The Duke will not.

COUNTESS.

He *will not* what he *must!*

ILLO.

It lies with you now.   Try.   For I am silenced,
When folks begin to talk to me of conscience,
And of fidelity.

COUNTESS.

                    How! then, when all
Lay in the far-off distance, when the road
Stretch'd out before thine eyes interminably,
Then hadst thou courage and resolve; and now,
Now that the dream is being realised,
The purpose ripe, the issue ascertain'd,
Dost thou begin to play the dastard now?
Plann'd merely, 't is a common felony;
Accomplish'd, an immortal undertaking:
And with success comes pardon hand in hand;
For all event is God's arbitrement.

SERVANT (*enters*).

The colonel Piccolomini.

COUNTESS (*hastily*).

                    —Must wait.

WALLENSTEIN.

I cannot see him now.   Another time.

SERVANT.

But for two minutes he entreats an audience:
Of the most urgent nature is his business.

WALLENSTEIN.

Who knows what he may bring us! I will hear him.

COUNTESS (*laughs*).

Urgent for him, no doubt! but thou mayst wait.

WALLENSTEIN.

What is it?

COUNTESS.

                    Thou shalt be inform'd hereafter.
First let the Swede and thee be compromised.

                              ‚ [*Exit* Servant.

WALLENSTEIN.

If there were yet a choice! if yet some milder
Way of escape were possible—I still
Will choose it, and avoid the last extreme.

COUNTESS.

Desirest thou nothing further? Such a way
Lies still before thee.   Send this Wrangel off.
Forget thou thy old hopes, cast far away
All thy past life; determine to commence
A new one.   Virtue hath her heroes too,
As well as Fame and Fortune.—To Vienna—
Hence—to the Emperor—kneel before the throne;
Take a full coffer with thee—say aloud,
Thou didst but wish to prove thy fealty;
Thy whole intention but to dupe the Swede.

ILLO.

For that too 't is too late.   They know too much;
He would but bear his own head to the block.

COUNTESS.

I fear not that.   They have not evidence
To attaint him legally, and they avoid
The avowal of an arbitrary power.
They'll let the Duke resign without disturbance.
I see how all will end.   The King of Hungary
Makes his appearance, and 't will of itself
Be understood, that then the Duke retires.
There will not want a formal declaration:
The young King will administer the oath
To the whole army; and so all returns
To the old position.   On some morrow morning
The Duke departs; and now 't is stir and bustle
Within his castles.   He will hunt, and build;
Superintend his horses' pedigrees,
Creates himself a court, gives golden keys,
And introduceth strictest ceremony
In fine proportions, and nice etiquette.
Keeps open table with high cheer: in brief,
Commenceth mighty King—in miniature.
And while he prudently demeans himself,
And gives himself no actual importance,
He will be let appear whate'er he likes:
And who dares doubt, that Friedland will appear
A mighty Prince to his last dying hour?
Well now, what then! Duke Friedland is as others,
A fire-new Noble, whom the war hath raised
To price and currency, a Jonah's gourd,
An over-night creation of court-favour,
Which with an undistinguishable ease
Makes Baron or makes Prince.

WALLENSTEIN (*in extreme agitation*).

                              Take her away.
Let in the young Count Piccolomini.

COUNTESS.

Art thou in earnest? I I entreat thee! Canst thou
Consent to bear thyself to thy own grave,
So ignominiously to be dried up?
Thy life, that arrogated such an height
To end in such a nothing! To be nothing,
When one was always nothing, is an evil
That asks no stretch of patience, a light evil;
But to become a nothing, having been——

WALLENSTEIN (*starts up in violent agitation*).

Show me a way out of this stifling crowd,
Ye powers of Aidance! Show me such a way
As *I* am capable of going.—I
Am no tongue-hero, no fine virtue-prattler;
I cannot warm by thinking; cannot say
To the good luck that turns her back upon me,

Magnanimously : " Go ; I need thee not.''
Cease I to work, I am annihilated.
Dangers nor sacrifices will I shun,
If so I may avoid the last extreme ;
But ere I sink down into nothingness,
Leave off so little, who began so great,
Ere that the world confuses me with those
Poor wretches, whom a day creates and crumbles,
This age and after ages[1] speak my name
With hate and dread ; and Friedland be redemp-
For each accursed deed ! [tion

COUNTESS.
            What is there here, then,
So against nature ! Help me to perceive it !
*O let not Superstition's nightly goblins
Subdue thy clear bright spirit ! Art thou bid
To murder !—with abhorr'd accursed poniard,
To violate the breasts that nourish'd thee ?
That *were* against our nature, that might aptly
Make thy flesh shudder, and thy whole heart sicken[2].
Yet not a few, and for a meaner object,
Have ventured even this, ay, and perform'd it.
What is there in thy case so black and monstrous ?
Thou art accused of treason—whether with
Or without justice is not now the question—
Thou art lost if thou dost not avail thee quickly
Of the power which thou possessest—Friedland !
  Duke !
Tell me where lives that thing so meek and tame,
That doth not all his living faculties
Put forth in preservation of his life ?
What deed so daring, which necessity
And desperation will not sanctify ?

WALLENSTEIN.
Once was this Ferdinand so gracious to me :
He loved me ; he esteem'd me ; I was placed
The nearest to his heart. Full many a time
We like familiar friends, both at one table,
Have banqueted together. He and I—
And the young kings themselves held me the bason
Wherewith to wash me—and is 't come to this !

COUNTESS.
So faithfully preservest thou each small favour,
And hast no memory for contumelies ?
Must I remind thee, how at Regensburg
This man repaid thy faithful services ?
All ranks and all conditions in the empire
Thou hadst wrong'd, to make him great,—hadst
  loaded on thee,
On *thee*, the hate, the curse of the whole world.
No friend existed for thee in all Germany,
And why ? because thou hadst existed only
For the Emperor. To the Emperor alone
Clung Friedland in that storm which gather'd
  round him
At Regensburg in the Diet—and he dropp'd thee !
He let thee fall ! he let thee fall a victim
To the Bavarian, to that insolent !
Deposed, stript bare of all thy dignity
And power, amid the taunting of thy foes,

[1] Could I have hazarded such a Germanism, as the use
of the word after-world, for posterity,—" Es spreche Welt
und *Nachwelt* meinen Namen "—might have been rendered with more literal fidelity :—Let world and after-
world speak out my name, etc.
[2] I have not ventured to affront the fastidious delicacy
of our age with a literal translation of this line,
                      werth
      Die Eingeweide schaudernd aufzuregen.

Thou wert let drop into obscurity.—
Say not, the restoration of thy honour
Has made atonement for that first injustice.
No honest good-will was it that replaced thee ;
The law of hard necessity replaced thee,
Which they had fain opposed, but that they could
WALLENSTEIN. [not.
Not to their good wishes, that is certain,
Nor yet to his affection I'm indebted
For this high office ; and if I abuse it,
I shall therein abuse no confidence.

COUNTESS.
Affection ! confidence !—they *needed* thee.
Necessity, impetuous remonstrant !
Who not with empty names, or shows of proxy,
Is served, who'll have the thing and not the symbol
Ever seeks out the greatest and the best,
And at the rudder places *him*, e'en though
She had been forced to take him from the rabble—
She, this Necessity, it was that placed thee
In this high office ; it was she that gave thee
Thy letters patent of inauguration.
For, to the uttermost moment that they can,
This race still help themselves at cheapest rate
With slavish souls, with puppets ! At the approach
Of extreme peril, when a hollow image
Is found a hollow image and no more,
Then falls the power into the mighty hands
Of Nature, of the spirit giant-born,
Who listens only to himself, knows nothing
Of stipulations, duties, reverences,
And, like the emancipated force of fire,
Unmaster'd scorches, ere it reaches them,
Their fine-spun webs, their artificial policy.

WALLENSTEIN.
'T is true ! they saw me always as I am—
Always ! I did not cheat them in the bargain.
I never held it worth my pains to hide
The bold all-grasping habit of my soul.

COUNTESS.
Nay rather—thou hast ever shown thyself
A formidable man, without restraint ;
Hast exercised the full prerogatives
Of thy impetuous nature, which had been
Once granted to thee. Therefore, Duke, not *thou*
Who hast still remain'd consistent with thyself,
But *they* are in the wrong, who fearing thee,
Entrusted such a power in hand they fear'd.
For, by the laws of Spirit, in the right
Is every individual character
That acts in strict consistence with itself.
Self-contradiction is the only wrong.
Wert thou another being, then, when thou
Eight years ago pursuedst thy march with fire,
And sword, and desolation, through the Circles
Of Germany, the universal scourge,
Didst mock all ordinances of the empire,
The fearful rights of strength alone exertedst,
Trampledst to earth each rank, each magistracy,
All to extend thy Sultan's domination ?
Then was the time to break thee in, to curb
Thy haughty will, to teach thee ordinance.
But no, the Emperor felt no touch of conscience ;
What served him pleased him, and without a murmur
He stamp'd his broad seal on these lawless deeds.
What at that time was right, because thou didst it
For him, to day is all at once become
Opprobrious, foul because it is directed
Against him.—O most flimsy superstition !

WALLENSTEIN (*rising*).
I never saw it in this light before,
'T is even so. The Emperor perpetrated
Deeds through my arm, deeds most unorderly.
And even this prince's mantle, which I wear,
I owe to what were services to him,
But most high misdemeanors 'gainst the empire.

COUNTESS.

Then betwixt thee and him (confess it Friedland!)
The point can be no more of right and duty,
Only of power and the opportunity.
That opportunity, lo! it comes yonder
Approaching with swift steeds; then with a swing
Throw thyself up into the chariot-seat,
Seize with firm hand the reins, ere thy opponent
Anticipate thee, and himself make conquest
Of the now empty seat. The moment comes;
It is already here, when thou must write
The absolute total of thy life's vast sum.
The constellations stand victorious o'er thee,
The planets shoot good fortune in fair junctions,
And tell thee, "Now's the time!" The starry courses
Hast thou thy life-long measured to no purpose!
The quadrant and the circle, were they playthings!
[*Pointing to the different objects in the room.*
The zodiacs, the rolling orbs of heaven,
Hast pictured on these walls, and all around thee
In dumb. foreboding symbols hast thou placed
These seven presiding Lords of Destiny—
For toys! Is all this preparation nothing!
Is there no marrow in this hollow art,
That even to thyself it doth avail
Nothing, and has no influence over thee
In the great moment of decision?——

WALLENSTEIN (*during this last speech walks up and down with inward struggles, labouring with passion; stops suddenly, stands still, then interrupting the Countess*).
Send Wrangel to me—I will instantly
Despatch three couriers——

ILLO (*hurrying out*).
God in heaven be praised!

WALLENSTEIN.

It is *his* evil genius and *mine*.
Our evil genius! It chastises *him*
Through me, the instrument of his ambition;
And I expect no less, than that Revenge
E'en now is whetting for *my* breast the poniard.
Who sows the serpent's teeth, let him not hope
To reap a joyous harvest. Every crime
Has, in the moment of its perpetration,
Its own avenging angel—dark misgiving,
An ominous sinking at the inmost heart.
He can no longer trust me—Then no longer
Can I retreat—so come that which must come.—
Still destiny preserves its due relations,
The heart within us is its absolute
Vicegerent. [*To* TERTSKY.
Go, conduct you Gustave Wrangel
To my state-cabinet.—Myself will speak to
The couriers.—And despatch immediately
A servant for Octavio Piccolomini.
[*To the* COUNTESS, *who cannot conceal her triumph*
No exultation! woman, triumph not!
For jealous are the Powers of Destiny.
Joy premature, and shouts ere victory,
Encroach upon their rights and privileges.
We sow the seed, and they the growth determine.
[*While he is making his exit the curtain drops*

ACT V.

SCENE I.

Scene, as in the preceding Act.

WALLENSTEIN, OCTAVIO PICCOLOMINI.

WALLENSTEIN (*coming forward in conversation*).
He sends me word from Linz, that he lies sick;
But I have sure intelligence, that he
Secretes himself at Frauenburg with Galas.
Secure them both, and send them to me hither.
Remember, thou takest on thee the command
Of those same Spanish regiments,—constantly
Make preparation, and be never ready;
And if they urge thee to draw out against me,
Still answer YES, and stand as thou wert fetter'd.
I know, that it is doing thee a service
To keep thee out of action in this business.
Thou lovest to linger on in fair appearances;
Steps of extremity are not thy province,
Therefore have I sought out this part for thee.
Thou wilt this time be of most service to me
By thy inertness. The mean time, if fortune
Declare itself on my side, thou wilt know
What is to do.

Enter MAX. PICCOLOMINI.

Now go, Octavio.
This night must thou be off, take my own horses:
Him here I keep with me—make short farewell—

Trust me, I think we all shall meet again
In joy and thriving fortunes.

OCTAVIO (*to his son*).
I shall see you
Yet ere I go.

———

SCENE II.

WALLENSTEIN, MAX. PICCOLOMINI.

MAX. (*advances to him*).
My General!

WALLENSTEIN.

That am I no longer, if
Thou stylest thyself the Emperor's officer.

MAX.

Then thou wilt leave the army, General!

WALLENSTEIN.

I have renounced the service of the Emperor.

MAX.

And thou wilt leave the army!

WALLENSTEIN.

Rather hope I
To bind it nearer still and faster to me.
[*He seats himself.*
Yes, Max., I have delay'd to open it to thee,
Even till the hour of acting 'gins to strike.
Youth's fortunate feeling doth seize easily

The absolute right, yea, and a joy it is
To exercise the single apprehension
Where the sums square in proof ;
But where it happens, that of two sure evils
One must be taken, where the heart not wholly
Brings itself back from out the strife of duties,
There 'tis a blessing to have no election,
And blank necessity is grace and favour.
—This is now present : do not look behind thee,—
It can no more avail thee. Look thou forwards !
Think not I judge not I prepare thyself to act I
The Court—it hath determined on my ruin,
Therefore I will to be beforehand with them.
We'll join the Swedes—right gallant fellows are
And our good friends. [they,
[He stops himself, expecting PICCOLOMINI's answer.
I have ta'en thee by surprise. Answer me not.
I grant thee time to recollect thyself.
[He rises, and retires at the back of the stage. MAX.
remains for a long time motionless, in a trance
of excessive anguish. At his first motion WAL-
LENSTEIN returns, and places himself before him.

MAX.
My General, this day thou makest me
Of age to speak in my own right and person,
For till this day I have been spared the trouble
To find out my own road. Thee have I follow'd
With most implicit unconditional faith,
Sure of the right path if I follow'd thee.
To-day, for the first time, dost thou refer
Me to myself, and forcest me to make
Election between thee and my own heart.

WALLENSTEIN.
Soft cradled thee thy Fortune till to day ;
Thy duties thou couldst exercise in sport,
Indulge all lovely instincts, act for ever
With undivided heart. It can remain
No longer thus. Like enemies, the roads
Start from each other. Duties strive with duties.
Thou must needs choose thy party in the war
Which is now kindling 'twixt thy friend and him
Who is thy Emperor.

MAX.
War ! is that the name !
War is as frightful as heaven's pestilence.
Yet it is good, is it heaven's will as that is.
Is that a good war, which against the Emperor
Thou wagest with the Emperor's own army ?
O God of heaven ! what a change is this.
Beseems it me to offer such persuasion
To thee, who like the fix'd star of the pole
Wert all I gazed at on life's trackless ocean ?
O ! what a rent thou makest in my heart !
The ingrain'd instinct of old reverence,
The holy habit of obediency,
Must I pluck live asunder from thy name !
Nay, do not turn thy countenance upon me—
It always was as a god looking at me !
Duke Wallenstein, its power is not departed :
The senses still are in thy bonds, although,
Bleeding, the soul hath freed itself.

WALLENSTEIN.
.Max. hear me.
MAX.
O ! do it not, I pray thee, do it not !
There is a pure and noble soul within thee,
Knows not of this unblest, unlucky doing.
Thy will is chaste, it is thy fancy only
Which hath polluted thee—and innocence,

It will not let itself be driven away
From that world-awing aspect. Thou wilt not,
Thou canst not, end in this. It would reduce
All human creatures to disloyalty
Against the nobleness of their own nature.
'Twill justify the vulgar misbelief,
Which holdeth nothing noble in free will,
And trusts itself to impotence alone,
Made powerful only in an unknown power.

WALLENSTEIN.
The world will judge me sternly, I expect it.
Already have I said to my own self
All thou canst say to me. Who but avoids
The extreme, can he by going round avoid it ?
But here there is no choice. Yes—I must use
Or suffer violence—so stands the case,
There remains nothing possible but that.

MAX.
O that is never possible for thee !
'Tis the last desperate resource of those
Cheap souls, to whom their honour, their good name
Is their poor saving, their last worthless keep,
Which having staked and lost, they stake themselves
In the mad rage of gaming. Thou art rich,
And glorious ; with an unpolluted heart
Thou canst make conquest of whate'er seems
But he, who once hath acted infamy, [highest !
Does nothing more in this world.

WALLENSTEIN (grasps his hand).
Calmly, Max. !
Much that is great and excellent will we
Perform together yet. And if we only
Stand on the height with dignity, 'tis soon
Forgotten, Max., by what road we ascended.
Believe me, many a crown shines spotless now,
That yet was deeply sullied in the winning.
To the evil spirit doth the earth belong,
Not to the good. All, that the powers divine
Send from above, are universal blessings :
Their light rejoices us, their air refreshes,
But never yet was man enrich'd by them :
In their eternal realm no property
Is to be struggled for—all there is general.
The jewel, the all-valued gold we win
From the deceiving Powers, depraved in nature,
That dwell beneath the day and blessed sun-light.
Not without sacrifices are they render'd
Propitious, and there lives no soul on earth
That e'er retired unsullied from their service.

MAX.
Whate'er is human, to the human being
Do I allow—and to the vehement
And striving spirit readily I pardon
The excess of action ; but to thee, my General !
Above all others make I large concession.
For thou must move a world, and be the master—
He kills thee, who condemns thee to inaction.
So be it then ! maintain thee in thy post
By violence. Resist the Emperor,
And if it must be, force with force repel :
I will not praise it, yet I can forgive it.
But not—not to the traitor—yes !—the word
Is spoken out——
Not to the traitor can I yield a pardon.
That is no mere excess ! that is no error
Of human nature—that is wholly different,
O that is black, black as the pit of hell !
[WALLENSTEIN betrays a sudden agitation.
Thou canst not hear it named, and wilt thou do it ?

O turn back to thy duty. That thou canst,
I hold it certain. Send me to Vienna:
I'll make thy peace for thee with the Emperor.
He knows thee not. But I do know thee. He
Shall see thee, Duke! with my unclouded eye,
And I bring back his confidence to thee.

WALLENSTEIN.

It is too late. Thou knowest not what has happen'd.

MAX.

Were it too late, and were things gone so far,
That a crime only could prevent thy fall,
Then—fall! fall honourably, even as thou stood'st,
Lose the command. Go from the stage of war.
Thou canst with splendour do it—do it too
With innocence. Thou hast lived much for others,
At length live thou for thy own self. I follow thee.
My destiny I never part from thine.

WALLENSTEIN.

It is too late! Even now, while thou art losing
Thy words, one after the other are the mile-stones
Left fast behind by my post couriers,
Who bear the order on to Prague and Egra.

[MAX. *stands as convulsed, with a gesture and
countenance expressing the most intense anguish.*

Yield thyself to it. We act as we are forced.
I cannot give assent to my own shame
And ruin. *Thou*—no—thou canst not forsake me!
So let us do, what must be done, with dignity,
With a firm step. What am I doing worse
Than did famed Cæsar at the Rubicon,
When he the legions led against his country,
The which his country had deliver'd to him!
Had he thrown down the sword, he had been lost,
As I were, if I but disarm'd myself.
I trace out something in me of his spirit;
Give me his luck, *that other thing* I'll bear.

[MAX. *quits him abruptly.* WALLENSTEIN, *startled
and overpowered, continues looking after him,
and is still in this posture when* TERTSKY *enters.*

SCENE III.

WALLENSTEIN, TERTSKY.

TERTSKY.

Max. Piccolomini just left you!

WALLENSTEIN.

Where is Wrangel?

TERTSKY.

He is already gone.

WALLENSTEIN.

In such a hurry!

TERTSKY.

It is as if the earth had swallow'd him.
He had scarce left thee, when I went to seek him.
I wish'd some words with him—but he was gone.
How, when, and where, could no one tell me. Nay,
I half believe it was the devil himself;
A human creature could not so at once
Have vanish'd.

ILLO (*enters*).

Is it true that thou wilt send
Octavio!

TERTSKY.

How, Octavio! Whither send him!

WALLENSTEIN.

He goes to Frauenburg, and will lead hither
The Spanish and Italian regiments.

ILLO.

No!

Nay, Heaven forbid!

WALLENSTEIN.

And why should Heaven forbid!

ILLO.

Him!—that deceiver! Wouldst thou trust to him
The soldiery! Him wilt thou let slip from thee,
Now, in the very instant that decides us——

TERTSKY.

Thou wilt not do this!—No! I pray thee, no!

WALLENSTEIN.

Ye are whimsical.

ILLO.

O but for this time, Duke,
Yield to our warning! Let him not depart.

WALLENSTEIN.

And why should I not trust him only this time,
Who have always trusted him! What, then, has
happen'd,
That I should lose my good opinion of him!
In complaisance to your whims, not my own,
I must, forsooth, give up a rooted judgment.
Think not I am a woman. Having trusted him
E'en till to-day, to-day too will I trust him.

TERTSKY.

Must it be he—he only! Send another.

WALLENSTEIN.

It must be he, whom I myself have chosen;
He is well fitted for the business. Therefore
I gave it him.

ILLO.

Because he's an Italian—
Therefore is he well fitted for the business!

WALLENSTEIN.

I know you love them not—nor sire nor son—
Because that I esteem them, love them—visibly
Esteem them, love them more than you and others,
E'en as they merit. Therefore are they eye-blights,
Thorns in your foot-path. But your jealousies,
In what affect they me or my concerns!
Are they the worse to *me* because you hate them!
Love or hate one another as you will,
I leave to each man his own moods and likings;
Yet know the worth of each of you to me.

ILLO.

Von Questenberg, while he was here, was always
Lurking about with this Octavio.

WALLENSTEIN.

It happen'd with my knowledge and permission.

ILLO.

I know that secret messengers came to him
From Galas——

WALLENSTEIN.

That's not true.

ILLO.

O thou art blind,
With thy deep-seeing eyes!

WALLENSTEIN.

Thou wilt not shake
My faith for me—my faith, which founds itself
On the profoundest science. If't is false,
Then the whole science of the stars is false;
For know, I have a pledge from Fate itself,
That he is the most faithful of my friends.

ILLO.

Hast thou a pledge, that this pledge is not false!

WALLENSTEIN.

There exist moments in the life of man,
When he is nearer the great Soul of the world
Than is man's custom, and possesses freely
The power of questioning his destiny:
And such a moment 't was, when in the night
Before the action in the plains of Lützen,
Leaning against a tree, thoughts crowding thoughts,
I look'd out far upon the ominous plain.
My whole life, past and future, in this moment
Before my mind's eye glided in procession,
And to the destiny of the next morning
The spirit, fill'd with anxious presentiment,
Did knit the most removed futurity.
Then said I also to myself, "So many
Dost thou command. They follow all thy stars,
And as on some great number set their All
Upon thy single head, and only man
The vessel of thy fortune. Yet a day
Will come, when Destiny shall once more scatter
All these in many a several direction:
Few be they who will stand out faithful to thee."
I yearn'd to know which one was faithfullest
Of all, this camp included. Great Destiny,
Give me a sign! And he shall be the man,
Who, on the approaching morning, comes the first
To meet me with a token of his love:
And thinking this, I fell into a slumber.
Then midmost in the battle was I led
In spirit. Great the pressure and the tumult!
Then was my horse kill'd under me: I sank;
And over me away all unconcernedly,
Drove horse and rider—and thus trod to pieces
I lay, and panted like a dying man;
Then seized me suddenly a saviour arm:
It was Octavio's—I awoke at once,
'T was broad day, and *Octavio* stood before me.
"My brother," said he, "do not ride to-day
The dapple, as you 're wont; but mount the horse
Which I have chosen for thee. Do it, brother!
In love to me. A strong dream warn'd me so."
It was the swiftness of this horse that snatch'd me
From the hot pursuit of Bannier's dragoons.
My cousin rode the dapple on that day,
And never more saw I or horse or rider.

ILLO.

That was a chance.

WALLENSTEIN (*significantly*).
There's no such thing as chance.
In brief, 't is sign'd and seal'd that this Octavio
Is my good angel—and now no word more.
[*He is retiring.*

TERTSKY.

This is my comfort—Max. remains our hostage.

ILLO.

And he shall never stir from here alive.

WALLENSTEIN (*stops and turns himself round*).
Are ye not like the women, who for ever
Only recur to their first word, although
One had been talking reason by the hour!
Know, that the human being's thoughts and deeds
Are not, like ocean billows, blindly moved.
The inner world, his microcosmus, is
The deep shaft, out of which they spring eternally.
They grow by certain laws, like the tree's fruit—
No juggling chance can metamorphose them.
Have I the human *kernel* first examined!
Then I know, too, the future will and action.
[*Exeunt.*

SCENE IV.

A Chamber in PICCOLOMINI's *Dwelling-House.*

OCTAVIO PICCOLOMINI, ISOLANI, *entering.*

ISOLANI.
Here am I—Well! who comes yet of the others!

OCTAVIO (*with an air of mystery*).
But, first, a word with you, Count Isolani.

ISOLANI (*assuming the same air of mystery*).
Will it explode, ha!—Is the Duke about
To make the attempt! In me, friend, you may place
Full confidence.—Nay, put me to the proof.

OCTAVIO.
That may happen.

ISOLANI.
Noble brother, I am
Not one of those men who in words are valiant,
And when it comes to action skulk away.
The Duke has acted towards me as a friend.
God knows it is so; and I owe him all——
He may rely on my fidelity.

OCTAVIO.
That will be seen hereafter.

ISOLANI.
Be on your guard,
All think not as I think; and there are many
Who still hold with the Court—yes, and they say
That those stolen signatures bind them to nothing.

OCTAVIO.
I am rejoiced to hear it.

ISOLANI.
You rejoice!

OCTAVIO.
That the Emperor has yet such gallant servants,
And loving friends.

ISOLANI.
Nay, jeer not, I entreat you.
They are no such worthless fellows, I assure you.

OCTAVIO.
I am assured already. God forbid
That I should jest!—In very serious earnest,
I am rejoiced to see an honest cause
So strong.

ISOLANI.
The Devil!—what!—why, what means this!
Are you not, then——For what, then, am I here!

OCTAVIO.
That you may make full declaration, whether
You will be call'd the friend or enemy
Of the Emperor.

ISOLANI (*with an air of defiance*).
That declaration, friend,
I'll make to him in whom a right is placed
To put that question to me.

OCTAVIO.
Whether, Count,
That right is mine, this paper may instruct you.

ISOLANI (*stammering*).
Why,—why—what! this is the Emperor's hand
and seal! [*Reads.*
"Whereas, the officers collectively
Throughout our army will obey the orders
Of the Lieutenant-general Piccolomini.

As from us ourselves."——*Hem!*—Yes! so!—
Yes! yes!—
I—I give you joy, Lieutenant-general!

OCTAVIO.

And you submit you to the order?

ISOLANI.

I——

But you have taken me so by surprise—
Time for reflection one *must* have——

OCTAVIO.

Two minutes.

ISOLANI.

My God! But then the case is——

OCTAVIO.

Plain and simple.
You must declare you, whether you determine
To act a treason 'gainst your Lord and Sovereign,
Or whether you will serve him faithfully.

ISOLANI.

Treason!—My God!—But who talks then of
treason?

OCTAVIO.

That is the case. The Prince-duke is a traitor—
Means to lead over to the enemy   [full—
The Emperor's army.—Now, Count!—brief and
Say, will you break your oath to the Emperor?
Sell yourself to the enemy?—Say, will you?

ISOLANI.

What mean you? I—I break my oath, d'ye say,
To his Imperial Majesty?
Did I say so!—When, when have I said that?

OCTAVIO.

You have not said it yet—not yet. This instant
I wait to hear, Count, whether you *will* say it.

ISOLANI.

Ay! that delights me now, that you yourself
Bear witness for me that I never said so.

OCTAVIO.

And you renounce the Duke then?

ISOLANI.

If he's planning
Treason—why, treason breaks all bonds asunder.

OCTAVIO.

And are determined, too, to fight against him?

ISOLANI.

He has done me service—but if he's a villain,
Perdition seize him!—All scores are rubb'd off.

OCTAVIO.

I am rejoiced that you are so well disposed.
This night, break off in the utmost secrecy
With all the light-arm'd troops—it must appear
As came the order from the Duke himself.
At Frauenburg's the place of rendezvous;
There will Count Galas give you further orders.

ISOLANI.

It shall be done.—But you'll remember me
With the Emperor—how well-disposed you found
me.

OCTAVIO.

I will not fail to mention it honourably.
              [*Exit* ISOLANI. *A Servant enters.*
What, Colonel Butler!—Show him up.

ISOLANI (*returning*).

Forgive me too my bearish ways, old father!
Lord God! how should I know, then, what a great
Person I had before me.

OCTAVIO.

No excuses!

ISOLANI.

I am a merry lad, and if at time
A rash word might escape me 'gainst the Court
Amidst my wine—You know no harm was meant.
              [*Exit.*

OCTAVIO.

You need not be uneasy on that score.
That has succeeded. Fortune favour us
With all the others only but as much.

——◆——

SCENE V.

OCTAVIO PICCOLOMINI, BUTLER.

BUTLER.

At your command Lieutenant-general.

OCTAVIO.

Welcome, as honour'd friend and visitor.

BUTLER.

You do me too much honour.

OCTAVIO (*after both have seated themselves*).

You have not   [day—
Return'd the advances which I made you yester-
Misunderstood them as mere empty forms.
That wish proceeded from my heart—I was
In earnest with you—for 'tis now a time
In which the honest should unite most closely.

BUTLER.——

'Tis only the like-minded can unite.

OCTAVIO.

True! and I name all honest men like-minded.
I never charge a man but with those acts
To which his character deliberately
Impels him; for alas! the violence
Of blind misunderstandings often thrusts
The very best of us from the right track. [Galas
You came through Frauenburg. Did the Count
Say nothing to you? Tell me. He's my friend.

BUTLER.

His words were lost on *me.*

OCTAVIO.

It grieves me sorely,
To hear it: for his counsel was most wise.
I had myself the like to offer.

BUTLER.

Spare
Yourself the trouble—me th' embarrassment,
To have deserved so ill your good opinion.

OCTAVIO.

The time is precious—let us talk openly.
You know how matters stand here. Wallenstein
Meditates treason—I can tell you further
He has committed treason; but few hours
Have past, since he a covenant concluded
With the enemy. The messengers are now
Full on their way to Egra and to Prague.
To-morrow he intends to lead us over
To the enemy. But he deceives himself;
For Prudence wakes—The Emperor has still
Many and faithful friends here, and they stand
In closest union, mighty though unseen.
This manifesto sentences the Duke—
Recalls the obedience of the army from him,
And summons all the loyal, all the honest,
To join and recognize in me their leader.

Choose—will you share with us an honest cause!
Or with the evil share an evil lot.

BUTLER (*rises*).

His lot is mine.

OCTAVIO.

Is that your last resolve!

BUTLER.

It is.

OCTAVIO.

Nay, but bethink you, Colonel Butler!
As yet you have time. Within my faithful breast
That rashly utter'd word remains interr'd.
Recal it, Butler! choose a better party:
You have not chosen the right one.

BUTLER (*going*).

Any other
Commands-for me, Lieutenant-general!

OCTAVIO.

See your white hairs: Recal that word!

BUTLER.

Farewell!

OCTAVIO.

What! Would you draw this good and gallant
In such a cause! Into a curse would you [sword
Transform the gratitude which you have earn'd
By forty years' fidelity from Austria!

BUTLER (*laughing with bitterness*).

Gratitude from the House of Austria. [*He is going.*

OCTAVIO (*permits him to go as far as the door, then calls after him*).

Butler!

BUTLER.

What wish you!

OCTAVIO.

How was't with the Count!

BUTLER.

Count! what!

OCTAVIO (*coldly*).

The title that you wish'd, I mean.

BUTLER (*starts in sudden passion*).

Hell and damnation!

OCTAVIO (*coldly*).

You petition'd for it—
And your petition was repell'd—Was it so!

BUTLER.

Your insolent scoff shall not go by unpunish'd.
Draw!

OCTAVIO.

Nay! your sword to 'ts sheath! and tell me calmly,
How all that happen'd. I will not refuse you
Your satisfaction afterwards.--Calmly, Butler!

BUTLER.

Be the whole world acquainted with the weakness
For which I never can forgive myself.
Lieutenant-general! Yes—I have ambition.
Ne'er was I able to endure contempt.
It stung me to the quick, that birth and title
Should have more weight than merit has in the army.
I would fain not be meaner than my equal,
So in an evil hour I let myself
Be tempted to that measure—It was folly!
But yet so hard a penance it deserved not.
It might have been refused; but wherefore barb
And venom the refusal with contempt?
Why dash to earth and crush with heaviest scorn
The grey-hair'd man, the faithful veteran!

Why to the baseness of his parentage
Refer him with such cruel roughness, only
Because he had a weak hour and forgot himself!
But nature gives a sting e'en to the worm
Which wanton Power treads on in sport and insult.

OCTAVIO.

You must have been calumniated. Guess you
The enemy who did you this ill service!

BUTLER.

Be't who it will—a most low-hearted scoundrel,
Some vile court-minion must it be, some Spaniard,
Some young squire of some ancient family,
In whose light I may stand, some envious knave,
Stung to his soul by my fair self-earn'd honours!

OCTAVIO.

But tell me! did the Duke approve that measure!

BUTLER.

Himself impell'd me to it, used his interest
In my behalf with all the warmth of friendship.

OCTAVIO.

Ay! are you sure of that!

BUTLER.

I read the letter.

OCTAVIO.

And so did I—but the contents were different.
[*BUTLER is suddenly struck.*
By chance I'm in possession of that letter—
Can leave it to your own eyes to convince you.
[*He gives him the letter.*

BUTLER.

Ha! what is this!

OCTAVIO.

I fear me, Colonel Butler,
An infamous game have they been playing with
you.
The Duke, you say, impell'd you to this measure!
Now, in this letter talks he in contempt
Concerning you, counsels the minister
To give sound chastisement to your conceit,
For so he calls it.
[*BUTLER reads through the letter, his knees tremble, he seizes a chair, and sinks down in it.*
You have no enemy, no persecutor;
There's no one wishes ill to you. Ascribe
The insult you received to the Duke only.
His aim is clear and palpable. He wish'd
To tear you from your Emperor—he hoped
To gain from your revenge what he well knew
(What your long-tried fidelity convinced him)
He ne'er could dare expect from your calm reason.
A blind tool would he make you, in contempt
Use you, as means of most abandon'd ends.
He has gained his point. Too well has he succeeded
In luring you away from that good path
On which you had been journeying forty years!

BUTLER (*his voice trembling*).

Can e'er the Emperor's Majesty forgive me!

OCTAVIO.

More than forgive you. He would fain compensate
For that affront, and most unmerited grievance
Sustain'd by a deserving, gallant veteran.
From his free impulse he confirms the present,
Which the Duke made you for a wicked purpose.
The regiment, which you now command, is your's.
[*BUTLER attempts to rise, sinks down again. He labours inwardly with violent emotions; tries to speak, and cannot. At length he takes his sword from the belt, and offers it to PICCOLOMINI.*

OCTAVIO.

What wish you! Recollect yourself, friend.

BUTLER.

Take it.

OCTAVIO.

But to what purpose! Calm yourself.

BUTLER.

O take it!

I am no longer worthy of this sword.

OCTAVIO.

Receive it then anew from my hands—and
Wear it with honour for the right cause ever.

BUTLER.

——Perjure myself to such a gracious Sovereign!

OCTAVIO.

You'll make amends. Quick! break off from the
Duke!

BUTLER.

Break off from him!

OCTAVIO.

What now! Bethink thyself.

BUTLER (no longer governing his emotion).
Only break off from him! He dies! he dies!

OCTAVIO.

Come after me to Frauenburg, where now
All who are loyal, are assembling under
Counts Altringer and Galas. Many others
I've brought to a remembrance of their duty :
This night be sure that you escape from Pilsen.

BUTLER (strides up and down in excessive agitation,
then steps up to OCTAVIO with resolved countenance).
Count Piccolomini! Dare that man speak
Of honour to you, who once broke his troth.

OCTAVIO.

He, who repents so deeply of it, dares.

BUTLER.

Then leave me here, upon my word of honour!

OCTAVIO.

What's your design!

BUTLER.

Leave me and my regiment.

OCTAVIO.

I have full confidence in you. But tell me
What are you brooding!

BUTLER.

That the deed will tell you.
Ask me no more at present. Trust to me.
Ye may trust safely. By the living God
Ye give him over, not to his good angel!
Farewell.   [Exit BUTLER.

SERVANT (enters with a billet).
A stranger left it, and is gone.
The Prince-Duke's horses wait for you below.
                                    [Exit Servant.

OCTAVIO (reads).
" Be sure make haste! Your faithful Isolan."
—O that I had but left this town behind me.
To split upon a rock so near the haven!—
Away! This is no longer a safe place for me!
Where can my son be tarrying!

SCENE VI.

OCTAVIO and MAX. PICCOLOMINI.

MAX. enters almost in a state of derangement from extreme
agitation, his eyes roll wildly, his walk is unsteady, and
he appears not to observe his father, who stands at a
distance, and gazes at him with a countenance expres-
sive of compassion. He paces with long strides through
the chamber, then stands still again, and at last throws
himself into a chair, staring vacantly at the object directly before him.

OCTAVIO (advances to him).
I am going off, my son.
          [Receiving no answer, he takes his hand.
                          My son, farewell.

MAX.

Farewell.

OCTAVIO.

Thou wilt soon follow me!

MAX.

I follow thee!
Thy way is crooked—it is not my way.
          [OCTAVIO drops his hand, and starts back.
O, hadst thou been but simple and sincere,
Ne'er had it come to this—all had stood otherwise.
He had not done that foul and horrible deed,
The virtuous had retain'd their influence o'er him :
He had not fallen into the snares of villains.
Wherefore so like a thief, and thief's accomplice
Didst creep behind him—lurking for thy prey !
O, unblest falsehood! Mother of all evil!
Thou misery-making dæmon, it is thou
That sink'st us in perdition. Simple truth,
Sustainer of the world, had saved us all !
Father, I will not, I cannot excuse thee!
Wallenstein has deceived me—O, most foully !
But thou hast acted not much better.

OCTAVIO.

Son !

My son, ah ! I forgive thy agony !

MAX. (rises, and contemplates his father with looks
of suspicion).
Was't possible! hadst thou the heart, my father,
Hadst thou the heart to drive it to such lengths,
With cold premeditated purpose! Thou—
Hadst thou the heart, to wish to see him guilty
Rather than saved! Thou risest by his fall.
Octavio, 'twill not please me.

OCTAVIO.

God in Heaven !

MAX.

O, woe is me! sure I have changed my nature.
How comes suspicion here—in the free soul !
Hope, confidence, belief, are gone ; for all
Lied to me, all that I e'er loved or honour'd.
No! no! not all! She—she yet lives for me,
And she is true, and open as the Heavens !
Deceit is everywhere, hypocrisy,
Murder, and poisoning, treason, perjury :
The single holy spot is our love,
The only unprofaned in human nature.

OCTAVIO.

Max.!—we will go together. 'Twill be better.

MAX.

What! ere I've taken a last parting leave,
The very last—no never !

OCTAVIO.
Spare thyself
The pang of necessary separation.
Come with me! Come, my son!
[*Attempts to take him with him.*

MAX.
No! as sure as God lives, no!

OCTAVIO (*more urgently*).
Come with me, I command thee! I, thy father.

MAX.
Command me what is human. I stay here.

OCTAVIO.
Max.! In the Emperor's name I bid thee come.

MAX.
No Emperor has power to prescribe   [me
Laws to the heart; and wouldst thou wish to rob
Of the sole blessing which my fate has left me,
Her sympathy? Must then a cruel deed
Be done with cruelty? The unalterable
Shall I perform ignobly—steal away,
With stealthy coward flight forsake her? No!
She shall behold my suffering, my sore anguish,
Hear the complaints of the disparted soul,
And weep tears o'er me. Oh! the human race
Have steely souls—but she is as an angel.
From the black deadly madness of despair
Will she redeem my soul, and in soft words
Of comfort, plaining, loose this pang of death!

OCTAVIO.
Thou wilt not tear thyself away; thou canst not.
O, come, my son! I bid thee save thy virtue.

MAX.
Squander not thou thy words in vain.
The heart I follow, for I dare trust to it.

OCTAVIO (*trembling, and losing all self-command*).
Max.! Max.! if that most damned thing could be,
If thou—my son—my own blood—(dare I *think* it!)
Do sell thyself to him, the infamous,
Do stamp this brand upon our noble house,
Then shall the world behold the horrible deed
And in unnatural combat shall the steel
Of the son trickle with the father's blood.

MAX.
O hadst thou always better thought of men,
Thou hadst then acted better. Curst suspicion!
Unholy miserable doubt! To him
Nothing on earth remains unwrench'd and firm,
Who has no faith.

OCTAVIO.
And if I trust thy heart,
Will it be always in thy power to follow it?

MAX.
The heart's voice *thou* hast not o'erpower'd—as
Will Wallenstein be able to o'erpower it.   [little

OCTAVIO.
O, Max.! I see thee never more again!

MAX.
Unworthy of thee wilt thou never see me.

OCTAVIO.
I go to Frauenburg—the Pappenheimers
I leave thee here, the Lothrings too; Tsokana
And Tiefenbach remain here to protect thee.
They love thee, and are faithful to their oath,
And will far rather fall in gallant contest
Than leave their rightful leader, and their honour.

MAX.
Rely on this, I either leave my life
In the struggle, or conduct them out of Pilsen.

OCTAVIO.
Farewell, my son!

MAX.
Farewell!

OCTAVIO.
How! not one look
Of filial love! No grasp of the hand at parting!
It is a bloody war to which we are going,
And the event uncertain and in darkness.
So used we not to part—it was not so!
Is it then true! I have a son no longer!
[MAX. *falls into his arms, they hold each other for
a long time in a speechless embrace, then go
away at different sides.*
(*The Curtain drops.*)

THE

DEATH OF WALLENSTEIN.

DRAMATIS PERSONÆ.

WALLENSTEIN, *Duke of Friedland, Generalissimo of the Imperial Forces in the Thirty-years' War.*
DUCHESS OF FRIEDLAND, *Wife of Wallenstein.*
THEKLA, *her Daughter, Princess of Friedland.*
The COUNTESS TERTSKY, *Sister of the Duchess.*
LADY NEUBRUNN.
OCTAVIO PICCOLOMINI, *Lieutenant General.*
MAX. PICCOLOMINI, *his Son, Colonel of a Regiment of Cuirassiers.*
COUNT TERTSKY, *the Commander of several Regiments, and Brother-in-law of Wallenstein.*
ILLO, *Field Marshal, Wallenstein's Confidant.*
BUTLER, *an Irishman, Commander of a Regiment of Dragoons.*

GORDON, *Governor of Egra.*
MAJOR GERALDIN.
CAPTAIN DEVEREUX.
CAPTAIN MACDONALD.
NEUMANN, *Captain of Cavalry, Aide-de-camp to Tertsky.*
SWEDISH CAPTAIN.
SENI.
BURGOMASTER *of Egra.*
ANSPESSADE *of the Cuirassiers.*
GROOM OF THE CHAMBER, } *Belonging to the Duke.*
A PAGE, }
Cuirassiers, Dragoons, Servants.

ACT I.

SCENE I.

A Chamber in the House of the Duchess of Friedland.

COUNTESS TERTSKY, THEKLA, LADY NEUBRUNN *(the two latter sit at the same table at work).*

COUNTESS *(watching them from the opposite side).*
So you have nothing to ask me—nothing !
I have been waiting for a word from you.
And could you then endure in all this time
Not once to speak his name !
　　　[THEKLA *remaining silent, the* COUNTESS *rises and advances to her.*
　　　　　　Why, how comes this !
Perhaps I am already grown superfluous,
And other ways exist, besides through me !
Confess it to me, Thekla : have you seen him !

THEKLA.
To-day and yesterday I have not seen him.

COUNTESS.
And not heard from him, either ! Come, be open.

THEKLA.
No syllable.

COUNTESS.
　　　And still you are so calm !

THEKLA.
I am.

COUNTESS.
　　May't please you, leave us, Lady Neubrunn.
　　　　　[*Exit* LADY NEUBRUNN.

SCENE II.

The COUNTESS, THEKLA.

COUNTESS.
It does not please me, Princess, that he holds
Himself so *still*, exactly at *this* time.

THEKLA.
Exactly at *this* time !

COUNTESS.
　　　　　He now knows all :
'Twere now the moment to declare himself.

THEKLA.
If I'm to understand you, speak less darkly.

COUNTESS.
'Twas for that purpose that I bade her leave us.
Thekla, you are no more a child. Your heart
Is now no more in nonage : for you love,
And boldness dwells with love—that *you* have proved.
Your nature moulds itself upon your father's
More than your mother's spirit. Therefore may you
Hear, what were too much for her fortitude.

THEKLA.
Enough : no further preface, I entreat you.
At once, out with it ! Be it what it may,
It is not possible that it should torture me
More than this introduction. What have you
To say to me ! Tell me the whole, and briefly !

COUNTESS.
You'll not be frighten'd——

THEKLA.

Name it, I entreat you.

COUNTESS.

It lies within your power to do your father
A weighty service——

THEKLA.

Lies within *my* power ?

COUNTESS.

Max. Piccolomini loves you. You can link him
Indissolubly to your father.

THEKLA.

I ?

What need of me for that ? And is he not
Already link'd to him ?

COUNTESS.

He was.

THEKLA.

And wherefore
Should he not be so now—not be so always ?

COUNTESS.

He cleaves to the Emperor too.

THEKLA.

Not more than duty
And honour may demand of him.

COUNTESS.

We ask
Proofs of his love, and not proofs of his honour.
Duty and honour !
Those are ambiguous words with many meanings.
You should interpret them for him : his love
Should be the sole definer of his honour.

THEKLA.

How !

COUNTESS.

The Emperor or you must he renounce.

THEKLA.

He will accompany my father gladly
In his retirement. From himself you heard,
How much he wish'd to lay aside the sword.

COUNTESS.

He must *not* lay the sword aside, we mean ;
He must unsheath it in your father's cause.

THEKLA.

He'll spend with gladness and alacrity
His life, his heart's-blood in my father's cause,
If shame or injury be intended him.

COUNTESS.

You will not understand me. Well, hear then :—
Your father has fallen off from the Emperor,
And is about to join the enemy
With the whole soldiery——

THEKLA.

Alas, my mother !

COUNTESS.

There needs a great example to draw on
The army after him. The Piccolomini
Possess the love and reverence of the troops ;
They govern all opinions, and wherever
They lead the way, none hesitate to follow.
The son secures the father to our interests—
You've much in your hands at this moment.

THEKLA.

Ah,
My miserable mother ! what a death-stroke
Awaits thee !—No ! she never will survive it.

COUNTESS.

She will accommodate her soul to that
Which is and must be. I do know your mother
The far-off future weighs upon her heart
With torture of anxiety ; but is it
Unalterably, actually present,
She soon resigns herself, and bears it calmly.

THEKLA.

O my foreboding bosom ! Even now,
E'en now 'tis here, that icy hand of horror !
And my young hope lies shuddering in its grasp ;
I knew it well—no sooner had I enter'd,
An heavy ominous presentiment
Reveal'd to me, that spirits of death were hovering
Over my happy fortune. But why think I
First of myself ? My mother ! O my mother !

COUNTESS.

Calm yourself ! Break not out in vain lamenting !
Preserve you for your father the firm friend,
And for yourself the lover, all will yet
Prove good and fortunate.

THEKLA.

Prove good ! What good ?
Must we not part ?—part ne'er to meet again ?

COUNTESS.

He parts not from you ! He can not part from you.

THEKLA.

Alas for his sore anguish ! It will rend
His heart asunder.

COUNTESS.

If indeed he loves you,
His resolution will be speedily taken.

THEKLA.

His resolution will be speedily taken—
O do not doubt of that ! A resolution !
Does there remain one to be taken ?

COUNTESS.

Hush !
Collect yourself ! I hear your mother coming.

THEKLA.

How shall I bear to see her ?

COUNTESS.

Collect yourself.

———◆———

SCENE III.

To them enter the DUCHESS.

DUCHESS (*to the* COUNTESS).

Who was here, sister ? I heard some one talking,
And passionately too.

COUNTESS.

Nay ! There was no one.

DUCHESS.

I am grown so timorous, every trifling noise
Scatters my spirits, and announces to me
The footstep of some messenger of evil.
And you can tell me, sister, what the event is ?
Will he agree to do the Emperor's pleasure,
And send the horse-regiments to the Cardinal ?
Tell me, has he dismiss'd Von Questenberg
With a favourable answer ?

COUNTESS.

No, he has not.

E

DUCHESS.

Alas! then all is lost! I see it coming,
The worst that can come! Yes, they will depose
      him;
The accursed business of the Regensburg diet
Will all be acted o'er again!

COUNTESS.
                    No! never!
Make your heart easy, sister, as to that.

[THEKLA, *in extreme agitation, throws herself upon
  her mother, and enfolds her in her arms, weeping.*

DUCHESS.

Yes, my poor child!
Thou too hast lost a most affectionate godmother
In the Empress. O that stern unbending man!
In this unhappy marriage what have I
Not suffer'd, not endured! For even as if
I had been link'd on to some wheel of fire
That restless, ceaseless, whirls impetuous onward,
I have pass'd a life of frights and horrors with him,
And ever to the brink of some abyss
With dizzy headlong violence he whirls me.
Nay, do not weep, my child! Let not my sufferings
Presignify unhappiness to thee,
Nor blacken with their shade the fate that waits
      thee.
There lives no second Friedland : thou, my child,
Hast not to fear thy mother's destiny.

THEKLA.

O let us supplicate him, dearest mother!
Quick! quick! here 's no abiding-place for us.
Here every coming hour broods into life
Some new affrightful monster.

DUCHESS.
                    Thou wilt share
An easier, calmer lot, my child! We too,
I and thy father, witness'd happy days.
Still think I with delight of those first years,
When he was making progress with glad effort,
When his ambition was a genial fire,
Not that consuming flame which now it is.
The Emperor loved him, trusted him : and all
He undertook could not but be successful.
But since that ill-starr'd day at Regensburg,
Which plunged him headlong from his dignity,
A gloomy uncompanionable spirit,
Unsteady and suspicious, has possess'd him.
His quiet mind forsook him, and no longer
Did he yield up himself in joy and faith
To his old luck, and individual power ;
But thenceforth turn'd his heart and best affections
All to those cloudy sciences, which never
Have yet made happy him who follow'd them.

COUNTESS.

You see it, sister! as your eyes permit you.
But surely this is not the conversation
To pass the time in which we are waiting for him.
You know he will be soon here. Would you have
Find *her* in this condition !   [him

DUCHESS.
                    Come, my child!
Come wipe away thy tears, and show thy father
A cheerful countenance. See, the tie-knot here
Is off—this hair must not hang so dishevell'd.
Come, dearest! dry thy tears up. They deform
Thy gentle eye.—Well now—what was I saying!
Yes, in good truth, this Piccolomini
Is a most noble and deserving gentleman.

COUNTESS.

That is he, sister!

THEKLA (*to the* COUNTESS, *with marks of great
      oppression of spirits*).
      Aunt, you will excuse me! (*Is going.*)

COUNTESS.

But whither! See, your father comes.

THEKLA.

I cannot see him now.

COUNTESS.
                    Nay, but bethink you.

THEKLA.

Believe me, I cannot sustain his presence.

COUNTESS.

But he will miss you, will ask after you.

DUCHESS.

What now! Why is she going!

COUNTESS.
                    She 's not well.

DUCHESS (*anxiously*).
What ails then my beloved child!
      [*Both follow the* PRINCESS, *and endeavour to detain
       her. During this* WALLENSTEIN *appears, engaged
       in conversation with* ILLO

———————•———————

SCENE IV.

WALLENSTEIN, ILLO, COUNTESS, DUCHESS, THEKLA.

WALLENSTEIN.

All quiet in the camp!

ILLO.
                    It is all quiet.

WALLENSTEIN.

In a few hours may couriers come from Prague
With tidings, that this capital is ours.
Then we may drop the mask, and to the troops
Assembled in this town make known the measure
And its result together. In such cases
Example does the whole. Whoever is foremost
Still leads the herd. An imitative creature
Is man. The troops at Prague conceive no other,
Than that the Pilsen army has gone through
The forms of homage to us ; and in Pilsen
They shall swear fealty to us, because
The example has been given them by Prague.
Butler, you tell me, has declared himself!

ILLO.

At his own bidding, unsolicited,
He came to offer you himself and regiment.

WALLENSTEIN.

I find we must not give implicit credence
To every warning voice that makes itself
Be listen'd to in the heart. To hold us back,
Oft does the lying Spirit counterfeit
The voice of Truth and inward Revelation,
Scattering false oracles. And thus have I
To intreat forgiveness, for that secretly
I 've wrong'd this honourable gallant man,
This Butler : for a feeling, of the which
I am not master (*fear* I would not call it),
Creeps o'er me instantly, with sense of shuddering,
At his approach, and stops love's joyous motion.

And this same man, against whom I am warn'd,
This honest man is he, who reaches to me
The first pledge of my fortune.

ILLO.
                        And doubt not
That his example will win over to you
The best men in the army.

WALLENSTEIN.
            Go and send
Isolani hither.   Send him immediately.
He is under recent obligations to me :
With him will I commence the trial.   Go.
                        [*Exit* ILLO.

WALLENSTEIN (*turns himself round to the females*).
Lo, there the mother with the darling daughter :
For once we 'll have an interval of rest—
Come ! my heart yearns to live a cloudless hour
In the beloved circle of my family.

COUNTESS.
'T is long since we 've been thus together, brother.

WALLENSTEIN (*to the* COUNTESS *aside*).
Can she sustain the news ! Is she prepared !

COUNTESS.
Not yet.

WALLENSTEIN.
        Come here, my sweet girl ! Seat thee by me,
For there is a good spirit on thy lips.
Thy mother praised to me thy ready skill ;
She says a voice of melody dwells in thee,
Which doth enchant the soul.   Now such a voice
Will drive away from me the evil dæmon
That beats his black wings close above my head.

DUCHESS.
Where is thy lute, my daughter ! Let thy father
Hear some small trial of thy skill.

THEKLA.
                        My mother !
I—

DUCHESS.
        Trembling ! Come, collect thyself.   Go, cheer
Thy father.

THEKLA.
        O my mother ! I—I cannot.

COUNTESS.
How, what is that, niece !

THEKLA (*to the* COUNTESS).
O spare me—sing—now—in this sore anxiety,
Of the o'erburthen'd soul—to sing to *him*,
Who is thrusting, even now, my mother headlong
Into her grave.

DUCHESS.
            How, Thekla ! Humoursome !
What ! shall thy father have express'd a wish
In vain !

COUNTESS.
Here is the lute.

THEKLA.
            My God ! how can I—
[*The orchestra plays.   During the ritornello* THEKLA
*expresses in her gestures and countenance the
struggle of her feelings ; and at the moment that
she should begin to sing, contracts herself together,
as one shuddering, throws the instrument down,
and retires abruptly.*

DUCHESS.
My child ! O she is ill—

WALLENSTEIN.
            What ails the maiden !
Say, is she often so !

COUNTESS.
            Since then herself
Has now betray'd it, I too must no longer
Conceal it.

WALLENSTEIN.
        What !

COUNTESS.
        She loves him !

WALLENSTEIN.
            Loves him ! Whom !

COUNTESS.
Max. does she love ! Max. Piccolomini
Hast thou ne'er noticed it ! Nor yet my sister !

DUCHESS.
Was it this that lay so heavy on her heart !
God's blessing on thee, my sweet child ! Thou
    need'st
Never take shame upon thee for thy choice.

COUNTESS.
This journey, if 't were not thy aim, ascribe it
To thine own self.   Thou shouldst have chosen
To have attended her.   [another

WALLENSTEIN.
            And does he know it !

COUNTESS.
Yes, and he hopes to win her.

WALLENSTEIN.
            Hopes to win her !
Is the boy mad !

COUNTESS.
            Well—hear it from themselves.

WALLENSTEIN.
He thinks to carry off Duke Friedland's daughter !
Ay !—The thought pleases me.
The young man has no grovelling spirit.

COUNTESS.
                        Since
Such and such constant favour you have shown him.

WALLENSTEIN.
He chuses finally to be my heir.
And true it is, I love the youth ; yea, honour him.
But must he therefore be my daughter's husband !
Is it daughters only ! Is it only children
That we must show our favour by !

DUCHESS.
His noble disposition and his manners—

WALLENSTEIN.
Win him my heart, but not my daughter.

DUCHESS.
                        Then
His rank, his ancestors—

WALLENSTEIN.
                Ancestors ! What !
He is a subject, and my son-in-law
I will seek out upon the thrones of Europe.

DUCHESS.
O dearest Albrecht ! Climb we not too high,
Lest we should fall too low.
                        E 2

WALLENSTEIN.
What! have I paid
A price so heavy to ascend this eminence,
And jut out high above the common herd,
Only to close the mighty part I play
In Life's great drama, with a common kinsman!
Have I for this—

[Stops suddenly, repressing himself.
She is the only thing
That will remain behind of me on earth;
And I will see a crown around her head,
Or die in the attempt to place it there.
I hazard all—all! and for this alone,
To lift her into greatness—
Yes, in this moment, in the which we are speaking—

[He recollects himself.
And I must now, like a soft-hearted father,
Couple together in good peasant-fashion
The pair, that chance to suit each other's liking—
And I must do it now, even now, when I
Am stretching out the wreath that is to twine
My full accomplish'd work—no! she is the jewel,
Which I have treasured long, my last, my noblest,
And 'tis my purpose not to let her from me
For less than a king's sceptre.

DUCHESS.
O my husband!
You're ever building, building to the clouds,
Still building higher, and still higher building,
And ne'er reflect, that the poor narrow basis
Cannot sustain the giddy tottering column.

WALLENSTEIN (*to the* COUNTESS).
Have you announced the place of residence
Which I have destined for her?

COUNTESS.
No! not yet.
'Twere better you yourself disclosed it to her.

DUCHESS.
How! Do we not return to Karn then?

WALLENSTEIN.
No.

DUCHESS.
And to no other of your lands or seats!

WALLENSTEIN.
You would not be secure there.

DUCHESS.
Not secure
In the Emperor's realms, beneath the Emperor's
Protection!

WALLENSTEIN.
Friedland's wife may be permitted
No longer to hope *that.*

DUCHESS.
O God in heaven!
And have you brought it even to this!

WALLENSTEIN.
In Holland
You'll find protection.

DUCHESS.
In a Lutheran country!
What! And you send us into Lutheran countries!

WALLENSTEIN.
Duke Franz of Lauenburg conducts you thither.

DUCHESS.
Duke Franz of Lauenburg!
The ally of Sweden, the Emperor's enemy.

WALLENSTEIN.
The Emperor's enemies are mine no longer.

DUCHESS (*casting a look of terror on the* DUKE *and
the* COUNTESS).
Is it then true! It is. You are degraded!
Deposed from the command! O God in heaven!

COUNTESS (*aside to the* DUKE).
Leave her in this belief. Thou seest she cannot
Support the real truth.

———◆———

SCENE V.

To them enter COUNT TERTSKY.

COUNTESS.
—Tertsky!
What ails him! What an image of affright!
He looks as he had seen a ghost.

TERTSKY (*leading* WALLENSTEIN *aside*).
Is it thy command that all the Croats—

WALLENSTEIN.
Mine!

TERTSKY.
We are betray'd.

WALLENSTEIN.
What!

TERTSKY.
They are off! This night
The Jägers likewise—all the villages
In the whole round are empty.

WALLENSTEIN.
Isolani!

TERTSKY.
Him thou hast sent away. Yes, surely.

WALLENSTEIN.
I!

TERTSKY.
No! Hast thou not sent him off! Nor Deodate!
They are vanish'd both of them.

———◆———

SCENE VI.

To them enter ILLO.

ILLO.
Has Tertsky told thee!

TERTSKY.
He knows all.

ILLO.
And likewise
That Esterhatzy, Goetz, Maradas, Kaunitz,
Kolatto, Palfi, have forsaken thee.

TERTSKY.
Damnation!

WALLENSTEIN (*winks at them*).
Hush!

COUNTESS (*who has been watching them anxiously
from the distance and now advances to them*).
Tertsky! Heaven! What is it! What has happen'd!

WALLENSTEIN (*scarcely suppressing his emotions*).
Nothing ! let us be gone !

TERTSKY (*following him*).
                          Theresa, it is nothing.

COUNTESS (*holding him back*).
Nothing ! Do I not see, that all the life-blood
Has left your cheeks—look you not like a ghost !
That even my brother but affects a calmness ?

PAGE (*enters*).
An Aide-de-Camp inquires for the Count Tertsky.
                    [TERTSKY *follows the* PAGE.

WALLENSTEIN.
Go, hear his business.
                               [*To* ILLO.
              This could not have happen'd
So unsuspected without mutiny.
Who was on guard at the gates ?

ILLO.
                    'Twas Tiefenbach.

WALLENSTEIN.
Let Tiefenbach leave guard without delay,
And Tertsky's grenadiers relieve him.

ILLO (*is going*).
                               Stop !
Hast thou heard aught of Butler ?

ILLO.
                          Him I met :
He will be here himself immediately.
Butler remains unshaken.
          [ILLO *exit*. WALLENSTEIN *is following him*.

COUNTESS.
Let him not leave thee, sister ! go, detain him !
There's some misfortune.

DUCHESS (*clinging to him*).
                    Gracious heaven ! What is it ?

WALLENSTEIN.
Be tranquil ! leave me, sister ! dearest wife !
We are in camp, and this is nought unusual ;
Here storm and sunshine follow one another
With rapid interchanges.   These fierce spirits
Champ the curb angrily, and never yet
Did quiet bless the temples of the leader.
If I am to stay, go you.   The plaints of women
Ill suit the scene where men must act.
                    [*He is going :* TERTSKY *returns*.

TERTSKY.
Remain here.   From this window must we see it.

WALLENSTEIN (*to the* COUNTESS).
Sister, retire !

COUNTESS.
No—never.

WALLENSTEIN.
                    'Tis my will.

TERTSKY (*leads the* COUNTESS *aside, and drawing
her attention to the* DUCHESS).
Theresa !

DUCHESS.
Sister, come ! since he commands it.

SCENE VII.

WALLENSTEIN, TERTSKY.

WALLENSTEIN (*stepping to the window*).
What now, then ?

TERTSKY.
There are strange movements among all the troops,
And no one knows the cause.   Mysteriously,
With gloomy silentness, the several corps
Marshal themselves, each under its own banners.
Tiefenbach's corps make threat'ning movements ;
The Pappenheimers still remain aloof   [only
In their own quarters, and let no one enter.

WALLENSTEIN.
Does Piccolomini appear among them ?

TERTSKY.
We are seeking him : he is no where to be met with.

WALLENSTEIN.
What did the Aide-de-Camp deliver to you ?

TERTSKY.
My regiments had despatch'd him ; yet once more
They swear fidelity to thee, and wait
The shout for onset, all prepared, and eager.

WALLENSTEIN.
But whence arose this larum in the camp ?
It should have been kept secret from the army,
Till fortune had decided for us at Prague.

TERTSKY.
O that thou hadst believed me ! Yester evening
Did we conjure thee not to let that skulker,
That fox, Octavio, pass the gates of Pilsen.
Thou gavest him thy own horses to flee from thee.

WALLENSTEIN.
The old tune still ! Now, once for all, no more
Of this suspicion—it is doting folly.

TERTSKY.
Thou didst confide in Isolani too ;
And lo ! he was the first that did desert thee.

WALLENSTEIN.
It was but yesterday I rescued him
From abject wretchedness.   Let that go by ;
I never reckon'd yet on gratitude.
And wherein doth he wrong in going from me ?
He follows still the god whom all his life
He has worshipp'd at the gaming-table.   With
My Fortune, and my seeming destiny,
He made the bond, and broke it not with me.
I am but the ship in which his hopes were stow'd,
And with the which well-pleased and confident
He traversed the open sea ; now he beholds it
In eminent jeopardy among the coast-rocks,
And hurries to preserve his wares.   As light
As the free bird from the hospitable twig
Where it had nested, he flies off from me :
No human tie is snapp'd betwixt us two.
Yea, he deserves to find himself deceived
Who seeks a heart in the unthinking man.
Like shadows on a stream, the forms of life
Impress their characters on the smooth forehead,
Nought sinks into the bosom's silent depth :
Quick sensibility of pain and pleasure
Moves the light fluids lightly ; but no soul
Warmeth the inner frame.

TERTSKY.
                    Yet, would I rather
Trust the smooth brow than that deep furrow'd one.

SCENE VIII.

WALLENSTEIN, TERTSKY, ILLO.

ILLO (*who enters agitated with rage*).
Treason and mutiny!

TERTSKY.
           And what further now!

ILLO.
Tiefenbach's soldiers, when I gave the orders
To go off guard—Mutinous villains!

TERTSKY.
                Well!

WALLENSTEIN.
What followed?

ILLO.
         They refused obedience to them.

TERTSKY.
Fire on them instantly! Give out the order.

WALLENSTEIN.
Gently! what cause did they assign?

ILLO.
                No other,
They said, had right to issue orders but
Lieutenant-General *Piccolomini*.

WALLENSTEIN (*in a convulsion of agony*).
What! How is that!

ILLO.
He takes that office on him by commission,
Under sign-manual of the Emperor.

TERTSKY.
From the Emperor—hear'st thou, Duke!

ILLO.
              At his incitement
The Generals made that stealthy flight—

TERTSKY.
           Duke! hear'st thou!

ILLO.
Caraffa too, and Montecuculi,
Are missing, with six other Generals,
All whom he had induced to follow him.
This plot he has long had in writing by him
From the Emperor; but 't was finally concluded
With all the detail of the operation
Some days ago with the Envoy Questenberg.

[WALLENSTEIN *sinks down into a chair and covers
his face.*

TERTSKY.
O hadst thou but believed me!

SCENE IX.

To them enter the COUNTESS.

COUNTESS.
            This suspense,
This horrid fear—I can no longer bear it.
For heaven's sake, tell me, what has taken place!

ILLO.
The regiments are all falling off from us.

TERTSKY.
Octavio Piccolomini is a traitor.

COUNTESS.
O my foreboding!

[*Rushes out of the room.*

TERTSKY.
           Hadst thou but believed me!
Now seest thou how the stars have lied to thee

WALLENSTEIN.
The stars lie not; but we have here a work
Wrought counter to the stars and destiny.
The science is still honest: this false heart
Forces a lie on the truth-telling heaven.
On a divine law divination rests;
Where nature deviates from that law, and stumbles
Out of her limits, there all science errs.
True, I did not suspect! Were it superstition
Never by such suspicion t' have affronted
The human form, O may that time ne'er come
In which I shame me of the infirmity.
The wildest savage drinks not with the victim,
Into whose breast he means to plunge the sword.
This, this, Octavio, was no hero's deed:
'T was not thy prudence that did conquer mine;
A bad heart triumph'd o'er an honest one.
No shield received the assassin stroke; thou
     plungest
Thy weapon on an unprotected breast—
Against such weapons I am but a child.

SCENE X.

To these enter BUTLER.

TERTSKY (*meeting him*).
O look there! Butler! Here we've still a friend!

WALLENSTEIN (*meets him with outspread arms, and
embraces him with warmth*).
Come to my heart, old comrade! Not the sun
Looks out upon us more revivingly
In the earliest month of spring,
Than a friend's countenance in such an hour.

BUTLER.
My General: I come—

WALLENSTEIN (*leaning on* BUTLER'S *shoulders*).
            Know'st thou already!
That old man has betray'd me to the Emperor.
What say'st thou? Thirty years have we together
Lived out, and held out, sharing joy and hardship.
We have slept in one camp-bed, drunk from one
     glass,
One morsel shared! I lean'd myself on *him*,
As now I lean me on *thy* faithful shoulder.
And now in the very moment, when, all love,
All confidence, my bosom beat to his,
He sees and takes the advantage, stabs the knife
Slowly into my heart.

[*He hides his face on* BUTLER'S *breast.*

BUTLER.
           Forget the false one.
What is your present purpose?

WALLENSTEIN.
           Well remember'd!
Courage, my soul! I am still rich in friends,
Still loved by Destiny; for in the moment,
That it unmasks the plotting hypocrite,
It sends and proves to me one faithful heart.

Of the hypocrite no more ! Think not, his loss
Was that which struck the pang : O no ! his treason
Is that which strikes this pang ! No more of him !
Dear to my heart, and honour'd were they both,
And the young man—yes—he did truly love me,
He—he—has not deceived me.   But enough,
Enough of this—Swift counsel now beseems us.
The Courier, whom Count Kinsky sent from Prague
I expect him every moment : and whatever
He may bring with him, we must take good care
To keep it from the mutineers.   Quick, then !
Despatch some messenger you can rely on
To meet him, and conduct him to me.

[ILLO *is going.*

BUTLER (*detaining him*).
My General, whom expect you then ?

WALLENSTEIN.
The Courier
Who brings me word of the event at Prague.

BUTLER (*hesitating*).
Hem !

WALLENSTEIN.
And what now ?

BUTLER.
You do not know it ?

WALLENSTEIN.
Well ?

BUTLER.
From what that larum in the camp arose ?

WALLENSTEIN.
From what ?

BUTLER.
That Courier——

WALLENSTEIN (*with eager expectation*).
Well ?

BUTLER.
Is already here.

TERTSKY and ILLO (*at the same time*).
Already here !

WALLENSTEIN.
My Courier ?

BUTLER.
For some hours.

WALLENSTEIN.
And I not know it ?

BUTLER.
The centinels detain him
In custody.

ILLO (*stamping with his foot*).
Damnation !

BUTLER.
And his letter
Was broken open, and is circulated
Through the whole camp.

WALLENSTEIN.
You know what it contains ?

BUTLER.
Question me not !

TERTSKY.
Illo ! alas for us.

WALLENSTEIN.
Hide nothing from me—I can hear the worst.
Prague then is lost.   It is.   Confess it freely.

BUTLER.
Yes ! Prague *is* lost.   And all the several regiments
At Budweiss, Tabor, Brannau, Konigingratz,
At Brun and Znaym, have forsaken you,
And ta'en the oaths of fealty anew
To the Emperor.   Yourself, with Kinsky, Tertsky,
And Illo have been sentenced.

[TERTSKY and ILLO *express alarm and fury.* WAL-
LENSTEIN *remains firm and collected.*

WALLENSTEIN.
'T is decided !
'T is well !   I have received a sudden cure
From all the pangs of doubt : with steady stream.
Once more my life-blood flows !   My soul's secure !
In the night only Friedland's stars can beam.
Lingering irresolute, with fitful fears
I drew the sword—'t was with an inward strife,
While yet the choice was mine.   The murderous
knife
Is lifted for my heart !   Doubt disappears !
I fight now for my head and for my life.

[*Exit* WALLENSTEIN ; *the others follow him.*

SCENE XI.

COUNTESS TERTSKY (*enters from a side-room*).
I can endure no longer.   No !

[*Looks around her.*
Where are they !
No one is here.   They leave me all alone,
Alone in this sore anguish of suspense.
And I must wear the outward show of calmness
Before my sister, and shut in within me
The pangs and agonies of my crowded bosom.
It is not to be borne.—If all should fail ;
If—if he must go over to the Swedes,
An empty-handed fugitive, and not
As an ally, a covenanted equal,
A proud commander with his army following ;
If we must wander on from land to land,
Like the Count Palatine, of fallen greatness
An ignominious monument—But no !
That day I will not see !   And could himself
Endure to sink so low, I would not bear
To see him so low sunken.

SCENE XII.

COUNTESS, DUCHESS, THEKLA.

THEKLA (*endeavouring to hold back the* DUCHESS).
Dear mother, do stay here !

DUCHESS.
No !   Here is yet
Some frightful mystery that is hidden from me.
Why does my sister shun me ?   Don't I see her
Full of suspense and anguish roam about
From room to room ?—Art thou not full of terror ?
And what import these silent nods and gestures
Which stealthwise thou exchangest with her ?

THEKLA.
Nothing, dear mother !

DUCHESS (*to the* COUNTESS).
Sister, I will know.

COUNTESS.
What boots it now to hide it from her ? Sooner
Or later she *must* learn to hear and bear it.
'T is not the time now to indulge infirmity ;
Courage beseems us now, a heart collect,
And exercise and previous discipline
Of fortitude. One word, and over with it !
Sister, you are deluded. You believe,
The Duke has been deposed—The Duke is not
Deposed—he is——

THEKLA (*going to the* COUNTESS).
What I do you wish to kill her ?

COUNTESS.
The Duke is——

THEKLA (*throwing her arms round her mother*).
O stand firm ! stand firm, my mother !

COUNTESS.
Revolted is the Duke ; he is preparing
To join the enemy ; the army leave him,
And all has fail'd.

ACT II.

SCENE I.

A spacious Room in the Duke of Friedland's Palace.

WALLENSTEIN (*in armour*).
Thou hast gain'd thy point, Octavio ! Once more
Almost as friendless as at Regensburg. [am I
There I had nothing left me, but myself—
But what one man can do, you have now experience.
The twigs have you hew'd off, and here I stand
A leafless trunk. But in the sap within
Lives the creating power, and a new world
May sprout forth from it. Once already have I
Proved myself worth an army to you—I alone !
Before the Swedish strength your troops had melted ;
Beside the Lech sunk Tilly, your last hope ;
Into Bavaria, like a winter torrent,
Did that Gustavus pour, and at Vienna
In his own palace did the Emperor tremble.
Soldiers were scarce, for still the multitude
Follow the luck : all eyes were turn'd on me,
Their helper in distress : the Emperor's pride
Bow'd itself down before the man he had injured.
'Twas I must rise, and with creative word
Assemble forces in the desolate camps.
I did it. Like a god of war, my name
Went through the world. The drum was beat—
and, lo !
The plough, the workshop is forsaken, all
Swarm to the old familiar long-loved banners ;
And as the wood-choir rich in melody
Assemble quick around the bird of wonder,
When first his throat swells with his magic song,
So did the warlike youth of Germany
Crowd in around the image of my eagle.
I feel myself the being that I was.
It is the soul that builds itself a body,
And Friedland's camp will not remain unfill'd.
Lead then your thousands out to meet me—true !
They are accustom'd under me to conquer,
But not against me. If the head and limbs
Separate from each other, 'twill be soon
Made manifest, in which the soul abode.

(ILLO *and* TERTSKY *enter.*)

Courage, friends ! Courage ! We are still unvan-
quish'd !
I feel my footing firm ; five regiments, Tertsky,
Are still our own, and Butler's gallant troops ;
And an host of sixteen thousand Swedes to-morrow.
I was not stronger, when nine years ago
I marched forth, with glad heart and high of hope,
To conquer Germany for the Emperor.

SCENE II.

WALLENSTEIN, ILLO, TERTSKY. (*To them enter* NEUMANN, *who leads* TERTSKY *aside, and talks with him.*)

TERTSKY.
What do they want ?

WALLENSTEIN.
What now !

TERTSKY.
Ten Cuirassiers
From Pappenheim request leave to address you
In the name of the regiment.

WALLENSTEIN (*hastily to* NEUMANN).
Let them enter.
[*Exit* NEUMANN.
This
May end in something. Mark you. They are still
Doubtful, and may be won.

SCENE III.

WALLENSTEIN, TERTSKY, ILLO, ten Cuirassiers (*led by an* ANSPESSADE [1], *march up and arrange themselves, after the word of command, in one front before the Duke, and make their obeisance. He takes his hat off, and immediately covers himself again.*)

ANSPESSADE.
Halt ! Front ! Present !

WALLENSTEIN (*after he has run through them with his eye, to the* ANSPESSADE).
I know thee well. Thou art out of Brüggen in
Thy name is Mercy. [Flanders :

ANSPESSADE.
Henry Mercy.

WALLENSTEIN.
Thou wert cut off on the march, surrounded by
the Hessians, and didst fight thy way with an hundred and eighty men through their thousand.

ANSPESSADE.
'Twas even so, General !

WALLENSTEIN.
What reward hadst thou for this gallant exploit ?

[1] Anspessade, in German Gefreiter, a soldier inferior to a corporal, but above the sentinels. The German name implies that he is exempt from mounting guard.

ANSPESSADE.

That which I asked for : the honour to serve in this corps.

WALLENSTEIN (*turning to a second*).

Thou wert among the volunteers that seized and made booty of the Swedish battery at Altenburg.

SECOND CUIRASSIER.

Yes, General!

WALLENSTEIN.

I forget no one with whom I have exchanged words. (*A pause.*) Who sends you ?

ANSPESSADE.

Your noble regiment, the Cuirassiers of Picco-lomini.

WALLENSTEIN.

Why does not your colonel deliver in your request, according to the custom of service ?

ANSPESSADE.

Because we would first know *whom* we serve.

WALLENSTEIN.

Begin your address.

ANSPESSADE (*giving the word of command*).

Shoulder your arms !

WALLENSTEIN (*turning to a third*).

Thy name is Risbeck ; Cologne is thy birth-place.

THIRD CUIRASSIER.

Risbeck of Cologne.

WALLENSTEIN.

It was thou that broughtest in the Swedish colonel, Diebald, prisoner, in the camp at Nüremberg.

THIRD CUIRASSIER.

It was not I, General !

WALLENSTEIN.

Perfectly right ! It was thy elder brother : thou hadst a younger brother too : Where did he stay ?

THIRD CUIRASSIER.

He is stationed at Olmütz with the Imperial army.

WALLENSTEIN (*to the* ANSPESSADE).

Now then—begin.

ANSPESSADE.

There came to hand a letter from the Emperor Commanding us—

WALLENSTEIN (*interrupting him*).

Who chose you ?

ANSPESSADE.

Every company Drew its own man by lot.

WALLENSTEIN.

Now ! to the business.

ANSPESSADE.

There came to hand a letter from the Emperor Commanding us collectively, from thee
All duties of obedience to withdraw,
Because thou wert an enemy and traitor.

WALLENSTEIN.

And what did you determine ?

ANSPESSADE.

All our comrades
At Brannau, Budweiss, Prague and Olmütz, have

Obey'd already ; and the regiments here,
Tiefenbach and Toscano, instantly
Did follow their example. But—but we
Do not believe that thou art an enemy
And traitor to thy country, hold it merely
For lie and trick, and a trumped up Spanish story !
[*With warmth.*
Thyself shalt tell us what thy purpose is,
For we have found thee still sincere and true :
No mouth shall interpose itself betwixt
The gallant General and the gallant troops.

WALLENSTEIN.

Therein I recognise my Pappenheimers.

ANSPESSADE.

And this proposal makes thy regiment to thee :
Is it thy purpose merely to preserve
In thine own hands this military sceptre,
Which so becomes thee, which the Emperor
Made over to thee by a covenant ?
Is it thy purpose merely to remain
Supreme commander of the Austrian armies ?—
We will stand by thee, General ! and guarantee
Thy honest rights against all opposition.
And should it chance, that all the other regiments
Turn from thee, by ourselves will we stand forth
Thy faithful soldiers, and, as is our duty,
Far rather let ourselves be cut to pieces,
Than suffer thee to fall. But if it be
As the Emperor's letter says, if it be true,
That thou in traitorous wise wilt lead us over
To the enemy, which God in heaven forbid !
Then we too will forsake thee, and obey
That letter—

WALLENSTEIN.

Hear me, children !

ANSPESSADE.

Yes, or no !
There needs no other answer.

WALLENSTEIN.

Yield attention.
You're men of sense, examine for yourselves ;
Ye think, and do not follow with the herd :
And therefore have I always shown you honour
Above all others, suffer'd you to reason ;
Have treated you as free men, and my orders
Were but the echoes of your prior suffrage.—

ANSPESSADE.

Most fair and noble has thy conduct been
To us, my General ! With thy confidence
Thou hast honour'd us, and shown us grace and favour
Beyond all other regiments ; and thou seest
We follow not the common herd. We will
Stand by thee faithfully. Speak but one word—
Thy word shall satisfy us, that it is not
A treason which thou meditatest—that
Thou meanest not to lead the army over
To the enemy ; nor e'er betray thy country.

WALLENSTEIN.

Me, me are they betraying. The Emperor
Hath sacrificed me to my enemies,
And I must fall, unless my gallant troops
Will rescue me. See ! I confide in you.
And be your hearts my strong-hold ! At this breast
The aim is taken, at this hoary head.
This is your Spanish gratitude, this is our
Requital for that murderous fight at Lutzen !

For this we threw the naked breast against
The halbert, made for this the frozen earth
Our bed, and the hard stone our pillow! never
    stream
Too rapid for us, nor wood too impervious:
With cheerful spirit we pursued that Mansfeldt
Through all the turns and windings of his flight;
Yea, our whole life was but one restless march;
And homeless, as the stirring wind, we travell'd
O'er the war-wasted earth. And now, even now,
That we have well nigh finish'd the hard toil,
The unthankful, the curse-laden toil of weapons,
With faithful indefatigable arm
Have roll'd the heavy war-load up the hill,
Behold! this boy of the Emperor's bears away
The honours of the peace, an easy prize!
He'll weave, forsooth, into his flaxen locks
The olive branch, the hard-earned ornament
Of this grey head, grown grey beneath the helmet.

ANSPESSADE.
That shall he not, while we can hinder it!
No one, but thou, who hast conducted it
With fame, shall end this war, this frightful war.
Thou led'st us out into the bloody field
Of death; thou and no other shalt conduct us home,
Rejoicing to the lovely plains of peace—
Shalt share with us the fruits of the long toil—

WALLENSTEIN.
What! Think you then at length in late old age
To enjoy the fruits of toil? Believe it not.
Never, no never, will you see the end
Of the contest! you and me, and all of us,
This war will swallow up! War, war, not peace,
Is Austria's wish; and therefore, because I
Endeavour'd after peace, therefore I fall.
For what cares Austria, how long the war
Wears out the armies and lays waste the world!
She will but wax and grow amid the ruin,
And still win new domains.
    [The Cuirassiers express agitation by their gestures.
                    Ye're moved—I see
A noble rage flash from your eyes, ye warriors!
Oh that my spirit might possess you now
Daring as once it led you to the battle!
Ye would stand by me with your veteran arms,
Protect me in my rights; and this is noble!
But think not that you can accomplish it,
Your scanty number! to no purpose will you
Have sacrificed you for your General.
    [Confidentially.
No! let us tread securely, seek for friends;
The Swedes have proffer'd us assistance, let us
Wear for a while the appearance of good will,
And use them for your profit, till we both
Carry the fate of Europe in our hands,
And from our camp to the glad jubilant world
Lead Peace forth with the garland on her head!

ANSPESSADE.
'Tis then but mere appearances which thou
Dost put on with the Swede? Thou'lt not betray
The Emperor? Wilt not turn us into Swedes?
This is the only thing which we desire
To learn from thee.

WALLENSTEIN.
            What care I for the Swedes!
I hate them as I hate the pit of hell,
And under Providence I trust right soon
To chase them to their homes across their Baltic.

My cares are only for the whole: I have
A heart—it bleeds within me for the miseries
And piteous groaning of my fellow Germans.
Ye are but common men, but yet ye think
With minds not common; ye appear to me
Worthy before all others, that I whisper ye
A little word or two in confidence!
See now! already for full fifteen years
The war-torch has continued burning, yet
No rest, no pause of conflict. Swede and German,
Papist and Lutheran! neither will give way
To the other, every hand's against the other.
Each one is party and no one a judge.
Where shall this end? Where's he that will
    unravel
This tangle, ever tangling more and more.
It must be cut asunder.
I feel that I am the man of destiny,
And trust, with your assistance, to accomplish it.

                ———◆———

                SCENE IV.

            To these enter BUTLER.

BUTLER (passionately).
General! This is not right!

            WALLENSTEIN.
                    What is not right?

BUTLER.
It must needs injure us with all honest men.

            WALLENSTEIN.
But what?

            BUTLER.
            It is an open proclamation·
Of insurrection.

            WALLENSTEIN.
        Well, well—but what is it?

            BUTLER.
Count Tertsky's regiments tear the Imperial Eagle
From off the banners, and instead of it
Have rear'd aloft thy arms.

ANSPESSADE (abruptly to the Cuirassiers).
                Right about! March!

            WALLENSTEIN.
Cursed be this counsel, and accursed who gave it!
        [To the Cuirassiers, who are retiring.
Halt, children, halt! There's some mistake in this;
Hark!—I will punish it severely. Stop!
They do not hear. (To ILLO). Go after them, assure
    them,
And bring them back to me, cost what it may.
                [ILLO hurries out.
This hurls us headlong. Butler! Butler!
You are my evil genius, wherefore must you
Announce it in their presence? It was all
In a fair way. They were half won! those madmen
With their improvident over-readiness—
A cruel game is Fortune playing with me.
The zeal of friends it is that razes me,
And not the hate of enemies.

                ————

SCENE V.

To these enter the DUCHESS, who rushes into the Chamber. THEKLA and the COUNTESS follow her.

DUCHESS.
                    O Albrecht!
What hast thou done!

WALLENSTEIN.
            And now comes this beside.

COUNTESS.
Forgive me, brother! It was not in my power.
They know all.

DUCHESS.
        What hast thou done!

COUNTESS (*to* TERTSKY).
Is there no hope! Is all lost utterly!

TERTSKY.
All lost. No hope. Prague in the Emperor's hands,
The soldiery have ta'en their oaths anew.

COUNTESS.
That lurking hypocrite, Octavio!
Count Max. is off too.

TERTSKY.
            Where can he be! He's
Gone over to the Emperor with his father.

[THEKLA *rushes out into the arms of her mother, hiding her face in her bosom.*

DUCHESS (*enfolding her in her arms*).
Unhappy child! and more unhappy mother!

WALLENSTEIN (*aside to* TERTSKY).
Quick! Let a carriage stand in readiness
In the court behind the palace. Scherfenberg
Be their attendant; he is faithful to us;
To Egra he'll conduct them, and we follow.
            [*To* ILLO, *who returns.*
Thou hast not brought them back!

ILLO.
            Hear'st thou the uproar!
The whole corps of the Pappenheimers is
Drawn out: the younger Piccolomini,
Their colonel, they require: for they affirm,
That he is in the palace here, a prisoner;
And if thou dost not instantly deliver him,
They will find means to free him with the sword.
                    [*All stand amazed.*

TERTSKY.
What shall we make of this!

WALLENSTEIN.
            Said I not so!
O my prophetic heart! he is still here.
He has not betray'd me—he could not betray me.
I never doubted of it.

COUNTESS.
            If he be
Still here, then all goes well; for I know what
                    [*Embracing* THEKLA.
Will keep him here for ever.

TERTSKY.
            It can't be.
His father has betray'd us, is gone over
To the Emperor—the son could not have ventured
To stay behind.

THEKLA (*her eye fixed on the door*).
            There he is!

SCENE VI.

To these enter MAX. PICCOLOMINI.

MAX.
Yes! here he is! I can endure no longer
To creep on tiptoe round this house, and lurk
In ambush for a favourable moment:
This loitering, this suspense exceeds my powers.
    [*Advancing to* THEKLA, *who has thrown herself into her mother's arms.*
Turn not thine eyes away. O look upon me!
Confess it freely before all. Fear no one.
Let who will hear that we both love each other.
Wherefore continue to conceal it! Secrecy
Is for the happy—misery, hopeless misery,
Needeth no veil! Beneath a thousand suns
It dares act openly.
    [*He observes the* COUNTESS *looking on* THEKLA *with expressions of triumph.*
            No, Lady! No!
Expect not, hope it not. I am not come
To stay: to bid farewell, farewell for ever.
For this I come! 'Tis over! I must leave thee!
Thekla, I must—*must* leave thee! Yet thy hatred
Let me not take with me. I pray thee, grant me
One look of sympathy, only one look.
Say that thou dost not hate me. Say it to me,
Thekla!   [*Grasps her hand.*
O God! I cannot leave this spot—I cannot!
Cannot let go this hand. O tell me, Thekla!
That thou dost suffer with me, art convinced
That I can not act otherwise.
    [THEKLA, *avoiding his look, points with her hand to her father.* MAX. *turns round to the Duke, whom he had not till then perceived.*
Thou here! It was not thou, whom here I sought.
I trusted never more to have beheld thee.
My business is with her alone. Here will I
Receive a full acquittal from this heart—
For any other I am no more concern'd.

WALLENSTEIN.
Think'st thou, that fool-like, I shall let thee go,
And act the mock-magnanimous with thee!
Thy father is become a villain to me;
I hold thee for his son, and nothing more:
Nor to no purpose shalt thou have been given
Into my power. Think not, that I will honour
That ancient love, which so remorselessly
He mangled. They are now past by, those hours
Of friendship and forgiveness. Hate and ven-
geance
Succeed—'tis now their turn—I too can throw
All feelings of the man aside—can prove
Myself as much a monster as thy father!

MAX. (*calmly*).
Thou wilt proceed with me, as thou hast power.
Thou know'st, I neither brave nor fear thy rage.
What has detain'd me here, that too thou know'st.
                    [*Taking* THEKLA *by the hand.*
See, Duke! All—all would I have owed to thee,
Would have received from thy paternal hand
The lot of blessed spirits. This hast thou
Laid waste for ever—that concerns not thee.
Indifferent thou tramplest in the dust
Their happiness, who most are thine. The god
Whom thou dost serve, is no benignant deity.
Like as the blind irreconcileable

Fierce element, incapable of compact,
Thy heart's wild impulse only dost thou follow.[1]

WALLENSTEIN.

Thou art describing thy own father's heart.
The adder! O, the charms of hell o'erpower'd me.
He dwelt within me, to my inmost soul
Still to and fro he pass'd, suspected never!
On the wide ocean, in the starry heaven
Did mine eyes seek the enemy, whom I
In my heart's heart had folded! Had I been
To *Ferdinand* what Octavio was to *me*,
War had I ne'er denounced against him. No,
I never could have done it. The Emperor was
My austere master only, not my friend.
There was already war 'twixt him and me
When he deliver'd the Commander's Staff
Into my hands; for there's a natural
Unceasing war 'twixt cunning and suspicion;
Peace exists only betwixt confidence
And faith. Who poisons confidence, he murders
The future generations.

MAX.

              I will not
Defend my father. Woe is me, I cannot!

Hard deeds and luckless have ta'en place; one crime
Drags after it the other in close link.
But we are innocent: how have we fallen
Into this circle of mishap and guilt?
To whom have we been faithless? Wherefore must
The evil deeds and guilt reciprocal
Of our two fathers twine like serpents round us?
              Why must our fathers'
Unconquerable hate rend us asunder,
Who love each other?

WALLENSTEIN,
            Max., remain with me.
Go you not from me, Max.! Hark! I will tell thee—
How when at Prague, our winter-quarters, thou
Wert brought into my tent a tender boy,
Not yet accustom'd to the German winters;
Thy hand was frozen to the heavy colours;
Thou wouldst not let them go.—
At that time did I take thee in my arms,
And with my mantle did I cover thee;
I was thy nurse, no woman could have been
A kinder to thee; I was not ashamed
To do for thee all little offices,
However strange to me; I tended thee
Till life return'd; and when thine eyes first open'd,
I had thee in my arms. Since then, when have I
Alter'd my feelings towards thee? Many thousands
Have I made rich, presented them with lands;
Rewarded them with dignities and honours;
Thee have I *loved:* my heart, my self, I gave
To thee! They all were aliens: THOU wert
Our child and inmate.[2] Max.! Thou canst not
leave me;
It cannot be; I may not, will not think
That Max. can leave me.

MAX.
            O my God!

WALLENSTEIN.
              I have
Held and sustain'd thee from thy tottering child-
What holy bond is there of natural love, [hood.
What human tie, that does not knit thee to me?
I love thee, Max.! What did thy father for thee,
Which I too have not done, to the height of duty?
Go hence, forsake me, serve thy Emperor;
He will reward thee with a pretty chain
Of gold; with his ram's fleece will he reward thee;
For that the friend, the father of thy youth,
For that the holiest feeling of humanity,
Was nothing worth to thee.

MAX.
            O God! how can I
Do otherwise? Am I not forced to do it,
My oath—my duty—honour—

WALLENSTEIN.
            How? Thy duty?
Duty to whom? Who art thou? Max.! bethink thee
What duties mayst *thou* have? If I am acting
A criminal part toward the Emperor,
It is my crime, not thine. Dost thou belong

To thine own self? Art thou thine own commander?
Stand'st thou, like me, a freeman in the world,
That in thy actions thou shouldst plead free agency?
On me thou'rt planted, I am thy Emperor;
To obey *me*, to *belong* to me, this is
Thy honour, this a law of nature to thee!
And if the planet, on the which thou livest
And hast thy dwelling, from its orbit starts,
It is not in thy choice, whether or no
Thou'lt follow it. Unfelt it whirls thee onward
Together with his ring and all his moons.
With little guilt stepp'st thou into this contest;
Thee will the world not censure, it will praise thee,
For that thou heldst thy friend more worth to thee
Than names and influences more removed.
For justice is the virtue of the ruler,
Affection and fidelity the subject's.
Not every one doth it beseem to question
The far-off high Arcturus. Most securely
Wilt thou pursue the nearest duty—let
The pilot fix his eye upon the pole-star.

SCENE VII.

To these enter NEUMANN.

WALLENSTEIN.

What now?

NEUMANN.
The Pappenheimers are dismounted,
And are advancing now on foot, determined
With sword in hand to storm the house, and free
The Count, their colonel.

WALLENSTEIN (*to* TERTSKY).
Have the cannon planted.
I will receive them with chain-shot.
[*Exit* TERTSKY.
Prescribe to me with sword in hand! Go Neumann!
'T is my command that they retreat this moment,
And in their ranks in silence wait my pleasure.
[NEUMANN *exit.* ILLO *steps to the window.*

COUNTESS.
Let him go, I entreat thee, let him go.

ILLO (*at the window*).
Hell and perdition!

WALLENSTEIN.
What is it?

ILLO.
They scale the council-house, the roof's uncover'd
They level at this house the cannon——

MAX.
Madmen!

ILLO.
They are making preparations now to fire on us.

DUCHESS AND COUNTESS.
Merciful Heaven!

MAX. (*to* WALLENSTEIN).
Let me go to them!

WALLENSTEIN.
Not a step!
MAX. (*pointing to* THEKLA *and the* DUCHESS.)
But their life! Thine!

WALLENSTEIN.
What tidings bring'st thou, Tertsky?

SCENE VIII.

To these TERTSKY (*returning*).

TERTSKY.
Message and greeting from our faithful regiments.
Their ardour may no longer be curb'd in.
They intreat permission to commence the attack;
And if thou wouldst but give the word of onset,
They could now charge the enemy in rear,
Into the city wedge them, and with ease
O'erpower them in the narrow streets.

ILLO.
O come!
Let not their ardour cool. The soldiery
Of Butler's corps stand by us faithfully;
We are the greater number. Let us charge them,
And finish here in Pilsen the revolt.

WALLENSTEIN.
What! shall this town become a field of slaughter,
And brother-killing Discord, fire-eyed,
Be let loose through its streets to roam and rage?
Shall the decision be deliver'd over
To deaf remorseless Rage, that hears no leader?
Here is not room for battle, only for butchery.
Well, let it be! I have long thought of it,
So let it burst then!
[*Turns to* MAX.
Well, how is it with thee?
Wilt thou attempt a heat with me. Away!
Thou art free to go. Oppose thyself to me,
Front against front, and lead them to the battle;
Thou'rt skilled in war, thou hast learn'd somewhat
under me,
I need not be ashamed of my opponent,
And never had'st thou fairer opportunity
To pay me for thy schooling.

COUNTESS.
Is it then,
Can it have come to this?—What! Cousin, Cousin!
Have you the heart?

MAX.
The regiments that are trusted to my care
I have pledged my troth to bring away from Pilsen
True to the Emperor, and this promise will I
Make good, or perish. More than this no duty
Requires of me. I will not fight against thee,
Unless compell'd; for though an enemy,
Thy head is holy to me still.
[*Two reports of cannon.* ILLO *and* TERTSKY *hurry
to the window.*

WALLENSTEIN.
What's that?

TERTSKY.
He falls.

WALLENSTEIN.
Falls! Who?

ILLO.
Tiefenbach's corps
Discharged the ordnance.

WALLENSTEIN.
Upon whom?

ILLO.
On Neumann
Your messenger.

WALLENSTEIN (*starting up*).
    Ha! Death and hell! I will—

TERTSKY.
Expose thyself to their blind frenzy!

DUCHESS *and* COUNTESS.
               No!
For God sake, no!

ILLO.
    Not yet, my General!

COUNTESS.
O, hold him! hold him!

WALLENSTEIN.
        Leave me——

MAX.
          Do it not;
Not yet! This rash and bloody deed has thrown them
Into a frenzy-fit—allow them time—

WALLENSTEIN.
Away! too long already have I loiter'd.
They are embolden'd to these outrages,
Beholding not my face. They shall behold
My countenance, shall hear my voice—
Are they not *my* troops! Am I not their General,
And their long-fear'd commander! Let me see,
Whether indeed they do no longer know
That countenance, which was their sun in battle!
From the balcony (mark!), I show myself
To these rebellious forces, and at once
Revolt is mounded, and the high-swoln current
Shrinks back into the old bed of obedience.

[*Exit* WALLENSTEIN; ILLO, TERTSKY, *and*
BUTLER *follow*.

SCENE IX.

COUNTESS, DUCHESS, MAX. *and* THEKLA.

COUNTESS (*to the* DUCHESS).
Let them but see him—there is hope still, sister.

DUCHESS.
Hope! I have none!

MAX. (*who during the last scene has been standing
at a distance in a visible struggle of feelings,
advances*).
      This can I not endure.
With most determined soul did I come hither;
My purposed action seem'd unblameable
To my own conscience—and I must stand here
Like one abhorr'd, a hard inhuman being:
Yea, loaded with the curse of all I love!
Must see all whom I love in this sore anguish,
Whom I with one word can make happy—O!
My heart revolts within me, and two voices
Make themselves audible within my bosom.
My soul's benighted; I no longer can
Distinguish the right track. O, well and truly
Didst thou say, father, I relied too much
On my own heart. My mind moves to and fro—
I know not what to do.

COUNTESS.
      What! you know not!
Does not your own heart tell you! O! then I
Will tell it you. Your father is a traitor,
A frightful traitor to us—he has plotted

Against our General's life, has plunged us all
In misery—and you're his son! 'T is your's
To make the *amends*—Make you the son's fidelity
Outweigh the father's treason, that the name
Of Piccolomini be not a proverb
Of infamy, a common form of cursing
To the posterity of Wallenstein.

MAX.
Where is that voice of truth which I dare follow!
It speaks no longer in *my* heart. We all
But utter what our passionate wishes dictate:
O that an angel would descend from Heaven,
And scoop for me the right, the uncorrupted,
With a pure hand from the pure Fount of Light.

[*His eyes glance on* THEKLA.
What other angel seek I! To this heart,
To this unerring heart, will I submit it;
Will ask thy love, which has the power to bless
The happy man alone, averted ever
From the disquieted and guilty—canst thou
Still love me, if I stay! Say that thou canst,
And I am the Duke's——

COUNTESS.
        Think, niece——

MAX.
        Think nothing, Thekla!
Speak what thou *feelest*.

COUNTESS.
        Think upon your father.

MAX.
I did not question thee, as Friedland's daughter.
Thee, the beloved and the unerring god
Within thy heart, I question. What's at stake!
Not whether diadem of royalty
Be to be won or not—that mightest thou *think* on.
Thy friend, and his soul's quiet, are at stake;
The fortune of a thousand gallant men,
Who will all follow me; shall I forswear
My oath and duty to the Emperor!
Say, shall I send into Octavio's camp
The parricidal ball! For when the ball
Has left its cannon, and is on its flight,
It is no longer a dead instrument!
It lives, a spirit passes into it,
The avenging furies seize possession of it,
And with sure malice guide it the worst way

THEKLA.
O! Max.——

MAX. (*interrupting her*).
    Nay, not precipitately either, Thekla.
I understand thee. To thy noble heart
The hardest duty might appear the highest.
The human, not the great part, would I act.
Even from my childhood to this present hour,
Think what the Duke has done for me, how
    loved me,
And think too, how my father has repaid him.
O likewise the free lovely impulses
Of hospitality, the pious friend's
Faithful attachment, these too are a holy
Religion to the heart; and heavily
The shudderings of nature do avenge
Themselves on the barbarian that insults them.
Lay all upon the balance, all—then speak,
And let thy heart decide it.

THEKLA.
O, thy own
Hath long ago decided.   Follow thou
Thy heart's first feeling——

COUNTESS.
Oh ! ill-fated woman !

THEKLA.
Is it possible, that that can be the right,
The which thy tender heart did not at first
Detect and seize with instant impulse ?   Go,
Fulfil thy duty !   I should ever love thee.
Whate'er thou hadst chosen, thou wouldst still
   have acted
Nobly and worthy of thee—but repentance
Shall ne'er disturb thy soul's fair peace.

MAX.
Then I
Must leave thee, must part from thee !

THEKLA.
Being faithful
To thine own self, thou art faithful too to me :
If our fates part, our hearts remain united.
A bloody hatred will divide for ever
The houses Piccolomini and Friedland ;
But we belong not to our houses—Go !
Quick ! quick ! and separate thy righteous cause
From our unholy and unblessed one !
The curse of Heaven lies upon our head :
'T is dedicate to ruin.   Even me
My father's guilt drags with it to perdition.
Mourn not for me :
My destiny will quickly be decided.

[MAX. clasps her in his arms in extreme emotion.
There is heard from behind the Scene a loud wild,
long continued cry, Vivat Ferdinandus ! accompanied by warlike Instruments. MAX. and
THEKLA remain without motion in each other's
embraces.

———◆———

SCENE X.

To the above enter TERTSKY.

COUNTESS (meeting him).
What meant that cry ?   What was it !

TERTSKY.
All is lost !

COUNTESS.
What ! they regarded not his countenance ?

TERTSKY.
'T was all in vain.

DUCHESS.
They shouted Vivat !

TERTSKY.
To the Emperor.

COUNTESS.
The traitors !

TERTSKY.
Nay ! he was not once permitted
Even to address them.   Soon as he began,
With deafening noise of warlike instruments
They drown'd his words.   But here he comes.

SCENE XI.

To these enter WALLENSTEIN, accompanied by ILLO and
BUTLER.

WALLENSTEIN (as he enters).
Tertsky !

TERTSKY.
My General !

WALLENSTEIN.
Let our regiments hold themselves
In readiness to march ; for we shall leave
Pilsen ere evening.   [Exit TERTSKY.
Butler !

BUTLER.
Yes, my General.

WALLENSTEIN.
The Governor of Egra is your friend
And countryman.   Write to him instantly
By a post courier.   He must be advised,
That we are with him early on the morrow.
You follow us yourself, your regiment with you.

BUTLER.
It shall be done, my General !

WALLENSTEIN (steps between MAX. and THEKLA,
who have remained during this time in each
other's arms).
Part !

MAX.
O God !
[Cuirassiers enter with drawn swords, and assemble in
the back-ground.   At the same time there are heard from
below some spirited passages out of the Pappenheim March,
which seem to address MAX.

WALLENSTEIN (to the Cuirassiers).
Here he is, he is at liberty : I keep him
No longer.
[He turns away, and stands so that MAX. cannot
pass by him nor approach the PRINCESS.

MAX.
Thou know'st that I have not yet learnt to live
Without thee !   I go forth into a desert,
Leaving my all behind me.   O do not turn
Thine eyes away from me !   O once more show me
Thy ever dear and honour'd countenance.
[MAX. attempts to take his hand, but is repelled ;
he turns to the COUNTESS.
Is there no eye that has a look of pity for me ?
[The COUNTESS turns away from him ; he turns to
the DUCHESS.
My mother !

DUCHESS.
Go where duty calls you.   Haply
The time may come, when you may prove to us
A true friend, a good angel at the throne
Of the Emperor.

MAX.
You give me hope ; you would not
Suffer me wholly to despair.   No ! no !
Mine is a certain misery—Thanks to Heaven !
That offers me a means of ending it.
[The military music begins again.   The stage fills
more and more with armed men.   MAX. sees
BUTLER and addresses him.
And you here, Colonel Butler—and will you
Not follow me !   Well, then ! remain more faithful
To your new lord, than you have proved yourself

To the Emperor. Côme, Butler ! promise me,
Give me your hand upon it, that you 'll be
The guardian of his life, its shield, its watchman.
He is attainted, and his princely head
Fair booty for each slave that trades in murder.
Now he doth need the faithful eye of friendship,
And those whom here I see—

[*Casting suspicious looks on* ILLO *and* BUTLER.

ILLO.
                    Go—seek for traitors
In Galas', in your father's quarters. Here
Is only one. Away ! away ! and free us
From his detested sight ! Away !

[MAX. *attempts once more to approach* THEKLA.
WALLENSTEIN *prevents him.* MAX. *stands irresolute, and in apparent anguish. In the mean
time the stage fills more and more ; and the horns
sound from below louder and louder, and each
time after a shorter interval.*

MAX.
Blow, blow ! O were it but the Swedish Trumpets,

And all the naked swords, which I see here,
Were plunged into my breast ! What purpose you !
You come to tear me from this place ! Beware,
Ye drive me not to desperation.—Do it not !
Ye may repent it !

[*The stage is entirely filled with armed men.*
Yet more ! weight upon weight to drag me down !
Think what ye 're doing. It is not well done
To chuse a man despairing for your leader ;
You tear me from my happiness. Well, then,
I dedicate your souls to vengeance. Mark !
For your own ruin you have chosen me :
Who goes with me, must be prepared to perish.

[*He turns to the back-ground, there ensues a sudden
and violent movement among the Cuirassiers ;
they surround him, and carry him off in wild
tumult.* WALLENSTEIN *remains immovable.*
THEKLA *sinks into her mother's arms. The curtain falls. The music becomes loud and over-
powering, and passes into a complete war-march
—the orchestra joins it—and continues during
the interval between the second and third Act.*

ACT III.

SCENE I.

The BURGOMASTER'S *House at Egra.*

BUTLER (*just arrived*).

Here then he is, by his destiny conducted.
Here, Friedland ! and no farther ! From Bohemia
Thy meteor rose, traversed the sky awhile,
And here upon the borders of Bohemia
Must sink.
        Thou hast foresworn the ancient colours,
Blind man ! yet trustest to thy ancient fortunes.
Profaner of the altar and the hearth,
Against thy Emperor and fellow-citizens
Thou mean'st to wage the war. Friedland, be-
ware—
The evil spirit of revenge impels thee—
Beware thou, that revenge destroy thee not !

SCENE II.

BUTLER *and* GORDON.

GORDON.
                          Is it you ?
How my heart sinks ! The Duke a fugitive traitor !
His princely head attainted ! O my God !

BUTLER.
You have received the letter which I sent you
By a post-courier ?

GORDON.
              Yes ; and in obedience to it
Open'd the stronghold to him without scruple,
For an imperial letter orders me
To follow your commands implicitly.
But yet forgive me ! when even now I saw
The Duke himself, my scruples recommenced.
For truly, not like an attainted man,
Into this town did Friedland make his entrance ;

His wonted majesty beam'd from his brow,
And calm, as in the days when all was right,
Did he receive from me the accounts of office.
'Tis said, that fallen pride learns condescension :
But sparing and with dignity the Duke
Weigh'd every syllable of approbation,
As masters praise a servant who has done
His duty, and no more.

BUTLER.
                    'Tis all precisely
As I related in my letter. Friedland
Has sold the army to the enemy,
And pledged himself to give up Prague and Egra.
On this report the regiments all forsook him,
The five excepted that belong to Tertsky,
And which have follow'd him, as thou hast seen.
The sentence of attainder is pass'd on him,
And every loyal subject is required
To give him in to justice, dead or living.

GORDON.
A traitor to the Emperor—Such a noble !
Of such high talents ! What is human greatness !
I often said, this can't end happily.
His might, his greatness, and this obscure power
Are but a cover'd pit-fall. The human being
May not be trusted to self-government.
The clear and written law, the deep trod foot-marks
Of ancient custom, are all necessary
To keep him in the road of faith and duty.
The authority entrusted to this man
Was unexampled and unnatural,
It placed him on a level with his Emperor,
Till the proud soul unlearn'd submission. Wo
    is me ;
I mourn for him ! for where he fell, I deem
Might none stand firm. Alas ! dear General,
We in our lucky mediocrity
Have ne'er experienced, cannot calculate,
What dangerous wishes such a height may breed
In the heart of such a man.

BUTLER.

             Spare your laments
Till he need sympathy ; for at this present
He is still mighty, and still formidable.
The Swedes advance to Egra by forced marches,
And quickly will the junction be accomplish'd.
This must not be ! The Duke must never leave
This strong-hold on free footing ; for I have
Pledged life and honour here to hold him prisoner,
And your assistance 'tis on which I calculate.

GORDON.

O that I had not lived to see this day !
From his hand I received this dignity,
He did himself entrust this strong-hold to me,
Which I am now required to make his dungeon.
We subalterns have no will of our own :
The free, the mighty man alone may listen
To the fair impulse of his human nature.
Ah ! we are but the poor tools of the law,
Obedience the sole virtue we dare aim at !

BUTLER.

Nay ! let it not afflict you, that your power
Is circumscribed. Much liberty, much error !
The narrow path of duty is securest.

GORDON.

And all then have deserted him, you say ?
He has built up the luck of many thousands ;
For kingly was his spirit : his full hand
Was ever open ! Many a one from dust
             With a sly glance on BUTLER.
Hath he selected, from the very dust
Hath raised him into dignity and honour.
And yet no friend, not one friend hath he purchased,
Whose heart beats true to him in the evil hour.

BUTLER.

Here's one, I see.

GORDON.

             I have enjoy'd from him
No grace or favour. I could almost doubt,
If ever in his greatness he once thought on
An old friend of his youth. For still my office
Kept me at distance from him ; and when first
He to this citadel appointed me,
He was sincere and serious in his duty.
I do not then abuse his confidence,
If I preserve my fealty in that
Which to my fealty was first deliver'd.

BUTLER.

Say, then, will you fulfil the attainder on him ?

GORDON (*pauses, reflecting—then as in deep
         dejection*).

If it be so—if all be as you say—
If he've betray'd the Emperor, his master,
Have sold the troops, have purposed to deliver
The strong-holds of the country to the enemy—
Yea, truly !—there is no redemption for him !
Yet it is hard, that me the lot should destine
To be the instrument of his perdition ;
For we were pages at the court of Bergau
At the same period ; but I was the senior.

BUTLER.

I have heard so——

GORDON.

        'Tis full thirty years since then.
A youth who scarce had seen his twentieth year
Was Wallenstein, when he and I were friends :
Yet even then he had a daring soul :

His frame of mind was serious and severe
Beyond his years: his dreams were of great objects.
He walk'd amidst us of a silent spirit,
Communing with himself ; yet I have known him
Transported on a sudden into utterance
Of strange conceptions ; kindling into splendour,
His soul reveal'd itself, and he spake so
That we look'd round perplex'd upon each other,
Not knowing whether it were craziness,
Or whether it were a god that spoke in him.

BUTLER.

But was it where he fell two story high
From a window-ledge, on which he had fallen
    asleep ,
And rose up free from injury ? From this day
(It is reported) he betrayed clear marks
Of a distemper'd fancy.

GORDON.

            He became
Doubtless more self-enwrapt and melancholy ;
He made himself a Catholic. Marvellously
His marvellous preservation had transform'd him.
Thenceforth he held himself for an exempted
And privileged being, and, as if he were
Incapable of dizziness or fall,
He ran along the unsteady rope of life.
But now our destinies drove us asunder ;
He paced with rapid step the way of greatness,
Was Count, and Prince, Duke-regent, and Dictator.
And now is all, all this too little for him ;
He stretches forth his hands for a king's crown,
And plunges in unfathomable ruin.

BUTLER.

No more, he comes.

——◆——

SCENE III.

To these enter WALLENSTEIN, *in conversation with the*
    BURGOMASTER *of Egra.*

WALLENSTEIN.

You were at one time a free town. I see,
Ye bear the half eagle in your city arms.
Why the *half* eagle only ?

BURGOMASTER.

            We were free,
But for these last two hundred years has Egra
Remain'd in pledge to the Bohemian crown ;
Therefore we bear the half eagle, the other half
Being cancell'd till the empire ransom us,
If ever that should be.

WALLENSTEIN.

           Ye merit freedom.
Only be firm and dauntless. Lend your ears
To no designing whispering court-minions.
What may your imposts be ?

BURGOMASTER.

           So heavy that
We totter under them. The garrison
Lives at our costs.

WALLENSTEIN.

I will relieve you. Tell me,
There are some Protestants among you still ?
           [*The* BURGOMASTER *hesitates.*
Yes, yes ; I know it. Many lie conceal'd
Within these walls—Confess now—you yourself——
      [*Fixes his eye on him. The* BURGOMASTER *alarmed.*
Be not alarm'd. I hate the Jesuits.

F

Could my will have determined it, they had
Been long ago expell'd the empire. Trust me—
Mass-book or bible — 'tis all one to me.
Of that the world has had sufficient proof.
I built a church for the Reform'd in Glogan
At my own instance. Harkye, Burgomaster!
What is your name?

BURGOMASTER.
                    Pachhalbel, may it please you.

WALLENSTEIN.

Harkye!——
But let it go no further, what I now
Disclose to you in confidence.
[Laying his hand on the BURGOMASTER's shoulder with
a certain solemnity.
                    The times
Draw near to their fulfilment, Burgomaster!
The high will fall, the low will be exalted.
Harkye! But keep it to yourself! The end
Approaches of the Spanish double monarchy—
A new arrangement is at hand. You saw
The three moons that appear'd at once in the Heaven?

BURGOMASTER.
With wonder and affright!

WALLENSTEIN.
                    Whereof did two
Strangely transform themselves to bloody daggers,
And only one, the middle moon, remain'd
Steady and clear.   .

BURGOMASTER.
            We applied it to the Turks.

WALLENSTEIN.
The Turks! That all!—I tell you, that two empires
Will set in blood, in the East and in the West,
And Luth'ranism alone remain.
            [Observing GORDON and BUTLER.
                        I' faith,
'Twas a smart cannonading that we heard
This evening, as we journey'd hitherward;
'Twas on our left hand.   Did you hear it here?

GORDON.
Distinctly.   The wind brought it from the South.

BUTLER.
It seem'd to come from Weiden or from Neustadt.

WALLENSTEIN.
'Tis likely.   That's the route the Swedes are taking.
How strong is the garrison?

GORDON.
                    Not quite two hundred
Competent men, the rest are invalids.

WALLENSTEIN.
Good! And how many in the vale of Jochim?

GORDON.
Two hundred arquebusiers have I sent thither
To fortify the posts against the Swedes.

WALLENSTEIN.
Good! I commend your foresight.   At the works
You have done somewhat?   [too

GORDON.
                    Two additional batteries
I caused to be run up.   They were needless.
The Rhinegrave presses hard upon us, General!

WALLENSTEIN.
You have been watchful in your Emperor's service.
I am content with you, Lieutenant-Colonel.
                                    [To BUTLER.

Release the outposts in the vale of Jochim
With all the stations in the enemy's route.
                                    [To GORDON.
Governor, in your faithful hands I leave
My wife, my daughter, and my sister.   I
Shall make no stay here, and wait but the arrival
Of letters to take leave of you, together
With all the regiments.

SCENE IV.

To these enter COUNT TERTSKY.

TERTSKY.
Joy, General; joy! I bring you welcome tidings.

WALLENSTEIN.
And what may they be?

TERTSKY.
                    There has been an engagement
At Neustadt; the Swedes gain'd the victory.

WALLENSTEIN.
From whence did you receive the intelligence?

TERTSKY.
A countryman from Tirschenseil convey'd it.
Soon after sunrise did the fight begin!
A troop of the Imperialists from Fachau
Had forced their way into the Swedish camp;
The cannonade continued full two hours;
There were left dead upon the field a thousand
Imperialists, together with their Colonel;
Further than this he did not know.

WALLENSTEIN.
                    How came
Imperial troops at Neustadt!   Altringer,
But yesterday, stood sixty miles from there.
Count Galas' force collects at Frauenburg,
And have not the full complement.   Is it possible,
That Suys perchance had ventured so far onward?
It cannot be.

TERTSKY.
            We shall soon know the whole,
For here comes Illo, full of haste, and joyous.

SCENE V.

To these enter ILLO.

ILLO (*to* WALLENSTEIN).
A courier, Duke! he wishes to speak with thee.

TERTSKY (*eagerly*).
Does he bring confirmation of the victory?

WALLENSTEIN (*at the same time*).
What does he bring?   Whence comes he?

ILLO
                    From the Rhinegrave.
And what he brings I can announce to you
Beforehand.   Seven leagues distant are the Swedes;
At Neustadt did Max. Piccolomini
Throw himself on them with the cavalry;
A murderous fight took place! o'erpower'd by
                                    numbers
The Pappenheimers all, with Max. their leader,
            [WALLENSTEIN *shudders and turns pale.*
Were left dead on the field.

WALLENSTEIN (*after a pause in a low voice*).
Where is the messenger? Conduct me to him.
[WALLENSTEIN *is going, when* LADY NEUBRUNN *rushes
into the room. Some servants follow her and run
across the stage.*

NEUBRUNN.
Help! Help!

ILLO *and* TERTSKY (*at the same time*).
What now?

NEUBRUNN.
The Princess!

WALLENSTEIN *and* TERTSKY.
Does she know it?

NEUBRUNN (*at the same time with them*).
She is dying!
[*Hurries off the stage, when* WALLENSTEIN *and* TERTSKY
follow her.

SCENE VI.

BUTLER *and* GORDON.

GORDON.
What's this?

BUTLER.
She has lost the man she loved—
Young Piccolomini who fell in the battle.

GORDON.
Unfortunate Lady!

BUTLER.
You have heard what Illo
Reporteth, that the Swedes are conquerors,
And marching hitherward.

GORDON.
Too well I heard it.

BUTLER.
They are twelve regiments strong, and there are five
Close by us to protect the Duke. We have
Only my single regiment; and the garrison
Is not two hundred strong.

GORDON.
'Tis even so.

BUTLER.
It is not possible with such small force
To hold in custody a man like him.

GORDON.
I grant it.

BUTLER.
Soon the numbers would disarm us,
And liberate him.

GORDON.
It were to be fear'd.

BUTLER (*after a pause*).
Know, I am warranty for the event;
With my head have I pledged myself for his,
Must make my word good, cost it what it will,
And if alive we cannot hold him prisoner,
Why—death makes all things certain!

GORDON.
Butler! What!
Do I understand you? Gracious God! *You* could—

BUTLER.
He must not live.

GORDON.
And *you* can do the deed!

BUTLER.
Either you or I. This morning was his last.

GORDON.
You would assassinate him.

BUTLER.
'Tis my purpose.

GORDON.
Who leans with his whole confidence upon you!

BUTLER.
Such is his evil destiny!

GORDON.
Your General!
The sacred person of your General!

BUTLER.
My General he *has* been.

GORDON.
That 't is only
An *"has been"* washes out no villany.
And without judgment pass'd?

BUTLER.
The execution
Is here instead of judgment.

GORDON.
This were murder,
Not justice. The most guilty should be heard.

BUTLER.
His guilt is clear, the Emperor has pass'd judg-
And we but execute his will. [ment,

GORDON.
We should not
Hurry to realize a bloody sentence.
A word may be recall'd, a life can never be.

BUTLER.
Despatch in service pleases sovereigns.

GORDON.
No honest man's ambition to press forward
To the hangman's service.

BUTLER.
And no brave man loses
His colour at a daring enterprise.

GORDON.
A brave man hazards life, but not his conscience.

BUTLER.
What then? Shall he go forth anew to kindle
The unextinguishable flame of war?

GORDON.
Seize him, and hold him prisoner—do not kill him!

BUTLER.
Had not the Emperor's army been defeated,
I might have done so.—But 'tis now past by.

GORDON.
O, wherefore open'd I the strong-hold to him?

BUTLER.
His destiny and not the place destroys him

GORDON.
Upon these ramparts, as beseem'd a soldier,
I had fallen, defending the Emperor's citadel!

BUTLER.
Yes! and a thousand gallant men have perish'd!

GORDON.
Doing their duty—that adorns the man!
But murder's a black deed, and nature curses it.

F 2

BUTLER (*brings out a paper*).
Here is the manifesto which commands us
To gain possession of his person. See—
It is addressed to you as well as me.
Are you content to take the consequences,
If through our fault he escape to the enemy?

GORDON.
I!—Gracious God!

BUTLER.
Take it on yourself.
Come of it what may, on you I lay it.

GORDON.
O God in heaven!

BUTLER.
Can you advise aught else
Wherewith to execute the Emperor's purpose?
Say if you can. For I desire his fall,
Not his destruction.

GORDON.
Merciful heaven! what must be
I see as clear as you. Yet still the heart
Within my bosom beats with other feelings!

BUTLER.
Mine is of harder stuff! Necessity   [Illo
In her rough school hath steel'd me. And this
And Tertsky likewise, they must not survive him.

GORDON.
I feel no pang for these. Their own bad hearts
Impell'd them, not the influence of the stars.
'Twas they who strew'd the seeds of evil passions
In his calm breast, and with officious villany
Water'd and nursed the pois'nous plants. May they
Receive their earnests to the uttermost mite!

BUTLER.
And their death shall precede his!
We meant to have taken them alive this evening
Amid the merry-making of a feast,
And keep them prisoners in the citadels.
But this makes shorter work. I go this instant
To give the necessary orders.

SCENE VII.

To these enter ILLO, *and* TERTSKY.

TERTSKY.
Our luck is on the turn. To-morrow come
The Swedes—twelve thousand gallant warriors,
Illo!
Then straightways for Vienna. Cheerily, friend!
What! meet such news with such a moody face!

ILLO.
It lies with us at present to prescribe   [traitors,
Laws, and take vengeance on those worthless
Those skulking cowards that deserted us;
One has already done his bitter penance,
The Piccolomini: be his the fate
Of all who wish us evil! This flies sure
To the old man's heart; he has his whole life long
Fretted and toil'd to raise his ancient house
From a Count's title to the name of Prince;
And now must seek a grave for his only son.

BUTLER.
'Twas pity, though! A youth of such heroic
And gentle temperament! The Duke himself,
'Twas easily seen, how near it went to his heart.

ILLO.
Hark ye, old friend! That is the very point
That never pleased me in our General—
He ever gave the preference to the Italians.
Yea, at this very moment, by my soul!
He'd gladly see us all dead ten times over,
Could he thereby recal his friend to life.

TERTSKY.
Hush, hush! Let the dead rest! This evening's
business
Is, who can fairly drink the other down—
Your regiment, Illo! gives the entertainment.
Come! we will keep a merry carnival—
The night for once be day, and 'mid full glasses
Will we expect the Swedish avant-garde.

ILLO.
Yes, let us be of good cheer for to-day,
For there's hot work before us, friends! This sword
Shall have no rest, till it be bathed to the hilt
In Austrian blood.

GORDON.
Shame, shame! what talk is this,
My Lord Field Marshal! Wherefore foam you so
Against your Emperor?

BUTLER.
Hope not too much
From this first victory. Bethink you, sirs!
How rapidly the wheel of Fortune turns;
The Emperor still is formidably strong.

ILLO.
The Emperor has soldiers, no commander,
For this King Ferdinand of Hungary
Is but a tyro. Galas? He's no luck,
And was of old the ruiner of armies.
And then this viper, this Octavio,
Is excellent at stabbing in the back,
But ne'er meets Friedland in the open field.

TERTSKY.
Trust me, my friends, it cannot but succeed;
Fortune, we know, can ne'er forsake the Duke!
And only under Wallenstein can Austria
Be conqueror.

ILLO.
The Duke will soon assemble
A mighty army: all comes crowding, streaming
To banners, dedicate by destiny,
To fame, and prosperous fortune. I behold
Old times come back again! he will become
Once more the mighty Lord which he has been.
How will the fools, who've now deserted him,
Look then? I can't but laugh to think of them,
For lands will he present to all his friends,
And like a King and Emperor reward
True services; but we've the nearest claims.
[*To* GORDON.
You will not be forgotten, Governor!
He'll take you from this nest, and bid you shine
In higher station: your fidelity
Well merits it.

GORDON.
I am content already,
And wish to climb no higher; where great height is,
The fall must needs be great. " Great height,
great depth."

ILLO.
Here you have no more business, for to-morrow
The Swedes will take possession of the citadel.
Come, Tertsky, it is supper-time. What think you?

Nay, shall we have the State illuminated
In honour of the Swede? And who refuses
To do it is a Spaniard and a traitor.

TERTSKY.

Nay! Nay! not that, it will not please the Duke—

ILLO.

What! we are masters here; no soul shall dare
Avow himself Imperial where we 've the rule.
Gordon! good night, and for the last time, take
A fair leave of the place. Send out patroles
To make secure, the watch-word may be alter'd
At the stroke of ten; deliver in the keys
To the Duke himself, and then you 've quit for ever
Your wardship of the gates, for on to-morrow
The Swedes will take possession of the citadel.

TERTSKY (*as he is going, to* BUTLER).
You come, though, to the castle?

BUTLER.
                    At the right time.
                    [*Exeunt* TERTSKY *and* ILLO.

—————◦—————

SCENE VIII.

GORDON *and* BUTLER.

GORDON (*looking after them*).
Unhappy men! How free from all foreboding!
They rush into the outspread net of murder,
In the blind drunkenness of victory;
I have no pity for their fate. This Illo,
This overflowing and fool-hardy villain,
That would fain bathe himself in his Emperor's
    blood.—

BUTLER.
Do as he order'd you. Send round patroles,
Take measures for the citadel's security;
When they are within I close the castle-gate
That nothing may transpire.

GORDON (*with earnest anxiety*).
                    Oh! haste not so!
Nay, stop; first tell me——

BUTLER.
                    You have heard already,
To-morrow to the Swedes belongs. This night
Alone is ours. They make good expedition.
But we will make still greater. Fare you well.

GORDON.
Ah! your looks tell me nothing good. Nay, Butler,
I pray you, promise me!

BUTLER.
                    The sun has set;
A fateful evening doth descend upon us,
And brings on their long night! Their evil stars
Deliver them unarm'd into our hands,
And from their drunken dream of golden fortunes
The dagger at their heart shall rouse them. Well,
The Duke was ever a great calculator;
His fellow-men were figures on his chess-board,
To move and station, as his game required.
Other men's honour, dignity, good name,
Did he shift like pawns, and made no conscience
Still calculating, calculating still;   [of it:
And yet at last his calculation proves
Erroneous; the whole game is lost; and lo!
His own life will be found among the forfeits.

GORDON.
O think not of his errors now! remember
His greatness, his munificence; think on all
The lovely features of his character,
On all the noble exploits of his life,
And let them, like an angel's arm, unseen
Arrest the lifted sword.

BUTLER.
                    It is too late.
I suffer not myself to feel compassion,
Dark thoughts and bloody are my *duty* now:
                    [*Grasping* GORDON's *hand.*
Gordon! 't is not my hatred (I pretend not
To love the Duke, and have no cause to love him)
Yet 't is not now my hatred that impels me
To be his murderer. 'Tis his evil fate.
Hostile concurrences of many events
Control and subjugate me to the office.
In vain the human being meditates
Free action. He is but the wire-work'd[1] puppet
Of the blind Power, which out of his own choice
Creates for him a dread necessity.
What too would it avail him, if there were
A something pleading for him in my heart—
Still I must kill him.

GORDON.
                    If your heart speak to you,
Follow its impulse. 'T is the voice of God.
Think you your fortunes will grow prosperous
Bedew'd with blood—his blood? Believe it not!

BUTLER.
You know not. Ask not! Wherefore should it
    happen,
That the Swedes gain'd the victory, and hasten
With such forced marches hitherward? Fain
    would I
Have given him to the Emperor's mercy.—Gordon!
I do not wish his blood—But I must ransom
The honour of my word,—it lies in pledge—
And he must die, or—
                    [*Passionately grasping* GORDON's *hand.*
                    Listen then, and know!
I am *dishonour'd* if the Duke escape us.

GORDON.
O! to save such a man——

BUTLER.
                    What!

GORDON.
                    It is worth
A sacrifice.—Come, friend! Be noble-minded!
Our own heart, and not other men's opinions,
Forms our true honour.

BUTLER (*with a cold and haughty air*).
                    He is a great Lord,
This Duke—and I am but of mean importance.
This is what you would say! Wherein concerns it
The world at large, you mean to hint to me,
Whether the man of low extraction keeps
Or blemishes his honour—
So that the man of princely rank be saved!
We all do stamp our value on ourselves:
The price we challenge for ourselves is given us.
There does not live on earth the man so station'd,
That I despise myself compared with him.

_____

[1] We doubt the propriety of putting so blasphemous a
sentiment in the mouth of any character. T.

Man is made great or little by his own will;
Because I am true to mine, therefore he dies.

GORDON.

I am endeavouring to move a rock.
Thou hadst a mother, yet no human feelings.
I cannot hinder you, but may some God
Rescue him from you! [*Exit* GORDON.

SCENE IX.

BUTLER (*alone*).

I treasured my good name all my life long;
The Duke has cheated me of life's best jewel,
So that I blush before this poor weak Gordon!

He prizes above all his fealty;
His conscious soul accuses him of nothing;
In opposition to his own soft heart
He subjugates himself to an iron duty.
Me in a weaker moment passion warp'd;
I stand beside him, and must feel myself
The worse man of the two. What, though the world
Is ignorant of my purposed treason, yet
One man does know it, and can prove it too—
High-minded Piccolomini!
There lives the man who can dishonour me!
This ignominy blood alone can cleanse!
Duke Friedland, thou or I—Into my own hands
Fortune delivers me—The dearest thing a man
has is himself.

(*The curtain drops.*)

ACT IV.

SCENE I.

Butler's Chamber.

BUTLER, MAJOR, and GERALDIN.

BUTLER.

Find me twelve strong Dragoons, arm them with
For there must be no firing—— [pikes,
Conceal them somewhere near the banquet-room,
And soon as the dessert is served up, rush all in
And cry—" Who is loyal to the Emperor?"
I will overturn the table—while you attack
Illo and Tertsky, and despatch them both.
The castle-palace is well barr'd and guarded,
That no intelligence of this proceeding
May make its way to the Duke.—Go instantly;
Have you yet sent for Captain Devereux
And the Macdonald?——

GERALDIN.

They 'll be here anon.
[*Exit* GERALDIN.

BUTLER.

Here 's no room for delay. The citizens
Declare for him, a dizzy drunken spirit
Possesses the whole town. They see in the Duke
A Prince of peace, a founder of new ages
And golden times. Arms too have been given out
By the town-council, and a hundred citizens
Have volunteer'd themselves to stand on guard.
Despatch! then be the word; for enemies
Threaten us from without and from within.

SCENE II.

BUTLER, CAPTAIN DEVEREUX, and MACDONALD.

MACDONALD.

Here we are, General.

DEVEREUX.

What 's to be the watchword?

BUTLER.

Long live the Emperor!

BOTH (*recoiling*).
How?

BUTLER.

Live the House of Austria!

DEVEREUX.

Have we not sworn fidelity to Friedland?

MACDONALD.

Have we not march'd to this place to protect him?

BUTLER.

Protect a traitor, and his country's enemy!

DEVEREUX.

Why, yes! in his name you administer'd
Our oath.

MACDONALD.

And followed him yourself to Egra.

BUTLER.

I did it the more surely to destroy him.

DEVEREUX.

So then!

MACDONALD.

An alter'd case!

BUTLER (*to* DEVEREUX).
Thou wretched man!
So easily leavest thou thy oath and colours?

DEVEREUX.

The devil!—I but follow'd your example,
If you could prove a villain, why not we?

MACDONALD.

We've nought to do with *thinking*—that's your
business.
You are our General, and give out the orders;
We follow you, though the track lead to hell.

BUTLER (*appeased*).
Good then! we know each other.

MACDONALD.
I should hope so.

DEVEREUX.

Soldiers of fortune are we—who bids most,
He has us.

MACDONALD.
'T is e'en so!

BUTLER.
Well, for the present
Ye must remain honest and faithful soldiers.

DEVEREUX.

We wish no other.

BUTLER.
Ay, and make your fortunes.

MACDONALD.

That is still better.

BUTLER.

Listen !

BOTH.

We attend.

BUTLER.

It is the Emperor's will and ordinance
To seize the person of the Prince-Duke Friedland,
Alive or dead.

DEVEREUX.

It runs so in the letter.

MACDONALD.

Alive or dead—these were the very words.

BUTLER.

And he shall be rewarded from the State
In land and gold, who proffers aid thereto.

DEVEREUX.

Ay ! that sounds well. The *words* sound always
well
That travel hither from the Court. Yes ! yes !
We know already what Court-words import.
A golden chain perhaps in sign of favour,
Or an old charger, or a parchment patent,
And such like.—The Prince-Duke pays better.

MACDONALD.

Yes,
The Duke's a splendid paymaster.

BUTLER.

All over
With that, my friends ! His lucky stars are set.

MACDONALD.

And is that certain ?

BUTLER.

You have my word for it.

DEVEREUX.

His lucky fortunes all past by ?

BUTLER.

For ever:
He is as poor as we.

MACDONALD.

As poor as we ?

DEVEREUX.

Macdonald, we'll desert him.

BUTLER.

We'll desert him !
Full twenty thousand have done that already ;
We must do more, my countrymen ! In short—
We—we must kill him.

BOTH (*starting back*).

Kill him !

BUTLER.

Yes, must kill him;
And for that purpose have I chosen you.

BOTH.

Us !

BUTLER.

You, Captain Devereux, and thee Macdonald.

DEVEREUX (*after a pause*).

Choose you some other.

BUTLER.

What ! art dastardly ?
Thou, with full thirty lives to answer for—
Thou conscientious, of a sudden ?

DEVEREUX.

Nay,
To assassinate our Lord and General—

MACDONALD.

To whom we 've sworn a soldier's oath—

BUTLER.

The oath
Is null, for Friedland is a traitor.

DEVEREUX.

No, no ! it is too bad !

MACDONALD.

Yes, by my soul !
It is too bad. One has a conscience too—

DEVEREUX.

If it were not our Chieftain, who so long
Has issued the commands, and claim'd our duty.

BUTLER.

Is that the objection ?

DEVEREUX.

Were it my own father,
And the Emperor's service should demand it of me,
It might be done perhaps—But we are soldiers,
And to assassinate our Chief Commander,
That is a sin, a foul abomination,
From which no Monk or Confessor absolves us.

BUTLER.

I am your Pope, and give you absolution.
Determine quickly !

DEVEREUX.

'T will not do.

MACDONALD.

'Twon't do !

BUTLER.

Well, off then ! and—send Pestalutz to me.

DEVEREUX (*hesitates*).

The Pestalutz—

MACDONALD.

What may you want with him ?

BUTLER.

If you reject it, we can find enough—

DEVEREUX.

Nay, if he must fall, we may earn the bounty
As well as any other. What think you,
Brother Macdonald ?

MACDONALD.

Why, if he *must* fall,
And *will* fall, and it can't be otherwise,
One would not give place to this Pestalutz.

DEVEREUX (*after some reflection*).

When do you purpose he should fall ?

BUTLER.

This night.
To-morrow will the Swedes be at our gates.

DEVEREUX.

You take upon you all the consequences ?

BUTLER.

I take the whole upon me.

DEVEREUX.

And it is
The Emperor's will, his express absolute will ?
For we have instances, that folks may like
The murder, and yet hang the murderer.

BUTLER.
The manifesto says—"alive or dead."
Alive—'t is not possible—you see it is not.

DEVEREUX.
Well, dead then! dead! But how can we come
at him!
The town is filled with Tertsky's soldiery.

MACDONALD.
Ay! and then Tertsky still remains, and Illo—
With these you shall begin—you understand me!

DEVEREUX.
How! And must they too perish!

BUTLER.
They the first.

MACDONALD.
Hear, Devereux! A bloody evening this.

DEVEREUX.
Have you a man for that! Commission me—

BUTLER.
'T is given in trust to Major Geraldin;
This is a carnival night, and there 's a feast
Given at the castle—there we shall surprise them,
And hew them down. The Pestalutz and Lesley
Have that commission—soon as that is finish'd—

DEVEREUX.
Hear, General! It will be all one to you—
Hark ye, let me exchange with Geraldin.

BUTLER.
'T will be the lesser danger with the Duke.

DEVEREUX.
Danger! The devil! What do you think me,
General!
'T is the Duke's eye, and not his sword, I fear.

BUTLER.
What can his eye do to thee!

DEVEREUX.
Death and hell!
Thou know'st that I'm no milk-sop, General!
But 't is not eight days since the Duke did send me
Twenty gold pieces for this good warm coat
Which I have on! and then for him to see me
Standing before him with the pike, his murderer,
That eye of his looking upon this coat—
Why—why—the devil fetch me! I'm no milk-sop!

BUTLER.
The Duke presented thee this good warm coat,
And thou, a needy wight, hast pangs of conscience
To run him through the body in return.
A coat that is far better and far warmer
Did the Emperor give to him, the Prince's mantle.
How doth he thank the Emperor! With revolt,
And treason.

DEVEREUX.
That is true. The devil take
Such thankers! I'll despatch him.

BUTLER.
And wouldst quiet
Thy conscience, thou hast nought to do but simply
Pull off the coat; so canst thou do the deed
With light heart and good spirits.

DEVEREUX.
You are right.
That did not strike me. I'll pull off the coat—
So there 's an end of it.

MACDONALD.
Yes, but there 's another
Point to be thought of.

BUTLER.
And what's that, Macdonald!

MACDONALD.
What avails sword or dagger against him?
He is not to be wounded—he is—

BUTLER (starting up).
What!

MACDONALD.
Safe against shot, and stab and flash! Hard frozen,
Secured, and warranted by the black art!
His body is impenetrable, I tell you.

DEVEREUX.
In Inglestadt there was just such another:
His whole skin was the same as steel; at last
We were obliged to beat him down with gunstocks.

MACDONALD.
Hear what I'll do.

DEVEREUX.
Well!

MACDONALD.
In the cloister here
There 's a Dominican, my countryman.
I 'll make him dip my sword and pike for me
In holy water, and say over them
One of his strongest blessings. That 's probatum!
Nothing can stand 'gainst that.

BUTLER.
So do, Macdonald!
But now go and select from out the regiment
Twenty or thirty able-bodied fellows,
And let them take the oaths to the Emperor.
Then when it strikes eleven, when the first rounds
Are pass'd, conduct them silently as may be
To the house—I will myself be not far off.

DEVEREUX.
But how do we get through Hartschier and Gordon,
That stand on guard there in the inner chamber!

BUTLER.
I have made myself acquainted with the place.
I lead you through a back-door that 's defended
By one man only. Me my rank and office
Give access to the Duke at every hour.
I 'll go before you—with one poniard-stroke
Cut Hartschier's windpipe, and make way for you.

DEVEREUX.
And when we are there, by what means shall we
gain
The Duke's bed-chamber, without his alarming
The servants of the Court: for he has here
A numerous company of followers!

BUTLER.
The attendants fill the right wing: he hates bustle,
And lodges in the left wing quite alone.

DEVEREUX.
Were it well over—hey, Macdonald! I
Feel queerly on the occasion, devil knows!

MACDONALD.
And I too. 'Tis too great a personage.
People will hold us for a brace of villains.

BUTLER.
In plenty, honour, splendour—You may safely
Laugh at the people's babble.

DEVEREUX.

If the business
Squares with one's honour — if that be quite
certain—

BUTLER.

Set your hearts quite at ease. Ye save for Ferdi-
nand
His Crown and Empire. The reward can be
No small one.

DEVEREUX.

And 'tis his purpose to dethrone the Emperor?

BUTLER.

Yes!—Yes!—to rob him of his Crown and Life.

DEVEREUX.

And he must fall by the executioner's hands,
Should we deliver him up to the Emperor
Alive?

BUTLER.

It were his certain destiny.

DEVEREUX.

Well! Well! Come then, Macdonald, he shall not
Lie long in pain.
          [*Exeunt* BUTLER *through one door,* MACDONALD *and*
          DEVEREUX *through the other.*

———◆———

SCENE III.

A Gothic and gloomy Apartment at the DUCHESS FRIED-
LAND'S. THEKLA *on a seat, pale, her eyes closed. The*
DUCHESS *and* LADY NEUBRUNN *busied about her.* WAL-
LENSTEIN *and the* COUNTESS *in conversation.*

WALLENSTEIN.

How knew she it so soon?

COUNTESS.

She seems to have
Foreboded some misfortune. The report
Of an engagement, in the which had fallen
A colonel of the Imperial army, frighten'd her.
I saw it instantly. She flew to meet
The Swedish Courier, and with sudden questioning,
Soon wrested from him the disastrous secret.
Too late we miss'd her, hasten'd after her,
We found her lying in his arms, all pale
And in a swoon.

WALLENSTEIN.

A heavy, heavy blow!
And she so unprepared! Poor child! How is it?
          [*Turning to the* DUCHESS.
Is she coming to herself?

DUCHESS.

Her eyes are opening.

COUNTESS.

She lives.

THEKLA (*looking around her*).
Where am I?

WALLENSTEIN (*steps to her, raising her up in*
his arms).
Come, cheerly, Thekla! be my own brave girl!
See, there's thy loving mother. Thou art in
Thy father's arms.

THEKLA (*standing up*).
Where is he? Is he gone?

DUCHESS.

Who gone, my daughter?

THEKLA.

He—the man who utter'd
That word of misery.

DUCHESS.

O! think not of it,
My Thekla!

WALLENSTEIN.

Give her sorrow leave to talk!
Let her complain—mingle your tears with hers,
For she hath suffer'd a deep anguish; but
She'll rise superior to it, for my Thekla
Hath all her father's unsubdued heart.

THEKLA.

I am not ill. See, I have power to stand.
Why does my mother weep? Have I alarm'd her?
It is gone by—I recollect myself—
          [*She casts her eyes round the room, as seeking some one.*
Where is he? Please you, do not hide him from me.
You see I have strength enough: now I will hear
    him.

DUCHESS.

No; never shall this messenger of evil
Enter again into thy presence, Thekla!

THEKLA.

My father—

WALLENSTEIN.

Dearest daughter!

THEKLA.

I'm not weak—
Shortly I shall be quite myself again.
You'll grant me one request?

WALLENSTEIN.

Name it, my daughter.

THEKLA.

Permit the stranger to be called to me,
And grant me leave, that by myself I may
Hear his report and question him.

DUCHESS.

No, never!

COUNTESS.

'Tis not adviseable—assent not to it.

WALLENSTEIN.

Hush! Wherefore wouldst thou speak with him, my
    daughter?

THEKLA.

Knowing the whole, I shall be more collected;
I will not be deceived. My mother wishes
Only to spare me. I will not be spared—
The worst is said already: I can hear
Nothing of deeper anguish!

COUNTESS *and* DUCHESS.
Do it not.

THEKLA.

The horror overpower'd me by surprise.
My heart betray'd me in the stranger's presence:
He was a witness of my weakness, yea,
I sank into his arms; and that has shamed me.
I must replace myself in his esteem,
And I must speak with him, perforce, that he,
The stranger, may not think ungently of me.

WALLENSTEIN.

I see she is in the right, and am inclined
To grant her this request of hers. Go, call him.
          [LADY NEUBRUNN *goes to call him.*

DUCHESS.

But I, thy mother, will be present—

THEKLA.

'Twere
More pleasing to me, if alone I saw him ;
Trust me, I shall behave myself the more
Collectedly.

WALLENSTEIN.

Permit her her own will.
Leave her alone with him : for there are sorrows,
Where of necessity the soul must be
Its own support. A strong heart will rely
On its own strength alone. In her own bosom,
Not in her mother's arms, must she collect
The strength to rise superior to this blow.
It is mine own brave girl. I'll have her treated
Not as the woman, but the heroine.   [Going.

COUNTESS (detaining him).

Where art thou going ? I heard Tertsky say
That 'tis thy purpose to depart from hence
To-morrow early, but to leave us here.

WALLENSTEIN.

Yes, ye stay here, placed under the protection
Of gallant men.

COUNTESS.

O take us with you, brother !
Leave us not in this gloomy solitude
To brood o'er anxious thoughts. The mists of
    doubt
Magnify evils to a shape of horror.

WALLENSTEIN.

Who speaks of evil ? I entreat you, sister,
Use words of better omen.

COUNTESS.

Then take us with you.
O leave us not behind you in a place
That forces us to such sad omens. Heavy
And sick within me is my heart——
These walls breathe on me, like a church-yard
    vault.
I cannot tell you, brother, how this place
Doth go against my nature. Take us with you.
Come, sister, join you your entreaty !—Niece,
Yours too. We all entreat you, take us with you !

WALLENSTEIN.

The place's evil omens will I change,
Making it that which shields and shelters for me
My best beloved.

LADY NEUBRUNN (returning).
The Swedish officer.

WALLENSTEIN.

Leave her alone with me.   [Exit.

DUCHESS (to THEKLA, who starts and shivers).
There—pale as death !—Child, 'tis impossible
That thou shouldst speak with him. Follow thy
    mother.

THEKLA.
The Lady Neubrunn then may stay with me.
        [Exeunt DUCHESS and COUNTESS.

SCENE IV.

THEKLA, THE SWEDISH CAPTAIN, LADY NEUBRUNN.

CAPTAIN (respectfully approaching her).

Princess—I must entreat your gentle pardon—
My inconsiderate rash speech—How could I—

THEKLA (with dignity).

You have beheld me in my agony.
A most distressful accident occasion'd
You from a stranger to become at once
My confidant.

CAPTAIN.

I fear you hate my presence,
For my tongue spake a melancholy word.

THEKLA.

The fault is mine. Myself did wrest it from you.
The horror which came o'er me interrupted
Your tale at its commencement. May it please
Continue it to the end.   [you,

CAPTAIN.

Princess, 'twill
Renew your anguish.

THEKLA.

I am firm,——
I will be firm. Well—how began the engagement ?

CAPTAIN.

We lay, expecting no attack, at Neustadt,
Entrench'd but insecurely in our camp,
When towards evening rose a cloud of dust
From the wood thitherward ; our vanguard fled
Into the camp, and sounded the alarm.
Scarce had we mounted, ere the Pappenheimers,
Their horses at full speed, broke through the lines,
And leapt the trenches ; but their heedless courage
Had borne them onward far before the others—
The infantry were still at distance, only
The Pappenheimers follow'd daringly
Their daring leader——
    [THEKLA betrays agitation in her gestures. The
    Officer pauses till she makes a sign to him to
    proceed.

CAPTAIN.

Both in van and flanks
With our whole cavalry we now received them ;
Back to the trenches drove them, where the foot
Stretch'd out a solid ridge of pikes to meet them.
They neither could advance, nor yet retreat ;
And as they stood on every side wedged in,
The Rhinegrave to their leader call'd aloud,
Inviting a surrender ; but their leader,
Young Piccolomini——
    [THEKLA, as giddy, grasps a chair.
Known by his plume,
And his long hair, gave signal for the trenches ;
Himself leapt first : the regiment all plunged after.
His charger, by a halbert gored, rear'd up,
Flung him with violence off, and over him
The horses, now no longer to be curbed,——
    [THEKLA, who has accompanied the last speech with
    all the marks of increasing agony, trembles
    through her whole frame, and is falling. The
    LADY NEUBRUNN runs to her, and receives her in
    her arms.

NEUBRUNN.

My dearest lady——

CAPTAIN.

I retire.

THEKLA.
                    'Tis over.
Proceed to the conclusion.

CAPTAIN.
                    Wild despair
Inspired the troops with frenzy when they saw
Their leader perish ; every thought of rescue
Wasspurn'd ; they fought like wounded tigers ; their
Frantic resistance roused our soldiery ;
A murderous fight took place, nor was the contest
Finish'd before their last man fell.

THEKLA (faltering).
                   And where——
Where is—You have not told me all.

CAPTAIN (after a pause).
                  This morning
We buried him. Twelve youths of noblest birth
Did bear him to interment ; the whole army
Follow'd the bier. A laurel deck'd his coffin ;
The sword of the deceased was placed upon it,
In mark of honour, by the Rhinegrave's self.
Nor tears were wanting ; for there are among us
Many, who had themselves experienced
The greatness of his mind, and gentle manners ;
All were affected at his fate. The Rhinegrave
Would willingly have saved him ; but himself
Made vain the attempt—'tis said he wish'd to die.

NEUBRUNN (to THEKLA, who has hidden her countenance).
Look up, my dearest lady——

THEKLA.
                Where is his grave ?

CAPTAIN.
At Neustadt, lady ; in a cloister church
Are his remains deposited, until
We can receive directions from his father.

THEKLA.
What is the cloister's name ?

CAPTAIN.
               Saint Catherine's.

THEKLA.
And how far is it thither ?

CAPTAIN.
             Near twelve leagues.

THEKLA.
And which the way ?

CAPTAIN.
          You go by Tirschenreit
And Falkenberg, through our advanced posts.

THEKLA.
                Who
Is their commander ?

CAPTAIN.
          Colonel Seckendorf.
[THEKLA steps to the table, and takes a ring from a
casket.

THEKLA.
You have beheld me in my agony,
And shown a feeling heart. Please you, accept
             [Giving him the ring.
A small memorial of this hour. Now go !

CAPTAIN (confused).
Princess——
[THEKLA silently makes signs to him to go, and turns
from him. The CAPTAIN lingers, and is about to
speak. LADY NEUBRUNN repeats the signal, and
he retires.

SCENE V.

THEKLA, LADY NEUBRUNN.

THEKLA (falls on LADY NEUBRUNN's neck).
Now, gentle Neubrunn, show me the affection
Which thou hast ever promised—prove thyself
My own true friend and faithful fellow-pilgrim.
This night we must away !

NEUBRUNN.
          Away ! and whither ?

THEKLA.
Whither ! There is but one place in the world.
Thither, where he lies buried ! To his coffin !

NEUBRUNN.
What would you do there ?

THEKLA.
             What do there ?
That wouldst thou not have ask'd, hadst thou e'er
   loved.
There, there is all that still remains of him !
That single spot is the whole earth to me.

NEUBRUNN.
That place of death——

THEKLA.
          Is now the only place,
Where life yet dwells for me : detain me not !
Come and make preparations : let us think
Of means to fly from hence.

NEUBRUNN.
          Your father's rage——

THEKLA.
That time is past——
And now I fear no human being's rage.

NEUBRUNN.
The sentence of the world ! The tongue of calumny !

THEKLA.
Whom am I seeking ? Him who is no more.
Am I then hastening to the arms——O God !
I haste but to the grave of the beloved.

NEUBRUNN.
And we alone, two helpless feeble women ?

THEKLA.
We will take weapons : my arm shall protect thee.

NEUBRUNN.
In the dark night-time ?

THEKLA.
         Darkness will conceal us.

NEUBRUNN.
This rough tempestuous night——

THEKLA.
         Had he a soft bed
Under the hoofs of his war-horses ?

NEUBRUNN.
             Heaven !
And then the many posts of the enemy !

THEKLA.
They are human beings. Misery travels free
Through the whole earth.

NEUBRUNN.
     The journey's weary length——

THEKLA.
The pilgrim, travelling to a distant shrine
Of hope and healing, doth not count the leagues.

NEUBRUNN.

How can we pass the gates?

THEKLA.

Gold opens them.

Go! do but go.

NEUBRUNN.

Should we be recognized—

THEKLA.

In a despairing woman, a poor fugitive,
Will no one seek the daughter of Duke Friedland.

NEUBRUNN.

And where procure we horses for our flight?

THEKLA.

My equerry procures them. Go and fetch him.

NEUBRUNN.

Dares he, without the knowledge of his lord?

THEKLA.

He will. Go, only go. Delay no longer.

NEUBRUNN.

Dear lady! and your mother?

THEKLA.

Oh! my mother!

NEUBRUNN.

So much as she has suffer'd too already;
Your tender mother—Ah! how ill prepared
For this last anguish!

THEKLA.

Woe is me! my mother!
[Pauses.

Go instantly.

NEUBRUNN.

But think what you are doing!

THEKLA.

What can be thought, already has been thought.

NEUBRUNN.

And being there, what purpose you to do?

THEKLA.

There a Divinity will prompt my soul.

NEUBRUNN.

Your heart, dear lady, is disquieted!
And this is not the way that leads to quiet.

THEKLA.

To a deep quiet, such as he has found.
It draws me on, I know not what to name it,
Resistless does it draw me to his grave.
There will my heart be eased, my tears will flow.
O hasten, make no further questioning!
There is no rest for me till I have left
These walls—they fall in on me—A dim power
Drives me from hence—Oh mercy! What a
feeling!
What pale and hollow forms are those! They fill,
They crowd the place! I have no longer room here!
Mercy! Still more! More still! The hideous
swarm!
They press on me; they chase me from these walls—
Those hollow, bodiless forms of living men!

NEUBRUNN.

You frighten me so, lady, that no longer
I dare stay here myself. I go and call
Rosenberg instantly. [Exit LADY NEUBRUNN.

———

SCENE VI.

THEKLA.

His spirit 'tis that calls me: 'tis the troop
Of his true followers, who offer'd up
Themselves to avenge his death: and they accuse
Of an ignoble loitering—they would not [me
Forsake their leader even in his death—they died
And shall I live!— [for him!
For me too was that laurel-garland twined
That decks his bier. Life is an empty casket:
I throw it from me. O! my only hope;—
To die beneath the hoofs of trampling steeds—
That is the lot of heroes upon earth!
[Exit THEKLA.[1]

(The Curtain drops.)

~~~~~~~~

ACT V.

SCENE I.

A Saloon, terminated by a Gallery which extends far into
the back-ground.

WALLENSTEIN (sitting at a table).

The SWEDISH CAPTAIN (standing before him).

WALLENSTEIN.

Commend me to your lord. I sympathize
In his good fortune; and if you have seen me
Deficient in the expressions of that joy,
Which such a victory might well demand,
Attribute it to no lack of good will,
For henceforth are our fortunes one. Farewell,
And for your trouble take my thanks. To-morrow
The citadel shall be surrender'd to you
On your arrival.

[The SWEDISH CAPTAIN retires. WALLENSTEIN sits
lost in thought, his eyes fixed vacantly, and his
head sustained by his hand. The COUNTESS
TERTSKY enters, stands before him awhile, un-
observed by him; at length he starts, sees her
and recollects himself.

WALLENSTEIN.

Comest thou from her! Is she restored! How is she!

COUNTESS.

My sister tells me, she was more collected
After her conversation with the Swede.
She has now retired to rest.

WALLENSTEIN.

The pang will soften,
She will shed tears.

COUNTESS.

I find thee alter'd too,
My brother! After such a victory
I had expected to have found in thee
A cheerful spirit. O remain thou firm!
Sustain, uphold us! For our light thou art,
Our sun.

---

[1] The soliloquy of Thekla consists in the original of six-
and-twenty lines, twenty of which are in rhymes of irregular recurrence. I thought it prudent to abridge it.
Indeed the whole scene between Thekla and Lady
Neubrunn might, perhaps, have been omitted without
injury to the play.

WALLENSTEIN.

Be quiet. I ail nothing. Where's
Thy husband?

COUNTESS.

At a banquet—he and Illo.

WALLENSTEIN (*rises and strides across the saloon*).
The night's far spent. Betake thee to thy chamber.

COUNTESS.
Bid me not go, O let me stay with thee!

WALLENSTEIN (*moves to the window*).
There is a busy motion in the Heaven,
The wind doth chase the flag upon the tower,
Fast sweep the clouds, the sickle [1] of the moon,
Struggling, darts snatches of uncertain light.
No form of star is visible! That one
White stain of light, that single glimmering yonder,
Is from Cassiopeia, and therein
Is Jupiter. (*A pause.*) But now
The blackness of the troubled element hides him!
[*He sinks into profound melancholy, and looks
vacantly into the distance.*

COUNTESS (*looks on him mournfully, then grasps
his hand*).
What art thou brooding on?

WALLENSTEIN.
Methinks,
If I but saw him, 'twould be well with me.
He is the star of my nativity,
And often marvellously hath his aspect
Shot strength into my heart.

COUNTESS.
Thou'lt see him again.

WALLENSTEIN (*remains for a while with absent
mind, then assumes a livelier manner, and turns
suddenly to the Countess*).
See him again! O never, never again!

COUNTESS.
How?

WALLENSTEIN.
He is gone—is dust.

COUNTESS.
Whom meanest thou then?

WALLENSTEIN.
He, the more fortunate! yea, he hath finish'd!
For him there is no longer any future,
His life is bright—bright without spot it *was*,
And cannot cease to be. No ominous hour
Knocks at his door with tidings of mishap.
Far off is he, above desire and fear;

---

[1] These four lines are expressed in the original with exquisite felicity.

  Am Himmel ist geschäftige Bewegung.
  Des Thurmes Fahne jagt der Wind, schnell geht
  Der Wolken Zug, die *Mondessichel wankt*,
  Und durch die Nacht zuckt ungewisse Helle.

The word "moon-sickle," reminds me of a passage in
Harris, as quoted by Johnson, under the word "falcated."
"The enlightened part of the moon appears in the form
of a sickle or reaping-hook, which is while she is moving
from the conjunction to the opposition, or from the new
moon to the full: but from full to a new again, the enlightened part appears gibbous, and the dark *falcated.*"
The words "wanken" and "schweben" are not easily
translated. The English words, by which we attempt to
render them, are either vulgar or pedantic, or not of sufficiently general application. So "der Wolken Zug"—The
Draft, the Procession of clouds.—The Masses of the Clouds
sweep onward in swift *stream.*

No more submitted to the change and chance
Of the unsteady planets. O 'tis well
With *him!* but who knows what the coming hour
Veil'd in thick darkness brings for us?

COUNTESS.
Thou speakest
Of Piccolomini. What was his death?
The courier had just left thee as I came.
[WALLENSTEIN *by a motion of his hand makes signs
to her to be silent.*
Turn not thine eyes upon the backward view,
Let us look forward into sunny days,
Welcome with joyous heart the victory,
Forget what it has cost thee. Not to-day,
For the first time, thy friend was to thee dead;
To thee he died, when first he parted from thee.

WALLENSTEIN.
This anguish will be wearied down,[1] I know;
What pang is permanent with man! From the
As from the vilest thing of every day [highest,
He learns to wean himself: for the strong hours
Conquer him. Yet I feel what I have lost
In him. The bloom is vanish'd from my life.
For O! he stood beside me, like my youth,
Transform'd for me the real to a dream,
Clothing the palpable and the familiar
With golden exhalations of the dawn.
Whatever fortunes wait my future toils,
The *beautiful* is vanish'd—and returns not.

COUNTESS.
O be not treacherous to thy own power.
Thy heart is rich enough to vivify
Itself. Thou lovest and prizest virtues in him,
The which thyself didst plant, thyself unfold.

WALLENSTEIN (*stepping to the door*).
Who interrupts us now at this late hour?
It is the Governor. He brings the keys
Of the Citadel. 'Tis midnight. Leave me, sister!

COUNTESS.
O 'tis so hard to me this night to leave thee—
A boding fear possesses me!

WALLENSTEIN.
Fear? Wherefore?

COUNTESS.
Shouldst thou depart this night, and we at waking
Never more find thee!

WALLENSTEIN.
Fancies!

COUNTESS.
O my soul
Has long been weigh'd down by these dark fore-
And if I combat and repel them waking, [bodings.
They still crush down upon my heart in dreams.
I saw thee yesternight with thy first wife
Sit at a banquet, gorgeously attired.

WALLENSTEIN.
This was a dream of favourable omen,
That marriage being the founder of my fortunes.

COUNTESS.
To-day I dreamt that I was seeking thee

---

[1] A very inadequate translation of the original:—

Verschmerzen werd' ich diesen Schlag, das weiss ich,
Denn was verschmerzte nicht der Mensch

LITERALLY.

I shall *grieve down* this blow, of that I'm conscious:
What does not man grieve down?

In thy own chamber. As I enter'd, lo !
It was no more a chamber : the Chartreuse
At Gitschin 'twas, which thou thyself hast founded,
And where it is thy will that thou shouldst be
Interr'd.

WALLENSTEIN.
Thy soul is busy with these thoughts.

COUNTESS.
What ! dost thou not believe that oft in dreams
A voice of warning speaks prophetic to us ?

WALLENSTEIN.
There is no doubt that there exist such voices.
Yet I would not call *them*
Voices of warning that announce to us
Only the inevitable. As the sun,
Ere it is risen, sometimes paints its image
In the atmosphere, so often do the spirits
Of great events stride on before the events,
And in to-day already walks to-morrow.
That which we read of the fourth Henry's death
Did ever vex and haunt me like a tale
Of my own future destiny. The king
Felt in his breast the phantom of the knife,
Long ere Ravaillac arm'd himself therewith.
His quiet mind forsook him : the phantasma
Started him in his Louvre, chased him forth
Into the open air : like funeral knells
Sounded that coronation festival ;
And still with boding sense he heard the tread
Of those feet that even then were seeking him
Throughout the streets of Paris.

COUNTESS.
And to *thee*
The voice within thy soul bodes nothing ?

WALLENSTEIN.
Nothing.
Be wholly tranquil.

COUNTESS.
And another time
I hasten'd after thee, and thou rann'st from me
Through a long suite, through many a spacious hall,
There seem'd no end of it : doors creak'd and
clapp'd ;
I follow'd panting, but could not o'ertake thee ;
When on a sudden did I feel myself
Grasp'd from behind—the hand was cold, that
grasp'd me—
'Twas thou, and thou didst kiss me, and there
seem'd
A crimson covering to envelop us.

WALLENSTEIN.
That is the crimson tapestry of my chamber.

COUNTESS (*gazing on him*).
If it should come to that—if I should see thee,
Who standest now before me in the fulness
Of life—   [*She falls on his breast and weeps.*

WALLENSTEIN.
The Emperor's proclamation weighs upon thee—
Alphabets wound not—and he finds no hands.

COUNTESS.
If he *should* find them, my resolve is taken—
I bear about me my support and refuge.
                    [*Exit* COUNTESS.

SCENE II.

WALLENSTEIN, GORDON.

WALLENSTEIN.
All quiet in the town ?

GORDON.
The town is quiet.

WALLENSTEIN.
I hear a boisterous music ! and the Castle
Is lighted up. Who are the revellers ?

GORDON.
There is a banquet given at the Castle
To the Count Tertsky, and Field Marshal Illo.

WALLENSTEIN.
In honour of the victory—This tribe
Can show their joy in nothing else but feasting.
            [*Rings. The* GROOM OF THE CHAMBER *enters.*
Unrobe me. I will lay me down to sleep.
            [WALLENSTEIN *takes the keys from* GORDON
So we are guarded from all enemies,
And shut in with sure friends.
For all must cheat me, or a face like this
                    [*Fixing his eye on* GORDON.
Was ne'er a hypocrite's mask.
        [*The* GROOM OF THE CHAMBER *takes off his mantle,
collar, and scarf.*

WALLENSTEIN.
Take care—what is that ?

GROOM OF THE CHAMBER.
The golden chain is snapped in two.

WALLENSTEIN.
Well, it has lasted long enough. Here—give it.
            [*He takes and looks at the chain.*
'Twas the first present of the Emperor.
He hung it round me in the war of Friule,
He being then Archduke ; and I have worn it
Till now from habit——
From superstition, if you will. Belike,
It was to be a Talisman to me ;
And while I wore it on my neck in faith,
It was to chain to me all my life long
The volatile fortune, whose first pledge it was.
Well, be it so ! Henceforward a new fortune
Must spring up for me : for the potency
Of this charm is dissolved.
        [GROOM OF THE CHAMBER *retires with the vestments,*
WALLENSTEIN *rises, takes a stride across the room,
and stands at last before* GORDON *in a posture of
meditation.*
How the old time returns upon me ! I
Behold myself once more at Burgau, where
We two were Pages of the Court together.
We oftentimes disputed : thy intention
Was ever good ; but thou wert wont to play
The Moralist and Preacher, and wouldst rail at
me—
That I strove after things too high for me,
Giving my faith to bold unlawful dreams,
And still extol to me the golden mean.
—Thy wisdom hath been proved a thriftless friend
To thy own self. See, it has made thee early
A superannuated man, and (but
That my munificent stars will intervene)
Would let thee in some miserable corner
Go out like an untended lamp.

GORDON.

My Prince!
With light heart the poor fisher moors his boat,
And watches from the shore the lofty ship
Stranded amid the storm.

WALLENSTEIN.

Art thou already
In harbour then, old man? Well! I am not.
The unconquer'd spirit drives me o'er life's billows;
My planks still firm, my canvas swelling proudly.
Hope is my goddess still, and Youth my inmate;
And while we stand thus front to front almost,
I might presume to say, that the swift years
Have passed by powerless o'er my unblanched hair.

[*He moves with long strides across the Saloon, and
remains on the opposite side over-against* GORDON

Who now persists in calling Fortune false?
To me she has proved faithful; with fond love
Took me from out the common ranks of men,
And like a mother goddess, with strong arm
Carried me swiftly up the steps of life.
Nothing is common in my destiny,
Nor in the furrows of my hand. Who dares
Interpret then my life for me as 't were
One of the undistinguishable many?
True, in this present moment I appear
Fallen low indeed; but I shall rise again.
The high flood will soon follow on this ebb;
The fountain of my fortune, which now stops
Repress'd and bound by some malicious star,
Will soon in joy play forth from all its pipes.

GORDON.

And yet remember I the good old proverb,
" Let the night come before we praise the day."
I would be slow from long-continued fortune
To gather hope: for Hope is the companion
Given to the unfortunate by pitying Heaven.
Fear hovers round the head of prosperous men:
For still unsteady are the scales of fate.

WALLENSTEIN (*smiling*).

I hear the very Gordon that of old
Was wont to preach to me, now once more preaching;
I know well, that all sublunary things
Are still the vassals of vicissitude.
The unpropitious gods demand their tribute.
This long ago the ancient Pagans knew:
And therefore of their own accord they offer'd
To themselves injuries, so to atone
The jealousy of their divinities:
And human sacrifices bled to Typhon.

[*After a pause, serious, and in a more subdued manner.*

I too have sacrificed to him—For me
There fell the dearest friend, and through my fault
He fell! No joy from favourable fortune
Can overweigh the anguish of this stroke.
The envy of my destiny is glutted:
Life pays for life. On his pure head the lightning
Was drawn off which would else have shatter'd me.

SCENE III.

To these enter SENI.

WALLENSTEIN.

Is not that Seni! and beside himself,
If one may trust his looks? What brings thee hither
At this late hour, Baptista?

SENI.

Terror, Duke!
On thy account.

WALLENSTEIN.

What now!

SENI.

Flee ere the day-break!
Trust not thy person to the Swedes!

WALLENSTEIN.

What now
Is in thy thoughts?

SENI (*with louder voice*).
Trust not thy person to these Swedes.

WALLENSTEIN.

What is it, then?

SENI (*still more urgently*).

O wait not the arrival of these Swedes!
An evil near at hand is threatening thee
From false friends. All the signs stand full of
horror!
Near, near at hand the net-work of perdition—
Yea, even now 't is being cast around thee!

WALLENSTEIN.

Baptista, thou art dreaming!—Fear befools thee.

SENI.

Believe not that an empty fear deludes me.
Come, read it in the planetary aspects;
Read it thyself, that ruin threatens thee
From false friends!

WALLENSTEIN.

From the falseness of my friends
Has risen the whole of my unprosperous for-
tunes.
The warning should have come before! At present
I need no revelation from the stars
To know that.

SENI.

Come and see! trust thine own eyes!
A fearful sign stands in the house of life—
An enemy; a fiend lurks close behind
The radiance of thy planet.—O be warn'd!
Deliver not thyself up to these heathens,
To wage a war against our holy church.

WALLENSTEIN (*laughing gently*).

The oracle rails that way! Yes, yes! Now
I recollect. This junction with the Swedes
Did never please thee—lay thyself to sleep,
Baptista! Signs like these I do not fear.

GORDON (*who during the whole of this dialogue
has shown marks of extreme agitation, and now
turns to* WALLENSTEIN).

My Duke and General! May I dare presume?
Speak freely.

WALLENSTEIN.

GORDON.

What if 't were no mere creation
Of fear, if God's high providence vouchsafed
To interpose its aid for your deliverance,
And made that mouth its organ?

WALLENSTEIN.

Ye 're both feverish!
How can mishap come to me from the Swedes!
They sought this junction with me—'t is their
interest.

GORDON (*with difficulty suppressing his emotion*).
But what if the arrival of these Swedes—
What if this were the very thing that wing'd
The ruin that is flying to your temples?
                    [*Flings himself at his feet.*
There is yet time, my Prince.

SENI.
                    O hear him! hear him!

GORDON (*rises*).
The Rhinegrave's still far off. Give but the orders,
This citadel shall close its gates upon him.
If then he will besiege us, let him try it.
But this I say; he'll find his own destruction
With his whole force before these ramparts, sooner
Than weary down the valour of our spirit.
He shall experience what a band of heroes,
Inspirited by an heroic leader,
Is able to perform. And if indeed
It be thy serious wish to make amend
For that which thou hast done amiss,—this, this
Will touch and reconcile the Emperor,
Who gladly turns his heart to thoughts of mercy;
And Friedland, who returns repentant to him,
Will stand yet higher in his Emperor's favour,
Than e'er he stood when he had never fallen.

WALLENSTEIN (*contemplates him with surprise, re-
mains silent awhile, betraying strong emotion*).
Gordon—your zeal and fervour lead you far.
Well, well—an old friend has a privilege.
Blood, Gordon, has been flowing. Never, never
Can the Emperor pardon me: and if he could,
Yet I—I ne'er could let myself be pardon'd.
Had I foreknown what now has taken place,
That he, my dearest friend, would fall for me,
My first death-offering: and had the heart
Spoken to me, as now it has done—Gordon,
It may be, I might have bethought myself.
It may be too, I might not. Might or might not,
Is now an idle question. All too seriously
Has it begun to end in nothing, Gordon!
Let it then have its course. [*Stepping to the window.*
All dark and silent—at the castle too
All is now hush'd—Light me, Chamberlain!
    [*The GROOM OF THE CHAMBER, who had entered dur-
    ing the last dialogue, and had been standing at a
    distance and listening to it with visible expres-
    sions of the deepest interest, advances in extreme
    agitation, and throws himself at the DUKE's feet.*
And thou too! But I know why thou dost wish
My reconcilement with the Emperor.
Poor man! he hath a small estate in Cärnthen,
And fears it will be forfeited because
He's in my service. Am I then so poor,
That I no longer can indemnify
My servants? Well! to no one I employ
Means of compulsion. If 't is thy belief
That fortune has fled from me, go! forsake me.
This night for the last time mayst thou unrobe me,
And then go over to thy Emperor.
Gordon, good night! I think to make a long
Sleep of it: for the struggle and the turmoil
Of this last day or two was great. May 't please you!
Take care that they awake me not too early.
    [*Exit WALLENSTEIN, the GROOM OF THE CHAMBER
    lighting him. SENI follows, GORDON remains on
    the darkened stage, following the DUKE with his
    eye, till he disappears at the farther end of the
    gallery: then by his gestures the old man expresses
    the depth of his anguish and stands leaning
    against a pillar.*

SCENE IV.

GORDON, BUTLER (*at first behind the scenes*).

BUTLER (*not yet come into view of the stage*).
Here stand in silence till I give the signal.

GORDON (*starts up*).
'T is he! he, has already brought the murderers.

BUTLER.
The lights are out. All lies in profound sleep.

GORDON.
What shall I do, shall I attempt to save him!
Shall I call up the house! Alarm the guards!

BUTLER (*appears, but scarcely on the stage*).
A light gleams hither from the corridor.
It leads directly to the Duke's bed-chamber.

GORDON.
But then I break my oath to the Emperor;
If he escape and strengthen the enemy,
Do I not hereby call down on my head
All the dread consequences?

BUTLER (*stepping forward*).
                    Hark! Who speaks there!

GORDON.
'T is better, I resign it to the hands
Of Providence. For what am I, that *I*
Should take upon myself so great a deed!
I have not murder'd him, if he be murder'd;
But all his rescue were *my* act and deed;
Mine—and whatever be the consequences,
I must sustain them.

BUTLER (*advances*).
                    I should know that voice.

GORDON.
Butler!

BUTLER.
                    'T is Gordon. What do *you* want here!
Was it so late then, when the Duke dismiss'd you!

GORDON.
Your hand bound up and in a scarf!

BUTLER.
                    'T is wounded.
That Illo fought as he was frantic, till
At last we threw him on the ground.

GORDON (*shuddering*).
                    Both dead!

BUTLER.
Is he in bed!

GORDON.
Ah, Butler!

BUTLER.
                    Is he! speak.

GORDON.
He shall *not* perish! Not through you! The Heaven
Refuses *your* arm. See—'t is wounded!—

BUTLER.
There is no need of *my* arm.

GORDON.
                    The most guilty
Have perish'd, and enough is given to justice.
    [*The GROOM OF THE CHAMBER advances from the
    Gallery with his finger on his mouth commanding
    silence.*

GORDON.

He sleeps! O murder not the holy sleep!

BUTLER.

No! he shall die awake. [Is going.

GORDON.

His heart still cleaves
To earthly things: he's not prepared to step
Into the presence of his God!

BUTLER (going).

God's merciful!

GORDON (holds him).

Grant him but this night's respite.

BUTLER (hurrying off).

The next moment
May ruin all.

GORDON (holds him still).

One hour!——

BUTLER.

Unhold me! What
Can that short respite profit him?

GORDON.

O—Time
Works miracles. In one hour many thousands
Of grains of sand run out; and quick as they,
Thought follows thought within the human soul.
Only one hour! Your heart may change its pur-
pose, [tidings
His heart may change its purpose—some new
May come; some fortunate event, decisive,
May fall from Heaven and rescue him. O what
May not one hour achieve!

BUTLER.

You but remind me,
How precious every minute is!

[He stamps on the floor.

SCENE V.

To these enter MACDONALD, and DEVEREUX, with the
HALBERDIERS.

GORDON (throwing himself between him and them).

No, monster!
First over my dead body thou shalt tread.
I will not live to see the accursed deed!

BUTLER (forcing him out of the way).

Weak-hearted dotard!

[Trumpets are heard in the distance.

DEVEREUX and MACDONALD.

Hark! The Swedish trumpets!
The Swedes before the ramparts! Let us hasten!

GORDON (rushes out).

O, God of Mercy!

BUTLER (calling after him).

Governor, to your post!

GROOM OF THE CHAMBER (hurries in).

Who dares make larum here? Hush! The Duke
sleeps.

DEVEREUX (with loud harsh voice).

Friend, it is time now to make larum.

GROOM OF THE CHAMBER.

Help!

Murder!

BUTLER.

Down with him!

GROOM OF THE CHAMBER (run through the body by
DEVEREUX, falls at the entrance of the Gallery).

Jesus Maria!

BUTLER.

Burst the doors open.

[They rush over the body into the Gallery—two doors
are heard to crash one after the other—Voices,
deadened by the distance—Clash of arms—then all
at once a profound silence.

SCENE VI.

COUNTESS TERTSKY (with a light).

Her bed-chamber is empty; she herself
Is no where to be found! The Neubrunn too,
Who watch'd by her, is missing. If she should
Be flown —— but whither flown? We must
call up
Every soul in the house. How will the Duke
Bear up against these worst bad tidings! O
If that my husband now were but return'd
Home from the banquet!—Hark! I wonder
whether
The Duke is still awake! I thought I heard
Voices and tread of feet here! I will go
And listen at the door. Hark! what is that!
'Tis hastening up the steps!

SCENE VII.

COUNTESS, GORDON.

GORDON (rushes in out of breath).

'Tis a mistake!
'Tis not the Swedes—Ye must proceed no further—
Butler!—O God! where is he?

GORDON (observing the COUNTESS).

Countess! Say——

COUNTESS.

You are come then from the castle! Where's my
husband?

GORDON (in an agony of affright).

Your husband!—Ask not!—To the Duke——

COUNTESS.

Not till
You have discover'd to me——

GORDON.

On this moment
Does the world hang. For God's sake! to the
Duke.
While we are speaking—— [Calling loudly.
Butler! Butler! God!

COUNTESS.

Why, he is at the castle with my husband.

[BUTLER comes from the Gallery

GORDON.

'Twas a mistake—'Tis not the Swedes—it is
The Imperialists' Lieutenant-General
Has sent me hither—will be here himself
Instantly.—You must not proceed.

G

SMITH'S STANDARD LIBRARY.

Already Published.

SCOTT'S LADY OF THE LAKE. 1s.
——— LAY OF THE LAST MINSTREL. 1s.
——— MARMION. 1s. 2d.
——— ROKEBY. 1s. 2d.
——— VISION OF DON RODERICK: BALLADS AND LYRICAL PIECES. 1s.
THE BOROUGH. By the Rev. G. Crabbe. 1s. 4d.
TALES. By the Rev. George Crabbe, LL.B. 2s.
THE MUTINY OF THE BOUNTY. 1s. 4d.
THE POETICAL WORKS OF H. KIRKE WHITE. 1s.
THE POETICAL WORKS OF ROBERT BURNS. 2s. 6d.
PAUL AND VIRGINIA, THE INDIAN COTTAGE, and ELIZABETH. 1s. 6d.
MEMOIRS OF THE LIFE OF COLONEL HUTCHINSON, Governor of Nottingham Castle during the Civil War. By his Widow, Mrs. Lucy Hutchinson. 2s. 6d.
THOMSON'S POEMS and PLAYS. Complete Edition. 5s.
——— SEASONS, and CASTLE of INDOLENCE. 1s.
LOCKE ON THE REASONABLENESS OF CHRISTIANITY. 1s.
GOLDSMITH'S POEMS AND PLAYS. 1s. 6d.
——— VICAR OF WAKEFIELD. 1s.
——— CITIZEN OF THE WORLD. 2s. 6d.
——— ESSAYS, &c. 2s.
KNICKERBOCKER'S HISTORY OF NEW YORK. 2s. 3d.
NATURE AND ART. By Mrs. Inchbald. 10d.
A SIMPLE STORY. By Mrs. Inchbald. 2s.
ANSON'S VOYAGE ROUND THE WORLD. 2s. 6d.
THE LIFE OF BENVENUTO CELLINI. 3s.
SCHILLER'S TRAGEDIES: THE PICCOLOMINI; and THE DEATH OF WALLENSTEIN. 1s. 8d.
THE POETICAL WORKS OF GRAY & COLLINS. 10d.
THE LIFE AND OPINIONS OF TRISTRAM SHANDY. By Laurence Sterne. 3s.
THE HISTORY OF CHARLES THE TWELFTH, KING OF SWEDEN. From the French of Voltaire. 1s. 10d.
HOME. By Miss Sedgwick. 9d.
INCIDENTS OF TRAVEL IN EGYPT, ARABIA PETRÆA, AND THE HOLY LAND. By J. L. Stephens, Esq. 2s. 6d.
INCIDENTS OF TRAVEL IN THE RUSSIAN AND TURKISH EMPIRES. By J. L. Stephens, Esq. 2s. 6d.

BEATTIE'S POETICAL WORKS, and BLAIR GRAVE. 1s.
THE LIFE AND ADVENTURES OF PETER WILKINS, a Cornish Man. 2s. 4d.
UNDINE: A miniature Romance. Translated from the German, by the Rev. Thomas Tracy. 9d.
THE ILIAD OF HOMER. Translated by Pope. 3s
ROBIN HOOD: a Collection of all the ancient Poems, Songs, and Ballads now extant, relative to that celebrated English Outlaw; to which are prefixed, historical Anecdotes of his Life. Carefully revised by Ritson. 2s. 6d.
THE LIVES OF DONNE, WOTTON, HOOKER, HERBERT, AND SANDERSON. Written by I. Walton. 2s. 6d.
THE LIFE OF PETRARCH. By Mrs. Dobson. 2s.
MILTON'S POETICAL WORKS, Complete. 4s.
——— PARADISE LOST. 1s. 10d.
——— PARADISE REGAINED, and MISCELLANEOUS POEMS. 2s.
RASSELAS. By Dr. Johnson. 9d.
ESSAYS ON TASTE. By Rev. A. Alison, LL.D. 2s. 5
THE POETICAL WORKS OF JOHN KEATS. 2s.
THE LINWOODS; or, "SIXTY YEARS SINCE IN AMERICA. By Miss Sedgwick. 2s. 8d.
PICCIOLA. From the French of X. B. Saintine. 2s. 4d.
THE POETICAL WORKS OF EDWARD YOUNG, LL.D. Complete. 5s.
THE POETICAL WORKS OF ALEXANDER POPE 5s.
POEMS, BY WILLIAM CULLEN BRYANT. 1s.
FAUST, A TRAGEDY, BY GOETHE. By Lewis Filmore. 1s. 10d.
LA FONTAINE'S FABLES. Translated by E. Wright.
TECUMSEH; or, THE WEST THIRTY YEARS SINCE. A Poem. By George H. Colton. 2s. 6d.
ESSAYS. By R. W. Emerson. 2s.
A JOURNEY ROUND MY ROOM; AND A NOCTURNAL EXPEDITION ROUND MY ROOM. Translated from the French of Count Xavier de Maistre. 1s.
STRIFE AND PEACE. From the Swedish of Frederika Bremer. 1s. 6d.
THE H——— FAMILY. From the Swedish of Frederika Bremer. 2s.

The publication of these Works will be immediately followed by others of a standard character: so that, in progress of time, many of those which are considered the Classics of this country, and others which deserve to be so, will, enriched by the productions of our French, German, and American brethren, be placed, in a handsome form, within the reach of all classes of the community. They will appear in no specified order, but being protected by a Wrapper, may be preserved and arranged in volumes, according to the taste of the purchaser.

Three objects have been kept in view in projecting these editions—first, *correctness*; secondly, *elegance of form and execution*; and thirdly, *lowness of price*. The latter has often been attained — but generally at the sacrifice of the two former.

The Publisher refers to the Works already published, as the best specimens he can give of his design. He confidently trusts that he shall be able to present to the public a series of works, suitable from their intrinsic merit, their mechanical excellence, and their cheapness, for the libraries of all classes.

[BRADBURY AND EVANS, PRINTERS, WHITEFRIARS.]

Printed in the USA
CPSIA information can be obtained
at www.ICGtesting.com
CBHW081001020624
9416CB00028B/583

9 781021 264909